CHASING PERFECTION

CHASING
PERFECTION

A Behind-the-Scenes Look at the
High-Stakes Game of Creating an
NBA Champion

ANDY GLOCKNER

DA CAPO PRESS

A Member of the Perseus Books Group

Copyright © 2016 by Andy Glockner

Designed by Jeff Williams
Set in 11.5-point Minion Pro by the Perseus Books Group

Cataloging-in-Publication data for this book is available from the Library of Congress.

First Da Capo Press edition 2016
Hardcover ISBN: 978-0-306-82402-9
E-book ISBN: 978-0-306-82403-6

Published by Da Capo Press
A Member of the Perseus Books Group
www.dacapopress.com

Note: The information in this book is true and complete to the best of our knowledge. This book is intended only as an informative guide for those wishing to know more about health issues. In no way is this book intended to replace, countermand, or conflict with the advice given to you by your own physician. The ultimate decision concerning care should be made between you and your doctor. We strongly recommend you follow his or her advice. Information in this book is general and is offered with no guarantees on the part of the authors or Da Capo Press. The authors and publisher disclaim all liability in connection with the use of this book.

10 9 8 7 6 5 4 3 2 1

To Bernard King, Chris Mullin, Walter Berry,
countless nights in the Palestra, and everything and
everyone else that made me fall in love with basketball,
a perfect sport filled with imperfections

CONTENTS

Perfected Players

One of the most important moments of the 2014–15 NBA season happened three months before it even started. Amid the myriad practices, meetings, and team functions related to the tryout camp for the US national team that was being put together to compete in the 2014 FIBA Basketball World Cup in Spain, one small thought on shooting technique was passed along from one world-class player to another. That disclosure set in motion improvements that amplified the latter player's impact on his whole team, and helped change the entire dynamic of the NBA's championship chase.

There was no way to know that at the time, though, as the focus of anyone who was observing the tryout camp at the University of Nevada-Las Vegas's glittering Mendenhall Center practice facility that July was on the battles to make the tournament roster. For five days, a sizable contingent of local, national, and international media looked on along with dozens of invited basketball luminaries as the nineteen hopefuls went through drills and scrimmages under the watchful eyes of USA Basketball chairman Jerry Colangelo, national team head coach Mike Krzyzewski, and his coaching staff. Despite a number of the NBA's elite players deciding to pass on trying out for the non-Olympics event, the roster still was loaded with young, world-class talent.

The headliner was Kevin Durant, the Oklahoma City Thunder's newly minted NBA most valuable player, who seemed to flow around the courts in all of his long-limbed scoring glory. There was former teammate, James Harden, now an established superstar for the Houston Rockets after a landmark 2012 trade that redefined both of those teams. There was emerging Indiana Pacers small forward Paul George, who had helped lead his team to the No. 1 seed in the Eastern Conference in 2014 despite the presence of two-time defending NBA champions LeBron James, Dwyane Wade, and others in Miami.

There also were the Golden State Warriors' "Splash Brothers," Stephen Curry and Klay Thompson; blossoming point guard studs like the Portland Trail Blazers' Damian Lillard, the Cleveland Cavaliers' Kyrie Irving, and the Washington Wizards' John Wall; prodigious post presences in the Detroit Pistons' Andre Drummond and the Sacramento Kings' DeMarcus Cousins; plus Chicago Bulls lead guard Derrick Rose, a former league MVP himself who was trying to get back from multiple knee injuries that had handcuffed a series of very good Bulls teams.

The energy levels during the scrimmages equaled the talent levels on the courts. Guys were going at each other hard. World-class players don't often get summer environments in which they can compete day after day against others of their caliber, and the opportunity to watch and learn from peers at the game's highest level can mean as much to the furthering of a career as making the final roster actually does.

One of the highlights of the camp was a post-practice series of one-on-one games between Durant, Harden, and George. Each of the trio took turns starting with the ball, with one attempt to score on the defender. If the bucket was made, the scorer stayed on the court to face the player sitting out, who would come on as the defender. If he missed, the defender then got the ball and the chance to score against the player who had been resting. Even with dozens of people milling around on the sidelines and baseline, just a few feet away from the action, the games were pretty focused and intense, with each star testing his best moves against two of the few equals they have.

There were plenty of these kinds of on-court battles at the camp. The whole week was somewhat of a referendum on the pecking order of the new generation of scoring point guards that were fueling the NBA's surge in watchability. The same was true of the big men. Traditional post players like Cousins and Drummond were testing each other against a legit foe, and the Denver Nuggets' hyperkinetic Kenneth Faried rebounded everything in sight. All the while, the specter of the NBA's Next Big Thing—the New Orleans Pelicans' Anthony Davis—loomed very large.

While all of these players battle for honors during the season, the communal goal of the national team setup makes the camps a lot less confrontational, and it's a chance for the best of the best to crib good stuff from others. It may be the way a dribbler sets up his crossover, or how to come off a screen to provide the extra inches of room that's all world-class players need to catch a pass and bury a jumper. Players at this level will see something they like, ask about it, and then quietly incorporate it into their games, making them even deadlier going forward.

A good example of this came to light in an ESPN.com column in January 2015, where Ethan Sherwood Strauss broke down some of the new things Klay Thompson had added to his offensive game for the 2014–15 season. One of them was dubbed the "Aussie-go-round," where Thompson cribbed from a USA Basketball teammate and learned to use his inside arm to grab big man Andrew Bogut around the waist when curling around a Bogut screen. The slingshot effect would propel Thompson forward too quickly for the trailing defender to recover. In the video clip embedded in the story, Thompson came up the right wing from the baseline and then tightly curled around Bogut, who was holding the ball. Defensive help wasn't able to rotate over quickly enough, and Bogut fed a simple pass to Thompson for a driving layup attempt, on which he was fouled.

Often, this type of adoption comes from players seeing something they like in a game or one of the practices. But sometimes, it's just a quick chat about basketball philosophy that does the trick.

Months after the national team camp had ended, one of the players who had participated was sitting on a metal folding chair off to the side of the practice court at his team's facility, recounting the conversation that had helped change him for the better.

"This is crazy, you'll like this," the player said. "So, I was talking to Kevin Durant—I ask people, from time to time, good shooters, 'When you're off, what is the thing you go back to?' Not that I ask everybody, just from time to time you just talk to someone and ask. And Kevin Durant said, 'I need to be in my heels. So when I'm in my heels, I'm stronger. I want my heels to be solid on the ground as I'm shooting.'

"I said, 'I've never heard that before.' This was just last summer at the USA thing, and so I was kind of playing around with it, and it was during that camp—which probably wasn't the time to play around with it—but I was trying to feel my heels while I was shooting, and there's something to it. Because when you're on your toes, your balance isn't there, but you don't want to be with your toes up, because you don't want to be fading back.

"That's why a lot of us miss all of our shots is because we get lazy in our core, and we're kind of curled back, or we've got our shoulders back, or our weight is somehow just a little bit back, and we [leave them] short. We miss our shots short all the time, and a lot of it's just because, I believe, of our body posture in our shot."

The player then rose from his chair and started to demonstrate what he was talking about, first leaning forward onto his forefeet, with his body slightly following suit, and then showing the difference in body posture when his heels were solid on the ground at the start of a shooting motion.

"I feel if I'm engaged, I like to try to be bent just barely forward—so it was really interesting," he said. "I was just like, 'Wow.' It was hard for me, kind of, to be in my heels to go. I mean, I can get on my heels, but to do it, it felt like everything was going to tip backwards. But sometimes, it would feel right. I would feel strong."

The player was interested in what he had been told and what he was feeling when he first tried it out, but he needed to figure out a way to make the movement natural to him, and allow him to incorporate it into his full-speed basketball actions. He felt some comfort immediately while doing it on catch-and-shoot chances, since on those plays you're already standing in the spot from where you will lift off. Working the new technique into his shots when he was on the move, though, took some significant alteration of his established workout routines.

"One of my movements that's been tough for me has been step-ups," he said, referencing longstanding issues he's had with one of his knees. "Usually, it'll hurt for the first two reps, and then I'll kind of get into a groove and then I can do them, but you can't do that in a game all the time. You don't always get a couple of reps; you kind of do because you're running around, but I need to feel good the first time. I want to feel good the first time I'm trying to do something, because you get stiff in a game, use a timeout, come out, and you gotta go shoot right away."

The player first incorporated heel-loading movements into his leg lifting routines. Then he began to practice them every time he went down the stairs in his house, reinforcing the weight distribution and technique of "being solid in his heels" to muscle memory. The technique changes eventually took, and not only did his shooting consistency improve in all aspects of his game, but unexpectedly, his knee felt increasingly better.

"I had no intention of [it helping my knee]," he said. "I was really just looking out about my shot. I'm just having a conversation, it wasn't even about trying to figure anything out. I was talking to someone, and then I was just playing with it, right? And then it turned into this."

"This" was one of the greatest shooting seasons in NBA history, and one of the stories this book is all about.

⌒

- Cleveland Cavaliers forward LeBron James, widely considered to be the best basketball player in the world, shot 22.7 percent on 110 3-point attempts during the playoffs.

- Stephen Curry, the league's most explosive shooter, shot five-for-twenty-three in a Finals loss, capping off a four-game stretch in which he converted just twenty-nine of eighty-three shot attempts.

- James Harden committed a playoff-record twelve turnovers in the Rockets' final game of the postseason.

These (with a hat-tip to Anthony Davis, the Pelicans' freak of nature) were the three best basketball players in the world during the 2014–15 NBA season. All three were named first-team All-NBA, Curry won the league's MVP award, and all three led their teams to the conference finals, with Curry and James meeting in the championship series. And yet, they are all capable of nights and stretches like those listed above, even when the games matter the most.

Yes, NBA superstars push as close to perfection as we're likely to see, but they are few and far between. There are 450 roster spots in the NBA each season, and the farther you get from the league's top echelon of talent (which includes maybe 10 percent of the players), the more it's up to the players—and their teams—to develop and utilize their strengths while diminishing and masking weaknesses as much as possible. There are no perfect basketball players, but there are plenty of *perfected* ones, who start with a basis of skill and physical ability and then are refined further and further in order to move closer and closer to their absolute potential.

The concept of players improving is as old as sport itself, but the current era of Big Data analytics the NBA finds itself in is transforming that process more quickly and aggressively than anything we have seen before. Players are learning more and more about themselves through video and data visualization, are seeing how things like diet and sleep can impact their performance, and are learning how having healthy joints and role-specific workout plans are lengthening and improving their careers. Teams are internalizing the same lessons, as well as figuring out how to better implement optimal on-court strategies, how to refine their different approaches to player procurement, and about the varying values and success rates of the different team-building components. It's an absolutely fascinating time to be a basketball fan, as we're in the early stages of where this all eventually will go, and the marriage of sports and technology brings two of our most popular and competitive worlds together in compelling fashion.

In the course of reporting and writing this book, I conducted over 125 interviews, watched nineteen of the NBA's thirty teams play live in eight different NBA arenas, worked as a color analyst on college games, watched elite high school events in multiple states, spent about a million hours watching NBA League Pass, repeatedly got lost in NBA.com's statistics sections, and dove headfirst into NBA Twitter in order to keep abreast of the latest smart writing going on.

Even with all of that preparation, the topic was a challenging one, both to report and to present. Basketball analysis and related technology keep evolving at a frantic pace, and as the NBA only has thirty franchises, with a very limited talent pool to draw from, any competitive advantages a franchise can establish are guarded ferociously. Many staffers are prohibited from talking about their team's personnel or anything to do with their internal analyses, and even if a person was allowed to broach the topic of analytics, most teams are so secretive and work in such silos that no one could really speak much about anyone else other than their own team. Third-party vendors are also very careful about identifying their clients, such is the level of secretiveness involved.

As such, the best way to attack the topic was to frame it within the 2014–15 NBA season and use detailed vignettes and case studies to attempt to explain what was happening. So, you will read about Gregg Popovich and the San Antonio Spurs—even though they (politely) refused to participate and wouldn't even guarantee me practice access in San Antonio. You will also read about the analytics-crazy Rockets and their general manager, Daryl Morey—even though he (through a team spokeswoman) declined to be interviewed. You will get much more inside perspective from other players, coaches, team management, service providers, and media that will piece together a comprehensive view of how analytics are shaping the basketball we watch, and how those who are behind in the technology race are already feeling the competitive hit.

It was impossible to get everyone, though, and perhaps the most perfect summation of the high level of protectiveness came from Dallas Mavericks owner Mark Cuban. Cuban typically is willing to converse with mostly anyone via e-mail or his Cyber Dust app, and he is an investor in at least two of the major analytics technologies now widely used in the NBA. Under Cuban, Dallas is widely considered to be a leading franchise in terms of both analytical focus and monetary investment, and Cuban himself has been quoted as saying the Mavericks have a huge number of data-related employees. It's not a secret that the Mavs are doing this, although what exactly they're doing is more of one.

His reply to an interview request: "Have to pass but I'll read it." Anything to get an edge.

CHAPTER 1

A Brief History of Modern Basketball Analytics

The similar revolution in baseball took a couple of decades, at least, and this took about half the time, in part because [baseball] helped pave the way.
—Kevin Pelton, NBA writer for ESPN Insider

Long before culling data from gigantic sets of inputs became a highly valued NBA front-office skill, and fans increasingly accepted various types of quantitative analysis as a growing necessity to better understand how the sport is played, an unknown economist may have spearheaded the first effort to use computers and statistics to project professional basketball performance.

Louis Guth was a senior vice president in the New York offices of National Economic Research Associates (NERA), an economics consulting firm, in the early 1980s. At the time, Guth was providing advisory services to the North American Soccer League in its antitrust lawsuit against the National Football League, one that alleged that the NFL's prohibition on cross-ownership (owning franchises in multiple sports leagues) was damaging the soccer league by denying it access to potential sports capital investment and operational expertise.

As part of his work for the lawsuit, Guth had to conduct economic analyses of the value of sports franchises. As detailed in a July 1980 *New York Times* article that Guth authored, he determined that sports franchises, especially those in major metropolitan areas with high levels of per capita income, such as New York City, were inherently undervalued based on how they were priced when they were bought and sold in that era.

Guth's analysis focused on the intrinsic, long-term values of franchises, which were based more heavily on factors like national TV revenues and the possible value of the home market at large, instead of ticket revenues and/or the current state of the franchise in terms of personnel. Those latter factors, Guth claimed (and was right about), were easily correctable with the hiring of better management and players, and had very little to do with the value of the franchise as an asset. Guth also smartly realized the unique position that sports franchises in that era had in terms of unpaid promotion through the major media entities in their respective cities.

"I said, 'Look, you guys are getting two to three pages of newspaper [every day].' Other businesses would kill for that," Guth recalled via phone from Florida, where he is now retired.

In the *Times* article, Guth used that era's New York Mets, who had just been purchased for what was an all-sports record price of $25 million by Nelson Doubleday and others, as a prime example. The Mets were terrible when they were purchased, but the club quickly developed a core of good players, traded for more, and eventually won the 1986 World Series. While that was happening, ticket sales for the team exploded, and the promise of the asset was realized.

When Guth was done with his work for the trial, the valuation analyses he had done made him think more specifically about how that type of work, aided by early-era computer technology, could be applied to sports themselves—and more specifically, to the monetary and performance value of players. While baseball already was in the early stages of its own statistical analysis revolution, driven by stats pioneer Bill James and the Society for American Baseball Research (SABR, which is the acronym that spawned the term *sabermetrics* for baseball analysis), Guth didn't see any comparable presence in professional basketball. That was in large part due to the inherent differences between the two sports. Baseball was a far more popular spectator sport than the NBA was during that era—one in which the NBA Finals were still shown late-night on tape delay—but more important was the nature of the sport and the history involved in its record keeping.

Baseball is a game of discrete, one-on-one, well-defined interactions between a hitter and a pitcher, and while current-era data analysis has expanded our understanding well beyond what was happening in 1980 (especially on the defensive side of the sport), it's still a much simpler sport to analyze than basketball, in which each play on the court involves ten players moving in dynamic, undefined, and unlimited patterns. It is quite easy to determine exactly how much offense a batter is able to produce or how effective a pitcher is in limiting opposing offenses. It is much more difficult to accurately assess the value of individuals in a sport of team-based actions.

That whole series of factors created a market opportunity that Guth was eager to step into.

"To my knowledge, there wasn't a heck of a lot of statistical analysis on basketball, and I migrated from other things I was doing because it looked like a wide-open field at the time," Guth said. "You had Bill James coming out with his baseball people and were looking at numbers a lot, and there was an early piece in the *American Economic Review* [about baseball]. But, to my knowledge, I'm not sure there were other things out there [about basketball]."

Guth set out to examine basketball through the lens of the economic principles that underscored his normal work. In his mind, a lot of the work at the time being done on baseball dealt with estimating the value of what he called the individual players' "marginal product," which, in economics parlance, is the output that results from one additional unit of a factor of production. Essentially, once you determined what a batter's capabilities were, it was reasonable to be able to project how he would do in a series of individual at-bats and to determine his composite product by adding up all of his estimated at-bats for a season. Additionally, while baseball games are constrained by outs, they are not constrained by a particular number of at-bats, or production "units," so to speak.

Because of its team-based, dynamic nature, basketball isn't nearly that linear and is much more complicated. The other four players on the court with a particular player directly impact his ability to produce, for better or worse. Also, because professional games are 48 minutes long, with five players on the court at any one time, you are constrained to 240 total minutes of production for a game. As a result, as Guth explains, "any time you add somebody, you can't say he brings all the talent he has. He also replaces somebody," which has to be accounted for in the analysis.

By 1982, Guth had created a database of all available NBA statistics from the league's most recent few seasons, and built a proprietary program first called FAMS (Free-Agent Market Simulator) and then FAME (Free-Agent [and Trades] Market Emulator) that crudely allowed him to determine a value for adding a new player to an existing team. It was groundbreaking stuff. As Guth noted with a chuckle during our phone conversation, his biggest mistake may have been in how he marketed his output.

"I should have called the stat 'wins against replacement,'" he said, paraphrasing a calculation that's now commonly used in sports in similar replacement analyses. "WAR is a fundamental Economics 1 concept, adapted to the reality of sports, which over the course of the season is pretty well set."

As detailed in an August 1982 *Sports Illustrated* article written by now-famed basketball writer Alexander Wolff, Guth became most well known for his analysis concerning Moses Malone, the league's reigning MVP and a future Hall of Fame center who at the time was a free agent after having completed his contract with the Houston Rockets. Thanks in part to collusive efforts of the NBA owners at the time, Malone was not receiving offers from franchises other than Houston, and Guth believed that to be a huge mistake on those other teams' parts.

Guth's economics roots shaped a system that focused on which teams should pursue a player like Malone based on the projected financial gain that player would give a new team, driven by improved performance on the court in relative terms. But when he focused more singularly on the projected on-court performance of the new player, exclusive of the monetary aspects, the story changed a bit in terms of where a specific player like Malone would make the most impact.

As detailed in a NERA company newsletter in 1984, much of Guth's system was based on proprietary formulas that tried to place values on teams' outputs at both ends of the floor. Offensive rebounds factored strongly into Guth's offensive formula, and in that era, there was one top-level team that seemed to have many of the ingredients of a world champion, but was relatively weak on the offensive glass: the Philadelphia 76ers.

Guth went and compared the 76ers to the two other premier teams in the league at that time: the Boston Celtics, who had won the 1981 NBA championship, and the Los Angeles Lakers, who had won the title over Philadelphia in both 1980 and 1982. Against both of those imposing foes, the 76ers had an offensive efficiency disadvantage, especially against the Lakers thanks to the dominant inside scoring of Hall of Fame center Kareem Abdul-Jabbar.

The easiest fix to that problem as Guth saw it, based on his formula, was for Philadelphia to improve its offensive rebounding.

During the 1981–82 season, the 76ers had only collected 1,031 offensive rebounds, which Guth calculated to be a 30 percent offensive rebound percentage. That was far below what the Celtics and Lakers were doing on that end, and something that could be fixed very quickly with the addition of a dominant offensive rebounder. It so happened that one was potentially available during the summer of 1982 in Moses Malone.

The free-agent rules at the time allowed a player's previous team to have right of first refusal on releasing a free agent that signed an offer sheet with another team. In a move that would make modern-day front-office personnel tip their caps in appreciation, the 76ers attempted to load their offer sheet for Malone with financial incentive clauses that were designed for the Rockets not to match, so Philadelphia could sign Malone without providing any compensation to Houston.

The case ultimately ended up in arbitration, where the 76ers were determined to have violated multiple league rules in the structure of their offer sheet, and the Rockets eventually matched the modified version. That then allowed the Rockets to trade Malone to the 76ers in exchange for forward Caldwell Jones and the 1983 first-round pick of the Cleveland Cavaliers, who were expected to be terrible and in contention for the No. 1 overall pick. (As it turns out, the Rockets collapsed without Malone, winning just fourteen games in 1982–83 and winning the coin flip for No. 1 themselves. They selected Ralph Sampson with that pick, and also got Rodney McCray at No. 3 with the pick obtained from the Cavaliers through the 76ers.)

Meanwhile, the 76ers had just acquired the big-time rebounder and defender they needed to add to a terrific core of Julius Erving, Andrew Toney, Bobby Jones, and Maurice Cheeks. From the outset, Philadelphia's new arrival, even though he was the reigning league MVP, seemed to understand his role.

"I know it's Doc's show," Malone told the *Philadelphia Inquirer* after the trade, referencing Julius "Dr. J" Erving's status as the team's main star, "and I'm happy to be part of Doc's show. . . . Doc'll still be the show, but maybe now it'll be a better show."

Indeed, it was. The expected uptick in offensive rebounding thanks to Malone's arrival helped close the projected offensive efficiency gap between the 76ers and Lakers in Guth's model, and bumped his regular-season forecast for the 76ers up to sixty-six wins. He was pretty much spot on. The 76ers ended up corralling 1,334 offensive rebounds (a top-50 total in NBA history), went 65–17, and rolled to their first world championship in sixteen seasons, going 12–1 in the playoffs and sweeping the Lakers in the Finals.

"The 76ers were not the one [Malone] would contribute the most to," Guth recalled when asked about the analysis, "but when he came to them, it led to the prediction that they would advance."

Had this happened maybe twenty years later, Guth would have received more recognition and interest in his work, but he said after the 76ers' projection panned out, he didn't hear from any NBA teams about his system. There just wasn't much interest at the time in computer analysis.

"It was almost a one-shot deal," Guth said. "We probably did it for a couple of years, then I got heavily involved in the baseball [antitrust] hearings, and also got involved with the PGA Tour."

Still, Guth thinks back to the days of the Hewlett-Packard mainframe and its findings, many of which turned out to be very prescient, even with the relatively limited amount of information at the time. Seeing what the industry has become today, with billion-dollar franchise values and entire submarkets built around Big Data analysis, he wonders what might have happened had he stuck with it and trusted his innate sense that all things in sports were undervalued in that era.

"If I applied my own analysis," Guth noted, "I should have built my own consulting firm."

The principal keeping of basketball statistics, basically since the beginning of the game, has centered around "counting" stats—the numbers observers can compile just by watching the game and adding. It's easy to track the number of points a team or player scores in a game, or their scoring averages, or how many shot attempts and makes there were. You can easily count rebounds for individual players, and sum them up for each team. You can track assists by whatever definition you create to identify one. Eventually, "steals" and "blocked shots" also became official categories. And all of those stats ended up being compiled into box scores that were printed in newspapers around the nation as a way to summarize what had happened in a game.

So-called advanced basketball statistics, in the way that we currently understand and continue to evolve them, date back at least as far as 1959, when then-North Carolina head coach Frank McGuire authored a book called *Defensive Basketball*. In it was a section written by then-assistant coach Dean Smith (who would go on to his own Hall of Fame career as the Tar Heels' head coach) that discussed how to evaluate the effectiveness of a team's offense and defense not by its raw totals of points scored or allowed, but by how many it tallied or conceded "per possession."

North Carolina set offensive and defensive scoring targets in that era on a per-possession basis, with Smith writing in the book that the Tar Heels wanted to keep teams below 0.63 points per possession while scoring more than that figure. Their methodology at the time considered an offensive rebound to create a new possession, and the book emphasized that defensive rebounding was crucial so the Tar Heels would end up with more possessions—read: more chances to score—than the opponent. Those "extra" possessions on both ends lowered the points-per-possession target below modern averages, as any possession that ended with an offensive rebound would be included as worth zero points. Today, in order to keep the number of possessions as equal as possible for both teams, offensive rebounds are considered part of the same offensive possession.

However North Carolina was defining possessions, Smith is widely cited as the first person to understand that the pace of a game had a significant role in determining just how good or bad a team was on either end of the floor, because composite statistics and averages don't take into account how many opportunities a team had during the course of a game. If two different teams each average eighty points a game, but one plays at a pace of seventy possessions per game and the other plays at ninety possessions per game, the team with the slower tempo has a much more effective offense (rounded to 1.13 points per possession) than the faster team (0.89 points per possession). The most lethal offensive teams (like the 2014–15 Golden State Warriors) play at high-possession tempos while registering great points-per-possession numbers, but most teams have a tradeoff on tempo versus efficiency once they speed up to a certain level.

The modern origins of basketball analysis, though, stem from baseball—more specifically from the work and impact of Bill James, widely considered to be the Godfather of advanced sports statistical analysis. Shortly after graduating from the University of Kansas in the early 1970s, James began positing about baseball in new and unusual ways. After finding resistance from traditional media outlets who didn't really understand or appreciate his work, James started self-publishing his now-famous annual *Baseball Abstract* in 1977 (and continued doing so until 1988). From there, James went on to publish a sizable number of additional books, and was hired by the Boston Red Sox as a consultant in late 2002. As of August 2015, he was still with the club in an advisory role.

James is responsible for a huge number of statistics that either have maintained their relevance or served as a launching point for additional study, and in the process, his baseball work spurred others to try to mimic significant parts of it for basketball. Among James's most famous concepts were runs created, which attempted to identify a specific player's responsibility for his team's run-scoring; Pythagorean winning percentage, which used run differential to establish what a team's record "should be" versus what it actually was; and win shares, which was a catch-all statistic designed to gauge a player's contribution to his team's success, allowing for cross-position and cross-era comparisons of players.

Right as James was coming to his decision to cease publication of his annual abstracts, a handful of basketball-related analysts started working on what became dubbed as APBRmetrics—honoring the Association for Professional Basketball Research—with many of the earliest practitioners working on offshoots of James's seminal stats that could apply to basketball. Here are some of the biggest names in the early advancement of basketball analytics, in approximate order of their time of prime impact:

- **Dave Heeren** is considered one of the forefathers of the basketball analytics movement. He created and further adapted TENDEX, which is credited with being the first linear-weight basketball metric. A linear-weight metric assigns positive values for good events and subtracts value for negative events to come up with a relative figure for player performance. It is fairly easy to calculate and understand even if it is not as nuanced or complete as a nonlinear calculation like wins over replacement value. Heeren once worked as a statistician for the New York Knicks but is better known for his annual basketball books called *Basketball Abstract* that were popular in the early 1990s.

- **Martin Manley** became prominent in the same time period that Heeren did, and published his own annual books called *Basketball Heaven*. The output of his player evaluation formula, which was nearly identical to Heeren's but also included the impact of turnovers committed by a player, was dubbed "Manley Credits," and became the basis for the NBA's own efficiency rating. Sadly, Manley, who also wrote for the *Kansas City Star*, may be most well known for how he died, committing a meticulously planned suicide outside an Overland Park, Kansas, police station on his sixtieth birthday in 2013, and leaving behind a detailed website that explained why he took his own life.

- **Bob Bellotti** was the inventor of the points-created metric, an offshoot of James's runs-created formulation for baseball, which attempted to define a player's contributions in a single calculation. He also wrote a series of books starting in the late 1980s, with a 1988 publication called *Basketball's Hidden Game* earning him initial entrance into the NBA with the Milwaukee Bucks. He consulted for Milwaukee for nineteen years before switching to the Washington Wizards when Bucks general manager Ernie Grunfeld moved to that franchise.

- **Bob Chaikin** created a computer analysis/simulation program called B-Ball, which used statistics to try to suss out player impact and successful lineup combinations. Beginning in 1992, Chaikin has worked as a statistical consultant, analyst, and/or scout at various times for the (then) New Jersey Nets, Miami Heat, and Portland Trail Blazers. Since 2008, he's been back with the Heat, where he also does college and NBA Development League statistical evaluations.

- **Jeff Sagarin** and **Wayne Winston** are former MIT undergraduate classmates who worked together to create WINVAL, which is credited as the first attempt at an adjusted plus-minus metric for players. Sagarin is best known for his college football (and other) rankings systems that get prominent play at *USA*

Today. Winston is a statistics professor at Indiana University who once taught Dallas Mavericks owner Mark Cuban in college. The Mavericks adopted the WINVAL metric shortly after Cuban bought the team in 2000, and Cuban credits the system for part of the Mavericks' subsequent success in that era.

- **Dean Oliver** is considered basketball's best proxy for Bill James. The Caltech-trained statistician was one of the forefathers of the APBR movement, first breaking new ground in his writing at his own site, the Journal of Basketball Studies, in the mid-1990s, and later as the author of the seminal basketball analytics book, *Basketball on Paper,* which he published in 2003. The book brought significant attention to what Oliver called the four factors of basketball success: effective field goal percentage, turnover percentage, offensive rebounding percentage, and free throw rate, as well as adjusting player and team analyses for possession-based game tempo, and assigning varying fractional credit for team wins and losses to individual players.

  Oliver also was a pioneer in bringing basketball analysis to the digital world, first as a leader on the Usenet group rec.sport.basketball in the text-heavy Internet era of the mid-1990s, and then on the APBR analysis group on Yahoo! groups in the early 2000s. Oliver posted the initial message in that forum, which saw a total of twenty-seven posts that February, and the first question he talked about exploring was whether "Hack-a-Shaq," the strategy to intentionally foul poor free throw shooters, actually worked. (Fourteen years later, this discussion became a frenzy during the Western Conference semifinal series between the Los Angeles Clippers and Houston Rockets, with both teams using the strategy so much that a rule change was discussed, but not enacted, in the summer of 2015.)

Oliver subsequently served front-office roles with the Seattle SuperSonics (where he was the first full-time NBA analytics hire), the Denver Nuggets and, after a stint as director of production analytics at ESPN, the Sacramento Kings.

- **John Hollinger** is another of the APBRmetricians who moved on to high-profile roles. After first founding a basketball writing site called AlleyOop.com in 1996, Hollinger spent three years working at *The Oregonian* newspaper in Portland, Oregon. In 2002, he was hired by SI.com and also started publishing *Pro Basketball Prospectus,* which later changed its name to *Pro Basketball Forecast.* In the mid-2000s, Hollinger started writing for ESPN.com, eventually moving all of his annual print publication work to ESPN's Insider premium online product.

  He is the creator of the player efficiency rating (PER) statistical metric that attempts to quantify everything a basketball player does in one composite number, and calibrates it against the rest of the league every season. It's considered to include an incomplete valuation of a player's defensive contributions, but remains one of the most widely known tools, thanks to Hollinger's writing platforms and subsequent success. In late 2012, Hollinger was hired by the Memphis Grizzlies to be their vice president of basketball operations.

- **Roland Beech** launched the impactful website 82Games.com during the 2002–03 NBA season, making advanced NBA stats easily available and consumable for the public. In 2009, Beech was hired by the Dallas Mavericks as their director of basketball analytics, with a pioneering role as part of the team's coaching staff, not the front office. Beech traveled with the team on the road, sat behind the bench during games, and liaised with cerebral and stats-friendly head coach Rick

Carlisle. Beech played a crucial role in the 2011 NBA Finals, where his lineup analysis allowed Carlisle and his staff to make crucial adjustments against the Miami Heat that helped the Mavericks win the title. In August 2015, Beech moved to the Sacramento Kings to lead their analytics department, replacing Oliver, who was pushed out in the aftermath of a team management shakeup.

As renowned as they were (and some still are), these men were not the only ones playing around with advanced basketball statistics in the early 2000s. Another prominent member of the APBR community during that formative era was Kevin Pelton, who as of August 2015 was an NBA writer for ESPN Insider. He also was the lead writer on ESPN.com's February 2015 ranking of all thirty NBA teams in terms of their analytics commitment and implementation.

Pelton traces his own statistical leanings back to his childhood reading of *Rick Barry's Pro Basketball Bible,* and has spent much of his writing career trying to make advanced statistics more accessible to mainstream readership. At one point he was a moderator of the APBR forum, he wrote for 82Games.com, and he worked as a consultant for the Indiana Pacers. He also created the WARP (wins above replacement player) quantitative model.

Before all of that, though, he was just trying to find some people like him who wanted to talk about basketball in new, mathematical ways.

"I went looking [around] and found Dean's stuff on the Internet—obviously, far and away the most advanced and most prominent work at that point—and then I think sometime around 2001, [I] stumbled into the APBR analysis discussion group," Pelton said of his initiation into the world of advanced basketball thinking. "At that point, [that] is where Dean was posting. Hollinger, I think, showed up at some point that year, in 2001–02, because that's when he started back writing about the NBA after he was at *The Oregonian*. Roland Beech was in the next couple of years, Justin Kubatko (founder of Basketball-Reference.com), people like that. That's sort of when the stuff started to take its modern shape around that point.

"That was the only place where you could have these kinds of discussions, with people who were on the same page, that had the same level of interest. Now that's pretty easy on Twitter to find that kind of community because there's enough people, but back then, it really was a small group. A lot of it was kinda trying to figure stuff out as you went. Around that time is when you had the first version of adjusted plus-minus from Wayne Winston and Jeff Sagarin. And what does this mean? Does this actually tell us something useful? There was no data or background at that point. We just had to use our intuition and discuss it amongst several of us and figure it out as we went."

Digging through the old posts on the Yahoo! ABPR group, it's striking how many concepts being discussed back in 2001 are topics that are still being explored today. Just in Oliver's posts alone, he broaches the concepts of individual player defensive value, defense effects on shooting percentages, why the Charlotte Hornets tended to play better without star forward Derrick Coleman, how to translate college statistics to the pros, and whether teams can actually win championships based on specific personnel strategies—in this case, a "twin towers" approach with two centers.

Today, thanks to modern technology and a couple of decades of thinking about these types of questions, we're moving closer to legitimate answers. In 2001, though, things really boiled down to a handful of really smart people bouncing numbers and ideas and theories off each other; given the much more limited data available at the time, there was no real way to test accuracy. In one of Oliver's posts, he wrote about tracking a specific game for defensive stats analysis purposes, and "hoping TNT doesn't cut away" from the game so he wouldn't lose any of his data.

So, whenever a new stat or approach came along, there was significant exploration—and disagreement—about its meaning, especially when it came to outlier cases.

"One of the memorable discussions that I've talked about in the past was the Timberwolves PR crew—the person who does their game notes was a friend of mine—they started including Kevin Garnett's net plus-minus in their game notes," Pelton said. "This was around his MVP season, and it was preposterous. It was like a plus-20 differential when he was on the court versus off the court. And people were like 'No, this is preposterous. There's no way one player can be that valuable,' so it was kind of difficult to wrap your mind around that at the time because there was no context for it. There was no history to compare it to. Obviously, there is now, and [it] quickly became [available] when Roland Beech started putting it on the 82games.com site. So that's sort of [an example] of breakthroughs and difficulties that these different concepts created.

"I think [discussions] could certainly be a bit contentious. There are a lot of opinionated people in this field. That certainly hasn't changed. A fundamental level of respect [existed, though]—especially for those who had contributed over an extended period of time and we'd seen the way their thought process worked."

While in today's professional sports, teams are more frequently hiring independent researchers and/or writers to help with their analytics evaluations, many of these formative discussions were happening prior to the Red Sox hiring James and well before Oliver was hired by the SuperSonics. The idea of moving these types of analyses into the mainstream and then getting hired to implement them for a sports franchise wasn't very reasonable at the time.

"I'm sure it was for some people, but it seemed too big of a goal," Pelton said of the sentiments of those participating. "The idea of getting people that understand the concept of true shooting percentage in there would be a big thing. And obviously, *Moneyball* kind of accelerated things and showed the possibilities in another sport, and that kind of raised the bar in a way.

"There was a discussion in the intro [of the first Basketball Prospectus we did for the 2009–10 season]—I wrote my own intro—and I think there were eight teams at that point who had someone working for them in the front office or as a consultant to the organization. Now it's probably twenty-eight or something like that, in a really short period of time."

Despite all of the brainpower working to unlock basketball's deepest secrets, implementation hasn't been the smoothest path. There are so many hurdles to overcome beyond whether someone can actually collect and analyze the data properly to come up with new, innovative solutions to a basketball problem. Many of those challenges involve communication across nonmath specialists and, at the end of the day, impacting an extremely dynamic sport played by human actors who are not capable of flawless implementation of strategy, even if the strategy itself somehow is flawless.

Still, Pelton thinks back to the formative days on the board, where everything was new and exciting and still really foreign in a lot of ways, and appreciates how far things have already come.

"It's kind of easy sometimes in the process to just see incremental changes and not notice them that much," he said, "and also see the setbacks and get discouraged by them, but when you actually take those opportunities and can step back and look at the bigger picture and the context of everything, it's really crazy how quickly this has happened.

"I mean, the similar revolution in baseball took a couple of decades, at least, and this took about half the time, in part because [baseball] helped pave the way."

An October 2005 article in *Sports Illustrated* by Chris Ballard helped announce the arrival of what we now accept as the modern analytics-enhanced basketball world, and the piece doubles as a genealogy of many of today's top NBA coaching and management thinkers.

Beyond discussing some of Oliver's work with Seattle, the article mentions twenty-nine-year-old Sam Presti, who was an assistant general manager with the San Antonio Spurs at the time and now is the general manager with the Oklahoma City Thunder. He's widely cited as one of the sharpest front office people in the league, has an extremely strong draft track record, and also was at the center of perhaps the most impactful trade decision of this decade. It also introduces twenty-seven-year-old Sam Hinkie, who then was a special assistant to Houston Rockets owner Carroll Alexander, and now is the general manager of the Philadelphia 76ers, where he has been the chief protagonist in one of professional sports' most debated team-rebuild strategies.

Additionally, it mentions San Antonio Spurs head coach Gregg Popovich. Popovich, of course, is in the discussion as the greatest head coach in NBA history, having won five NBA championships in San Antonio while churning out annual fifty- and sixty-win seasons. He's also responsible for the NBA's newfound appreciation of resting players and more balanced minute distributions across his roster, and is the figurehead for what is the most secretive analytics-friendly franchise in the league.

It also goes into some depth about thirty-one-year-old Boston Celtics senior vice president of operations Daryl Morey, who has since become the public face of NBA analytics. He helped found the wildly popular and influential Sloan Sports Analytics Conference (Morey has an MBA from MIT's Sloan School of Management) while implementing increasingly sophisticated playing and personnel strategies as the general manager of the Houston Rockets.

In the subsequent decade or so since that article ran, the entire landscape has continued to evolve and morph into what we see today (with much of it continuing to be proprietary and unseen by the public). There's way more money involved in the NBA today than even ten years ago, and teams have to work harder and harder to find and maintain competitive edges. How they're doing so varies wildly from team to team, and heavily involves state-of-the-art technology to try to move ever closer to solving an impossibly complex and nuanced sport.

CHAPTER 2

The Basketball Technology Revolution

The power of having good algorithms is that it's like you have a million pairs of eyes watching every single game. . . . It's as if you have someone who has watched every single second of your opponent's game and you can get very complete scouting, or every single second of a particular player that you're trying to scout.

—Rajiv Maheswaran, CEO and cofounder, Second Spectrum

O ne of the major epicenters of basketball's ongoing technology movement spent some of its formative months in 2014 about a mile or so from Staples Center, in a hybrid work/ live high rise on Los Angeles's tony Wilshire Boulevard. While the building's marble-adorned lobby with the make-your-own-espresso machine, as well as the rooftop pool and Jacuzzi, suggested hints of decadence, the crowded second-floor office of Second Spectrum didn't match that anticipated standard.

The hall the office was located on was more traditionally apartment building-esque, with rows of closed doors on either side, and the sounds of hip hop pulsating from a room a few doors down. Inside, the one-room headquarters already was straining to handle the company's growth. It was shaped like a flat-bottomed *U*, with a reception desk (*sans* receptionist on this occasion) somewhat awkwardly lodged near the doorway in front of the right prong. Rows of minimalist desks lined the walls on both sides of that prong. In the back right corner was tucked Rajiv Maheswaran, the company's CEO and cofounder, who with his team is starting to fundamentally change the way many think about professional basketball, from teams and players to fans watching the games.

Maheswaran and Yu-Han Chang were both computer science faculty at University of Southern California when they brainstormed an idea to track NBA player data, which turned into a research paper submission for the 2012 Sloan Sports Analytics Conference. The paper, which used player- and shot-tracking data along with machine-learning techniques, redefined what was then known about rebounding. It broke down the process of collecting missed shots into functions of initial on-court positioning, the hustle to pursue the ball once it came off the rim, and the conversion of opportunities to secure a rebound. The work won the conference's best paper honors, and helped earn the duo the attention of some NBA teams. They and a third colleague, Jeff Su, formally launched Second Spectrum in 2013.

Feeding off the NBA's new initiative with SportVU motion capture cameras that capture every movement on the court, Second Spectrum set out to interpret mountains of raw data, then layer video and/or graphics over it to serve a variety of constituents. By August 2015, the company, which has a staff literally composed of rocket scientists, was employed by nine of the NBA's thirty teams, and was starting to marry data, technology, and presentation in landmark and visually unique ways.

Teams were using them as a third-party provider to help enhance on-court strategy, and Second Spectrum also was translating in-game plays into statistic-heavy motion-enhanced graphics, so fans attending games could see things like the projected point values of the various pass and shot options as the ball moved around to different players and spots on the court. In-arena work started with the hometown Los Angeles Clippers, and the company also has had its graphics product (called DataFX) used on ESPN's *SportsCenter,* NBA TV, Fox Sports, and other national outlets.

But while his products focus extensively on ultra-micro analysis, the high-energy Maheswaran takes a very practical, high-level view of what makes his company's work so potentially valuable.

"When computers understand anything, good things happen for everyone in that ecosystem," he said while seated at an oversized conference table wedged into limited space in the left prong of the office. "A good example is when computers understood music, you got things like Pandora and Shazam, right? And so the equivalent is when computers understand sports, lots of good things happen. One of the fundamental premises for the technologies that we're trying to develop is the ability for a computer to understand sports."

But, Maheswaran notes, technical sophistication in the handling and processing of data is not enough to make for a good consumer product, even when you're targeting a highly specialized internal audience of NBA teams and their coaching staffs. As good as the information may be, you have to be able to serve it in a way that will make sense to the end users, and won't force them outside of the way they currently process information.

"So what we try to do is put numbers to words that people already use," he said. "People already know that a shot is either a good shot or a bad shot, and we have mathematical models that actually quantify the shot—or the shot quality and the shooting ability. We also break down rebounding as not one thing; it's three things. It's positioning, attack, and hustle. So, words that coaches already use. But the biggest thing that we do is we use pattern recognition to identify things that happen in a game. So a pick and roll, and reject a screen, and a blitz, an ICE, all these things."

The biggest hurdle for any external service like Second Spectrum is the potential for distrust of its findings. As longtime NBA coach

Stan Van Gundy (who took over both the head coaching and person-nel functions for the Detroit Pistons in 2014) famously railed on at the 2014 Sloan Sports Analytics Conference, many basketball lifers are reluctant to believe what a computer tells them. Van Gundy's own hesitation was centered around his perception of the integrity of data input, specifically the qualifications of the people who were assigned to tag plays that fuel the systems of earlier market entrants like Synergy Sports Technology (more on them in a little bit, too).

As Van Gundy argued, there is potential for error when manually identifying and tagging data, especially if the operator is not really sophisticated in understanding the NBA game. Not everything is a straight pick and roll or an isolation or a catch-and-shoot jump shot. There are offensive actions that lead to other actions, which makes it somewhat inaccurate to label them as one specific thing. There are also many defensive tactics that aren't cut and dry at all, especially when you don't know the specific context of what the team was ask-ing its players to do. Without knowing more specifics, it can be diffi-cult to identify where a defensive mistake occurred, or why.

For coaches to get value from data, they have to have this kind of exactness. Otherwise, it doesn't fully conform to their own qualita-tive ideology on both ends of the court, and can create dissonance when a data report presents information that may counter the coach's intuition. The ramp-up of this kind of basketball understanding and precision as Maheswaran's team developed their algorithms was the most crucial piece to building Second Spectrum from an academic idea into a successful commercial business.

"You can do tests against humans and say, 'Here's what our com-puter said, and here's what a bunch of people said. [What] your stats said.' And you can go against their staff, and maybe it's not as good as their staff, but if it's close, very very close, then you save them a lot of time," Maheswaran said.

"The hard part about it is this concept of accuracy, both in terms of precision—if I say it's a pick and roll, is it really a pick and roll?—and recall—how many of them do I actually catch? So there's a balance. Because I could say, 'Every single second of the game is a pick and roll,' and I've gotten all of them, but my accuracy isn't very good, or I could find the one pick and roll I'm *sure* is a pick and roll and say, 'that's a pick and roll,' and my precision is perfect, but I missed a bunch. So how do you get high [marks] in both those areas?

"It turns out [for] a variety of people, it's pretty easy to get 80–80. We had an undergrad who was able to get 80 percent precision and 80 percent recall in like three, four days. . . . The question is would that be OK for people who have large numbers [of data points]? And, there's also bias. [If] you're getting the 80 easiest ones, so you're missing all the rejections and the slips [of screens], well, that's a big deal. So the thing that we have brought to the table is the fact that we understand [these distinctions]. Our algorithms tend to be in the high 90s for [both] precision and recall. So we're missing very, very few things. We're basically better than most human beings, if you look at a collection of analysts. We can watch to an almost-human level."

The result is Second Spectrum's platform can parse anything from any number of games, and display the information in both digital and video form. The power of their output is staggering.

To give me an example, Maheswaran turned and started fidgeting with a laptop that was feeding a picture onto a large wall-mounted projection screen near the conference table. He tapped into the company's Eagle system and queued up every pick and roll Clippers point guard Chris Paul had run so far in the 2014–15 season, and requested to see the plays unfold on video from three seconds before the actual screen was set (so we could see how Paul sets up the screens) through one second after the pick (to see what his initial decision would be).

These four-second plays looped continuously, one after another on the screen, and in a matter of a few minutes, we had visually consumed Chris Paul's entire pick-and-roll repertoire from the current season. Work that would have taken a team's video coordinator hours to compile a decade ago, now is available in seconds with a few mouse clicks. Maheswaran said that his system can even assuage the fears of the Van Gundys of the world, because it also can log actions that aren't the final action of a play. It can essentially track anything you enable it to learn.

"The power of having good algorithms is that it's like you have a million pairs of eyes watching every single game," he said. "You can scale. Whenever [you] want to know about the game, it's as if you have someone who has watched every single second of your opponent's game and you can get very complete scouting, or every single second of a particular player that you're trying to scout.

"It's not that you go back and watch the last three, five games and have a video staff chop it up. You can basically get information about every single moment of the game. Every single pick that led to a post up, that led to a layup. The things that happened—maybe a pick and roll that was stopped, that's something that you might want information about. Or a pick and roll that was defended well [and] that might've led to something else, that led to an iso, that led to a score, and somebody might report, 'Well, there was an iso,' but you don't talk about all the other things that we stuffed."

So far, Maheswaran's bet on his and his colleagues' technological chops—specifically the discipline of spatiotemporal pattern recognition, which he oversimplifies as the science of "moving dots"—is paying significant dividends. With around 30 percent of the NBA as clients, Second Spectrum started adapting its technology for other sports, including professional football and soccer. The group also found a new home quickly after the aforementioned visit, shedding the U-shaped office for much bigger space near City Hall, a couple of miles northeast of Staples Center.

While the technology is complicated, Maheswaran and his team have simplified the output to make for an elegant end-user experience. The use of language that basketball people actually use provides staffs with subject comfort as they seek out information that they think will help them make decisions. Knowing that coaches and their staffs often are less receptive when data is pushed onto them, Second Spectrum's technology promotes the pulling of only the data that they're interested in.

"We have not tried to necessarily generate a whole new class of things," Maheswaran said. "We go to the coaches and say, 'What is it that you would want to know that you cannot know right now? Or what is it that you want to do that you cannot do right now?' And we use the fact that a computer understands to get that to them. We don't come up and say, 'We've got seven new magic metrics that tell you what you should do,' because coaches really, I think, if given the information, know their teams well, know their constraints well, and will figure out what the right thing is to do.

"The question is: Do you have all the information you need, when you're making your decision? And one of our things is the most informed make the best decisions, and there is a bottleneck in terms of how well informed you can be based on the technology and the manpower you have. And what we do is just give you basically one hundred times the power of having way more information, or one thousand times the power. I'm not sure quite how to measure this. The other thing we can do is because we have a computer that understands the data, we've also done some algorithms that allow the computers to understand the video.

"So here, now, coaches have the initiative to look at numbers," he added, "[and since] we've used the power of the fact that the computer understands both the video and the data, you could essentially ask a question and get the answer both in numbers and in video, instantaneously. So that is a very, very powerful thing."

⌒

Second Spectrum (and similarly oriented analysis businesses, such as MOCAP, a Silicon Valley company that works with the Golden State Warriors) is a next-generation development of the NBA's original data and video compilation technology provider, Synergy Sports

Technology. That company was founded by former college and NBA assistant coach Garrick Barr back in 2005, and the origins of his service, which continues to thrive and is used by all thirty NBA teams and virtually every Division I men's and women's basketball program, come from very serendipitous roots.

As Barr explains it, back when he was a Phoenix Suns assistant coach in 1992, he had walked into a store to buy some music equipment. Inside the store, Barr noticed that the retailer also sold audio/video equipment, and his interest was piqued by a low-end, first-generation AVID nonlinear digital video editing machine. Tape cutting at the time was very laborious, and the state-of-the-art equipment was extremely large and impossible to bring on the road, so teams weren't able to replicate the film work they did at their own facilities when they were on road trips. If anything was put together, it would come from the home office and be sent out via FedEx or a similar carrier.

Beyond a reduction in size and the ability to potentially travel with the new equipment, Barr also understood the advantages of being able to streamline the tape-cutting process, potentially allowing the Suns to splice tape during games for use in halftime meetings and in-game strategy adjustments. He asked the store owner if he thought the AVID editor could be built into a protective travel case. It could, and it was, and Barr suddenly had provided the Suns with a very significant advantage while starting to push pro basketball out of the deck-to-deck tape era (with AVID forming its own business called AVID Sports Pro to leverage the idea). Barr also says that the Suns at that time built the first comprehensive team-scouting database, which was phone-synced so everyone was able to see the same data and could review each other's reports.

These developments helped steer Barr away from a potential coaching career and toward a career creating technology designed to help coaches. In 1998, Barr partnered with another college basketball coach, Scott Mossman, to create Quantified Scouting Service, which produced computer-generated data reports based off of the company's screening of game videos. This was still much too early for video streaming that could layer clips on top of numerical data being generated. Instead, Mossman and his wife used VCRs and a satellite dish to capture as many games as they could, and then farmed the tapes out to "loggers," who tagged every play for their system. Barr's clients then were able to use dial-up modems to access the reports.

A few years later, with video streaming at a level where it was reasonable to create a platform that paired video with the plays the loggers were tagging, Barr partnered with engineer Nils Lahr and rechristened the company as Synergy Sports Technology. By 2008, they had a licensing agreement in place with the NBA to provide their data to the league's television and digital arms. Today, Synergy is a market-dominating, cross-sport technology phenomenon.

"The benefit of Synergy was that you were no longer tied to a local piece of equipment where you do all the work," Barr said. "Instead, [now] it's cloud-based and we do all the work. We do 80 percent of the tagging. You can still tag things and those can be associated and cross-pollinated with our data in custom reports. Now they can pull up any game that we've tagged. They can go through and tag all the play calls: fist, two out, fist down. It's like baseball. Every team has a different set, so we can't resolve that. We can't figure out thirty different teams' playbooks and the calls that they have. The plays tend to be the same, but they call it different things.

"So if the team will take fifteen to twenty minutes and tag a team's play calls, the result is staggering. They end up with a report that shows the breakdown of what happens each time they run those plays, what play types are run as a result [of the set]: pick and roll, post up, iso, whatever. You can see where your stars are getting points or not. You may be running something that you think is designed to help your star get off, to get him a touch when you really need it, but it might turn out that he doesn't get that and you don't even know that. You can see which plays result in offensive rebounds or threes.

You can see the proportions on everything, the points per possession on everything.

"You're essentially taking three data sets and combining them to produce that report. There's the stuff that we logged, the stuff that they logged, and the stuff the scorer's table logged, so you got points, assists, and rebounds and all that stuff; you have shot locations—in college, based upon us tagging it; in the pros, they do it, so we just use their locations. And then you have all the play-type information we log, as well as the defensive side of the ball—who was guarding the play and what happened. Who the players are, what the play type was, where on the floor were they, what direction did they go, what was the move that was used. And then what was the ultimate result, and that's all tied to the scorer's table data—the stats feed—so we know who had the assist, whether it was a three or a two. We don't have to tag all of that since it's integrated data feeds.

"The result is you have a report that tells you what your team or the opposing team does, what proportion, how good they are, what they get out of it, how they set up, etc. And any way you want to, you can click on a matching data point and get the related video."

Barr said he is aware of what companies like Second Spectrum are doing—in fact, Dallas Mavericks owner Mark Cuban, an investor in Synergy, brought the two parties together for a bit for potential collaboration—and, really, Synergy is providing similar types of data, similar access to video clips, and similar ease of use/accessibility for the end user. Barr makes sure his loggers also use "coachspeak," so coaches are comfortable with the terminology returned in the queries.

While neither CEO specified his exact price points, conversations with teams that utilize their products confirm that Synergy is more affordable than Second Spectrum's solution, which certainly has some appeal. There also are differences in the outputs. Synergy's output, while really robust and increasingly aided by data visualization, doesn't have Second Spectrum's same granularity, as plays on Synergy are tagged according to the final action that leads to a shot, foul, or turnover, rather than breaking down the possession into multiple elements. Also, while you are able to pull up sequences of video like the Chris Paul example earlier, each clip is of the entire possession. If you want to carve out more specific time periods within a possession, you would need to go into Synergy's nice video-editing capabilities to do that.

The quality of any output, though, is dictated by the quality of the data being used to generate it, and as such, the principal discussion in comparing the products of machine learning versus human loggers centers around the concept of "what is good enough?" While there are a few NBA teams that have brought most things in-house and hired a slew of programmers and data scientists to extract value from all of the different data being collected, most NBA teams don't require—or want, for now—that level of rigorousness. A comprehensive outsourced solution with an acceptable standard of quality is a perfectly fine solution for them. They get much of the benefit without a lot of the operational headaches of hiring up and maintaining a database that still requires integration across other platforms to match the capabilities of top third-party providers.

Barr believes his loggers' accuracy is more than good enough. He touts the company's rigorous standards for quality assurance, where data tags go through a series of second checks and global spot-checking for accuracy, and also he knows that if his work wasn't accurate enough, he would hear about it directly from the thousands of coaches he works with. That said, Barr also understands the benefits of better technology, so he's interested in the ongoing tech-driven processes that are converting SportVU motion data into valuable output. (As of August 2015, Synergy had not yet incorporated SportVU into its overall product.)

"One of the first things Lars asked me [when they started this] was 'Can this be automated?' And that would be great. That's the Holy Grail. I get it," Barr said. "Ultimately, human beings are fallible, and if you can perfect machine recognition, maybe you can eliminate the fallibility, although I think our error margin is completely acceptable by all coaches at this point, and pretty much all along.

"Like zone recognition: I will concede we were terrible at that for a while, but we made it a much bigger emphasis and we're doing much better on it now. It's still a tough one, but we're doing it.

"With respect to the computer, the machine-type recognition, maybe it will give you better accuracy, and I suppose that's inevitable given the way technology marches forward. I'll concede that. And when that happens, I'll be the first one standing in line and using that technology instead of the people, because of the second benefit: it's cheaper."

That's not to say that Synergy is shying away from technological innovation. During our conversation, Barr noted that Synergy was on the brink of introducing a more integrated product where NBA teams will be able to operate their own databases behind Synergy's firewall. That will allow the teams to seamlessly integrate their work with Synergy's data, along with Synergy's video editing and other capabilities, instead of the team having to implement that kind of integration on their end. As part of that push, Synergy will start enabling SportVU data intake within their own products. Barr believes a total turnkey solution on that level will be really appealing to almost every one of Synergy's existing customers.

"A lot of NBA teams don't want to build a database and hire programmers and do all of that themselves," he said. "It's very expensive and, ultimately, is inefficient. If you spend enough money on it, you get what Daryl [Morey in Houston] has. You get what Boston has. You get what Dallas has. There are some teams that are doing extraordinary things there. But I will bet that over 90 percent of the teams will end up operating their database, with their own proprietary tagging and services they buy into and import data, they're all going to do it within Synergy within the next five years. Probably quicker than that once we have it, because the price point is going to be so much sweeter. You don't need programmers to query the data. We allow methods where you can use an expression editor in order to create the queries without having any particular expertise. I think it's going to be a game-changer.

"We are not logging everything we could log [currently]," Barr added. "We're going to identify several new things to make our data set more robust, but clearly there's more stuff that can be identified. There is automated tracking like SportVU, which we are not currently working with in our system. So, yeah, if you have unlimited resources, and I think Daryl is the poster child for this, then you are going to be able to extract an nth degree of data, significant data and value into your applications and your ability ultimately to win games via the draft or scouting or trades or even your coach's development. All of that stuff. But I do agree that in the vast majority of cases, teams find what we offer to be enough."

⤸

While Synergy was nailing down an alliance with the NBA in 2008, that also was the year STATS, LLC, began investigating the merits of SportVU, a company that was repurposing Israeli missile-tracking technology for sporting applications. STATS ultimately decided to acquire SportVU, which had adapted a system originally created by military defense electronics manufacturer Elbit Technologies, and was, in 2008, using it to track the movements of soccer players.

The technology, which was created to analyze the actual paths of launched missiles against their anticipated trajectories, evolved to where cameras were hung above playing services to track the movements of players and the ball in three dimensions, and record all of that data in real time. When Brian Kopp, now the North American president of Catapult Sports, an Australia-based maker of wearable sports technology, arrived at STATS that year to work as a strategist, he was handed the task of figuring out how to translate this new soccer technology for other sports.

"So we looked at American football, [and worked with] the NFL for a while, and early on a couple of basketball teams [came down]— Houston and the guys at San Antonio and a couple others," Kopp said. "They reached out to me and took my calls because they were scouring what was going on in other sports, and they saw these camera technologies used in soccer, and they allowed me to put some cameras in the arena and start to go about building this technology.

"What's interesting about it is the technology didn't exist for basketball. We had to build it, but it's not like we had a basketball arena. So we had to go to the teams and say, 'Can I please put some cameras in, so that I can build this thing?' So when I first started [landing teams as clients], they didn't have anything [in place to use it]. It was just an idea. Their edge was to be the first ones to understand it, to be the first ones to get access to it, and then hopefully drive it forward . . . they knew that eventually the power would be getting it in every arena, but they were hoping that [they'd] have a first-mover advantage, and so we worked with a couple of teams.

"Our focus was the technology side, but early on I knew we had to build out the rest of the analytics off the back of it. It wasn't just going to be, 'OK, here's a bunch of X, Y coordinates, and I'm just going to dump it on your desk, and [say] 'go nuts . . . ' [although] that's all [then Houston Rockets vice president] Sam Hinkie wanted . . . and teams like the Mavericks didn't want me to work with anyone else.

"I remember clearly having a conversation with Mark Cuban, and he said, 'Well, I don't want you to get too many more teams.' And I said, 'Well, if it's OK with you, I'm going to try and get them all.' For them, they were, 'Wow, we don't want it to grow too big,' but to me, the advantage is never going to be an access to the data. It should be in what you do with it."

Kopp said that a lot of those early moments for SportVU were spent defining the basics of what was actually available from the data and what kinds of reports they could generate. Kopp believes that the creation of this more manageable information, combined with STATS management not supporting the development of more sophisticated data services off of its own data, is what led to the formation of companies like Second Spectrum and today's whole industry of third-party data solution providers. Instead of expanding STATS' own business, Kopp had to actively seek out external partners in order to get STATS' data, in manageable formats, into the hands of potential customers.

"To be very blunt with you . . . it's part of the reason I'm not at STATS [anymore]. They didn't support it from the beginning, so I had to go partner with other people," Kopp said. "They didn't allow me to build out my own Second Spectrum for a while, so I had to partner with people like that to broaden the aperture and exposure of the data. So I had to work with Kirk Goldsberry (a Harvard lecturer who also contributed to ESPN's *Grantland*) to give him data and get it out there and have it exposed to people.

"Ideally, you do that all in-house, you keep it all yourself. But I also knew that anybody who wanted to have access to this data would have to work through us. So, in a weird way, Second Spectrum, we gave them free data, they decide to—I like those guys, they're really smart, [but] I really don't like how they built their business, personally. Because they took data that I gave them for free, and they decided to run a business and I said, 'OK, we can work out some [deal] to get access to it,' and they decided, 'No, we don't need you anymore.'

"Certainly, it could've been handled in different ways, both by STATS and by some of those potential partners," Kopp added. "I could have kept it hidden in a vacuum, and people at Second Spectrum would argue, 'Well, you wouldn't have gotten certain clients without exposure to our data,' and I'm like, 'Nah, I'm pretty sure we would've gotten them anyway.'"

(Asked to respond to this, Second Spectrum's Maheswaran declined comment.)

Early in the SportVU buildout, Kopp tried to sell the product directly to the NBA, but the league wasn't interested at that point in widespread implementation. Instead, Kopp built an individual team client base from the couple of early adopters into fifteen of the league's thirty teams. At that point, the NBA decided to license the product at the league level, putting cameras in all twenty-nine NBA arenas (the Los Angeles Lakers and Clippers share Staples Center) and distributing the data to all of its franchises. The league, per an article by David Aldridge on NBA.com, actually started testing SportVU during the 2009 NBA Finals. In that series, the league used the technology to slow-motion check a crucial goaltending call, and it turned out that the referees had gotten the call correct. That sparked the realization at the league level of how powerful the technology could be.

The NBA's decision to install the cameras in every arena has pushed the league headfirst into the Big Data era, and much like it has with Synergy's products, the NBA has now incorporated a ton of SportVU's data into NBA.com, so fans (and media) can access it. The data portion of the league's website is remarkably robust, with users able to check traditional statistics as well as a litany of advanced analytics options, plus huge video libraries, dynamic player-tracking graphics, and much more. While what's accessible on NBA.com is just a fraction of the output generated, there really isn't very much even the hardest of hard core fans are missing if they know how to navigate the site and the myriad SAP-powered search options for each category.

Want to know the Bulls' best and worst player combinations? How about which two Cavaliers paired the best with LeBron? You can find how the Grizzlies did when Marc Gasol was on and off the court. You can slice up Steph Curry's 3-point shooting by court area. You can learn that Kobe Bryant shot just 32.9 percent on jump shots in 2014–15, and that DeAndre Jordan led the league in defensive rebound conversion rate. You can literally spend hours at a time combing through the various categories. The league also has a writer, John

Schuhmann, specifically dedicated to crafting analytics-based stories for the site, to add even more refinement.

Video availability is the gem of the revamped NBA.com site, though, especially with the disappearance of Synergy's independent, public-facing product called MySynergySports. (In August 2015, Barr hinted that it may return in a different form down the road.) Now, on NBA.com, with the help of Synergy, you can pull up all sorts of clips to complement the stats you're examining. For example, if you want to view, in sequence, all 202 baskets Curry made from five feet or closer to the rim in the 2014–15 season, you just need to click on the video option link for that particular stat, and they're cued up for you. Overall, the site is an incredible trove of numerical and visual information that brings users as deep as they want to go into the sport, and this reflects the pro-technology reign of newish league commissioner Adam Silver.

So, if fans now have this kind of access, just imagine what NBA teams *actually* have, and the many different ways they are using it in order to create and sustain competitive advantages.

CHAPTER 3

Analytics Believers and Doubters

Teams are trending towards taking less mid-range shots, and that appears to be a sound strategy. So, these teams' efficiency attacking the rim and knocking down perimeter shots should be a good indicator of the teams' success (at least on offense). If restricted area and 3-point shots are the most efficient looks on offense, and teams are trending towards taking more of these shots, then a team's ability to defend these areas must also increase in importance.

—**Dr. Stephen Shea, mathematician and coauthor of *Basketball Analytics:***
Objective and Efficient Strategies for Understanding How Teams Win

With every NBA team having equal access to the raw SportVU data and subscribing to some level of Synergy's service as well, it appears that Catapult's Brian Kopp was right: teams derive their advantages from what they can find in the data and how creatively they can implement ideas on and off the court. How they're doing it, though, varies very widely from team to team, and a lot depends on the amount of money invested and proprietary work being done at the franchise.

In Kevin Pelton's February 2015 NBA analytics rankings, he labeled twelve of the league's thirty teams as being either "believers" or "all-in" on analytics (which foots fairly closely to what research for this book determined independently). The four teams described as "all-in" were the Philadelphia 76ers, Houston Rockets, San Antonio Spurs, and Dallas Mavericks, all of whom also made the overall top ten in ESPN's 122-team combined ranking of NBA, NFL, MLB, and NHL teams. Those four NBA teams also double as perhaps the league's most secretive.

The difficulty in establishing long-term strategic advantages, though, stems from the simple fact that, eventually, you have to show people what you're doing (except in the areas of player health and wellness, which is why according to a growing number of NBA personnel, developments in that area ultimately will dwarf the current evolution of on-court strategy). Whether it's in player acquisition, draft philosophy, or on-court strategy, there's going to be a video and paper trail that everyone else in the league can dissect, and they can eventually figure out some part of your plan.

That ability to dissect applies to writers, as well, so below are breakdowns of some unique ways in which three of those four all-in teams are thinking differently about conventional NBA strategies.

The Spurs and (the One-Season Fall of) Strategic Roster Management

The cramped interview area tucked just outside the visitor's locker room at Denver's Pepsi Center felt like the perfect setting for legendarily gruff San Antonio Spurs head coach Gregg Popovich to discuss his team's highly compressed early-season schedule. It was mid-December, just six weeks into the 2014–15 season, but Popovich and the Spurs—who for years had been well ahead of the rest of the NBA in terms of managing their roster to endure the strains of an eighty-two-game regular season while still winning enough to position themselves for postseason success—seemed to be meeting their match in terms of balancing performance and player workloads.

The Spurs entered this particular tilt with the homestanding Nuggets with a perfectly reasonable record of 16–7, which projected to around fifty-seven wins, which was a typically normal Spurs haul in the Popovich era. Popovich's concern, though, was that the schedule, along with a spate of injuries, was already taxing his team—especially his aging core of Tim Duncan, Manu Ginobili, and Tony Parker—to a degree that was much worse than in previous seasons. November already had seen the Spurs play eleven games over an eighteen-day stretch, and this meeting with the Nuggets was in the midst of an absolutely punishing December run that, if you included a game on November 30 at Boston, featured nineteen games in thirty-two days, including seven sets of back-to-back contests. To make matters worse, none of those back-to-backs even featured two consecutive home games.

"The whole month is just ridiculous. We just have to deal with it," Popovich said, plainly.

While coaches often can trend toward both hyperbole and recency effect, there was ample reason to believe Popovich when he said that December was the worst schedule month he had ever seen in his two decades with the franchise. In addition to the sheer number of games, the travel, and the quick turnarounds, a rash of injuries had left him much shorter on personnel than the ordinarily deep Spurs liked to find themselves. Parker, the starting point guard, was struggling with a hamstring problem that had cost him some games, and he wouldn't play on this night. His primary backup, Patty Mills, still hadn't at this point returned from summer rotator cuff surgery, so the point guard role was nominally in the hands of the inexperienced Cory Joseph, with some help from Ginobili and other perimeter players.

The Spurs also had seen small forward Kawhi Leonard suffer a hand injury that cost him two games ahead of this particular contest (in which he played), and then soon after saw him miss fifteen more. San Antonio also had been without center Tiago Splitter for all but ten minutes of the season prior to his return on December 8, and on this night, he still hadn't completely been integrated back into the rotation as he got his fitness levels back to normal playing standard.

All of this meant Duncan, in particular, was finding himself playing more minutes than usual. Entering this particular game, Duncan had played at least thirty-six minutes in four of his last five appearances after not even averaging thirty minutes a game during the 2013–14 season. Two nights before, Duncan played a then season-high forty minutes against the Los Angeles Lakers; later in the week, he would play forty-eight and forty-three minutes, respectively, in triple-overtime losses to Memphis and Portland. Popovich ultimately found a way to rest Duncan for four separate games in December, but the thirty-eight-year-old still played in fourteen contests and averaged 34.5 minutes a game for the month. It was hardly ideal.

"It's a little tougher on us this year, you know?" Popovich said, expounding on the impact of the schedule and the personnel issues. "Patty Mills is such a big part of what we do, coming off the bench if Tony didn't play, because he scores. And Tiago's just coming back into the feel of the game. He hadn't played in, well, I don't know how long now. So we're doing OK. We're much better off with Tiago and Patty Mills [though] if we sit people."

Sitting players in strategic fashion has been a major part of how Popovich has extended the contention window for this Spurs team as its core ages. The team even made some light of the strategy late in the 2011–12 season, which was a compressed sixty-six-game schedule after extended negotiations over a new collective bargaining agreement cost the league part of the campaign. Box scores list the reason players who didn't enter a game received a "DNP" (did not play) in that particular contest, and against the 76ers on March 25, 2012, the Spurs listed Duncan's reason for his DNP as "old."

Some in the league office didn't find these types of roster manip-
ulations funny, and the issue came to a head early in the following
season, when the Spurs elected to send Duncan, Parker, Ginobili, and
swingman Danny Green home before the end of a six-game road trip,
having them miss the Spurs' lone game in Miami that season. It didn't
help the Spurs' cause that the game was a national TV broadcast, and
no league wants to irk its big-money broadcast partners. After playing shorthanded and losing a tough game to LeBron James, Dwyane
Wade, and the Heat, the Spurs were fined $250,000 by then-commis-
sioner David Stern for violating league rules by resting players in a
manner that was "contrary to the best interests of the NBA."

In a statement released by the league, Stern explained that "the
result here is dictated by the totality of the facts in this case. The
Spurs decided to make four of their top players unavailable for an
early-season game that was the team's only regular-season visit to
Miami. The team also did this without informing the Heat, the media,
or the league office in a timely way. Under these circumstances, I have
concluded that the Spurs did a disservice to the league and our fans."

Interestingly, it was James himself who triggered an initial discussion of the rights of a team to strategically rest its players when
Cleveland sat him for four straight games late in the 2009–10 season
to help him recover ahead of what was expected to be a lengthy playoff run. At a subsequent owners' meeting in New York, Stern discussed the issue with his constituents and noted that there was "no
conclusion reached, other than a number of teams thought it should
be at the sole discretion of the team, the coach, the general manager,
and I think it's fair to say I agree with that, unless that discretion is
abused."

Since the Miami incident, the Spurs and Popovich have become more prudent in the way they strategically utilize their roster,
but they continue to do so, and with good reason. At a base level,
Popovich, general manager RC Buford, and their lieutenants do a

masterful job of identifying players that will fit into the Spurs' culture and basketball systems, and then Popovich is able to achieve the equally difficult task of maintaining their readiness throughout the season. That successful nexus is how the Spurs annually seem to have quality depth options at bargain prices. The Spurs typically still play well when they're shorthanded, and research into the strategy—and the whole structure of the Spurs' roster—illuminates just how they manage to pull that off.

In a November 2014 column at *The Cauldron*, Ian Levy looked at the way the Spurs handled their minutes during the 2013–14 season (one in which the Spurs ended up winning the NBA title after no one on the roster averaged more than thirty minutes a game during the regular season), and noted that, while the top four players on the Spurs played fewer minutes on average than their counterparts on other NBA teams, the rest of the roster (players five through twelve) played more minutes than average. Levy detailed this in the graphic shown below:

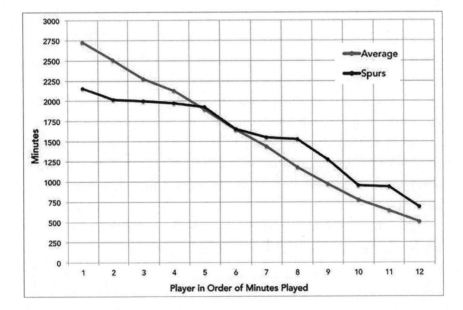

This in itself isn't a surprise for a team that has older stars, quality depth that allows them to go deeper into their bench, and finds itself in a fair number of blowout wins, which means they can pull their best players earlier in the contest. What was much more compelling, though, was that the Spurs were getting *significantly* more impact from their deeper rotation players than the average NBA team. Levy charted a stat called "box plus-minus" (which measures a player's approximate impact when he's on the floor), against the players' total minutes distributions, and painted a really interesting picture:

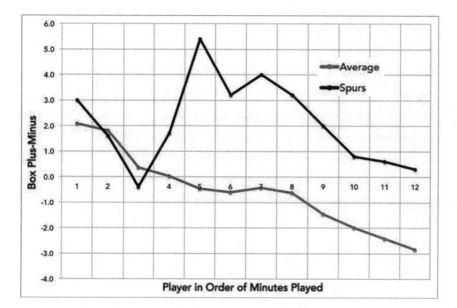

Levy's second chart shows that the Spurs basically got the same composite level of production from their top three players as other NBA teams do. San Antonio's top minutes guy (Duncan) was better overall than the NBA average while the second- and third-most heavy minutes guys (surprisingly, shooting guard Marco Belinelli and point guard Tony Parker) were slightly worse.

Look at the rest of that chart, though. Where the NBA at large sees a continued drop-off in on-court impact, with no average player from number four in minutes through the end of the bench even having a positive box plus-minus rating, *every single Spur* from four through twelve was positive, and the players in positions four through nine were *highly* positive contributors.

The initial jump in the Spurs' curve comes from the number two through five players being very close in minutes, along with Kawhi Leonard's (number five in overall minutes) emergence as a bona fide star. The curve beyond that, though, tracks on a path similar to the NBA average, just three to four net points above the trend for every spot. The result, according to Levy, is that "spreading minutes more evenly is not the sacrifice for the Spurs that it is for most other teams in the league. In fact, if you use the ratings of each Spurs player from last season, but redistribute their minutes so as to match the league average pattern, their projected net rating changes a whopping . . . 0.1 points per one hundred possessions. That difference is small enough that it wouldn't even affect San Antonio's win projection across the entire season. Their sacrifice really isn't a sacrifice at all."

Basically, because of San Antonio's quality of depth, the way in which they shaved minutes for their main players and allocated them to supposedly lesser ones didn't impact them at all during the regular season. Popovich, in 2013–14 at least, was able to make sure his best players got as much rest as they could, and saw no impact on the Spurs' overall record. That's an amazing advantage, especially in a league where being healthy in the playoffs is paramount. The relative freshness showed up in profound fashion in the final three games of that season's NBA Finals, when the Spurs played some of the best offensive basketball in recent memory to vaporize a worn-down Heat team, closing Miami out in five games for the franchise's fifth championship.

While the conclusions are compelling on paper, it still takes proper man management from Popovich and buy-in from all of his players to make things work. While it may seem from the outside that the Spurs make it easy, plugging and playing whomever to cover for the absence of someone else, it's not, and on this night in Denver, after a

99–91 Spurs victory, Duncan explained how the series of injuries—especially at the point guard position—was affecting these Spurs.

"It does impact us. It impacts us tremendously, but we find a way to adjust," he said. "We're not going to sit back and complain about our depth. Those guys are going to step up, and luckily we have some guys like Manu [Ginobili], who's been here for a long time and understands what [the team] wants and needs to be done. Marco [Belinelli]'s still figuring out his way, but we trust him with the ball, as well. And luckily, we run an offense where a lot of people touch the ball, so we're not needing one guy to sit there and set everything up for us, so that plays to our strengths."

Before the game, Popovich noted that he had been "managing" the Spurs through NBA seasons for two decades, so this particular one—while daunting—didn't provide any challenges he hadn't seen before. Duncan, who arrived for Popovich's second season on the bench and has never left, agreed that the way Popovich managed the team makes a lot of sense for them.

"Pop's a master of that," Duncan said about his coach's ability to strategically utilize the roster. "He's been through enough seasons that he understands what we want to do and we have to rest at times. The guys, the players, we want to go out there and play every game, but that's really going to wear us down at some point, so there's a happy medium there somewhere. We can keep minutes down and sometimes [when we] play back-to-backs, sometimes the older guys can't. We just have to play it by ear and see how everyone feels."

Does Duncan, who has forged one of sport's most powerful and successful bonds with his head coach, get any say in when he rests as the team's enduring superstar and eldest statesman?

"No, I've never gotten an opinion," he semi-deadpanned, going against published accounts of his relationship with Popovich. "I just show up for the games."

As much as the coach played it down and the star player joked about it, though, all of the injuries and the schedule and their age seemed to take a toll on the 2014–15 Spurs. While only Leonard ended up playing more than thirty minutes a game for the season (Duncan ended up at 28.9 minutes), there was a much bigger concentration of production in San Antonio's top three minutes guys (including Green) than the year before, along with a huge drop-off in support from the players in spots four through twelve.

All three of Leonard, Duncan, and Green finished with box plus-minuses (BPM) of at least 5, which placed all of them in the top thirteen in the entire NBA for players who played at least one thousand minutes. The trio more than tripled the previous season's combined BPM for the team's top three in minutes played. But after that, San Antonio was a mess.

Parker never really fully found his health or his stride and turned in the poorest season of his career, his diminished offensive productivity no longer offsetting his steadily worsening defense as he ages at what's now a very athletic position across the league. Boris Diaw, who had been a huge positive the season before, was barely positive at a BPM of 0.1, and four other players besides Parker also finished with a negative BPM for the season. The Spurs' BPM curve got much, much steeper than the season before, and the back end of the team's rotation became much closer to an average NBA bench than an elite one.

The combination of all of that ended up being too much to overcome. The Spurs lost at Memphis on the final night of the regular season to drop from the number two seed to number six in the ultra-compact Western Conference playoff order. They then were beaten in the first round after seven incredible games with the Los Angeles Clippers. In that series, neither Leonard's nor Green's performances were of the same caliber as their regular seasons, and Parker went from bad to abysmal, shooting just 36 percent from the field while not making a 3-pointer the entire series (on nine tries). And with Popovich distributing minutes in a more staggered fashion than during the regular season (Duncan and Leonard both played almost thirty-six minutes a game in the series), even improved play from the back of the rotation wasn't quite enough to save them against a very good opponent.

It's no coincidence that the Spurs subsequently re-signed Leonard and Green to long-term contracts, then lured former Portland Trail Blazers standout forward LaMarcus Aldridge in free agency. While no one knows when the Tim Duncan era will finally end in San Antonio, the Spurs did everything possible to make sure his supporting cast was much better than it was in 2014–15.

The 76ers and Tanking's Sneaky Side Benefits

The question was posed while sitting in the well-appointed office of Philadelphia 76ers (and New Jersey Devils) CEO Scott O'Neil, a handful of long outlet passes away from the Wells Fargo Center in the Philadelphia Navy Yards complex hard by the Delaware River. Would the team's notoriously tight-lipped and media-averse general manager, Sam Hinkie, be willing to discuss the club's analytics approach that's fueled the most hotly debated team rebuilding strategy in sports?

O'Neil pondered the request briefly before saying, somewhat matter-of-factly, "Yeah, Sam probably won't talk to you. He doesn't talk to anybody."

That much is unequivocally true. Hinkie, who came to the franchise from the Houston Rockets in 2013 after having worked under chattier statsmaster Daryl Morey, does not talk on the record (or, really, very much off the record, either) about the masterplan for the 76ers, who at the time of this conversation were moving through the second season of a radical long-term overhaul. Hinkie's reticence, though, didn't stop other people from talking about the 76ers, and those people had very strong opinions on what the team was doing.

After replacing Tony DiLeo in the aftermath of the 76ers' disastrous trade for Los Angeles Lakers center Andrew Bynum, who never played a game for Philadelphia thanks to injury, Hinkie's first major move came during the 2013 NBA Draft, when he traded All-Star point guard Jrue Holiday to the New Orleans Hornets (now Pelicans) in exchange for that year's No. 6 overall pick (Nerlens Noel) and a 2014 first-rounder. While Noel may have fit Hinkie's vision of the kind of prospect he wanted to rebuild the team with, the University of Kentucky big man also had additional "value" to the 76ers because he had torn the anterior cruciate ligament in his left knee late in his only college season and subsequently slid down some draft boards because he wouldn't be available to play in the 2013–14 season. That kind of delay was music to the 76ers' ears. Not only did they nab an undervalued talent (and collected an additional first-rounder for the following season for their trouble), but Noel's absence helped ensure that Philadelphia would be very bad in 2013–14, which likely would push its own first-round pick higher in the 2014 draft.

In that draft, the 76ers doubled down on this gambit, using the No. 3 overall pick on Kansas center Joel Embiid, who had foot and back issues in college and was, like Noel, at risk for missing a large piece of his first pro season. Philadelphia also spun a deal with Orlando with the pick it received from New Orleans, netting an additional second-round pick (more on this aspect of the strategy shortly), and an extra first-rounder down the road. With the twelfth overall pick, the 76ers then took Dario Saric, a two-time European youth player of the year who was not eligible to come to the NBA for *two* more seasons because of his professional contract in Spain.

So, over Hinkie's first two drafts, the 76ers used three of their four lottery selections on players who couldn't play immediately, two of whom were carrying significant injury risk. All three of those players were downgraded by other teams because of those concerns, but they made them more valuable to Philadelphia, which (a) thought the players had star potential; and (b) wanted to continue to be bad for the short term, in order to rack up even more high lottery picks.

This was the case again in 2014–15, when the 76ers went 18–64, with a start of the season that was so horrible (they went 0–17 before winning a game) that it launched a number of things:

- The team itself had head coach Brett Brown regularly meet season ticket holders in pregame forums to take direct questions about the franchise's plan. (I walked in on one of these before a November 2014 game against the Chicago Bulls.)

- The NBA brought in team management in December to answer questions about the so-called "tanking" strategy and the integrity of the 76ers' overall rebuilding plan.

- Most notably, the NBA also brought to a vote potential changes in the draft lottery system to disincentivize losing as a way of helping a team improve its chances at a top pick.

That vote, somewhat surprisingly based on sentiments described in pre-vote media reports, fell six yesses short of the required three-quarters needed to flatten out the draft lottery odds. That was, in part, because some teams felt changing rules that quickly midstream would be unjust when there were trades already on the books that included draft pick swaps as far out as 2020, and in part because some understood there was a method behind Hinkie's madness and that Philadelphia was operating within the rules, even if some found the 76ers' methods distasteful.

"I think, in essence, the owners were concerned about unintended consequences," NBA commissioner Adam Silver said after the results of the vote were announced. "I think we all recognize we need to find the right balance between creating the appropriate incentives on one hand for teams to, of course, win, and on the other hand allowing for appropriate rebuilding and the draft to work as it should in which the worst performing teams get the highest picks in the draft."

"I don't necessarily disagree with the way it works now," Silver added. "I'd say from a personal standpoint, what I'm most concerned about is perception out there right now and frankly the pressure on a lot of our teams, even from their very fans, to somehow underperform because it's in some peoples' view the most efficient and quickest way to get better. I think that's a corrosive perception out there."

Despite the draft root of the plan being upheld by franchise owner vote, the 76ers' strategy prompted a lengthy discussion as to whether the team was willfully warping the competitive spirit of the league for their own projected benefit. As *ESPN The Magazine*'s Pablo Torre detailed in an excellent February 2015 column looking at the 76ers' situation, criticism of the team was coming from so many directions that one of its players eventually authored a column debunking the claims.

From Torre's feature:

> "If you're in tanking mode," Lakers co-owner Jeanie Buss recently told ESPN, throwing shade in Hinkie's general direction, "I think that's unforgivable." SLAM magazine declared the team "a flesh-eating bacteria of sorts on the NBA's collective self-respect." The league's former deputy commissioner, Russ Granik, testified to *The New York Times*, "I don't understand this strategy at all." By November, the national backlash had grown so overwhelming that Philadelphia's point guard, 23-year-old Michael Carter-Williams, wrote a defiant essay for the Players' Tribune, Derek Jeter's online publishing concern, titled "Don't Talk to Me About Tanking." "Grown men are going to purposely mail it in for a 1-in-4 shot at drafting somebody who might someday take their job?" Carter-Williams wrote. "Nope."

O'Neil insists he roots for the 76ers to win every time they take the floor, even though it was obvious that losing benefited the team in the short term, and that the team was designed to lose games. His position is certainly plausible, because there's a difference between rooting against your own team and putting a group on the floor that simply isn't capable of winning very often. The 76ers weren't dogging games; the team actually played very hard. They just haven't been very good, by design, in order to forge a better path to get *really* good somewhere down the road.

Focusing solely on the losses and the overall strategy, though, made a lot of people miss more subtle signs of growth, along with the potential of the team's draft, trade, and contract strategies.

Statistically, the 76ers were the worst offensive team in the league in 2014–15, scoring a paltry 95.5 points per one hundred possessions, according to Basketball-Reference.com. As such, many fans assumed the 76ers had a bad offense, which is not the same thing, and was not true. Even with a really young, inexperienced roster that was shuttling players in and out, Brown was busy installing a modern offensive philosophy that should work as the team's talent level increases and stabilizes.

The Houston Rockets (as explained in more detail in a few pages) have set an extreme standard for NBA shot selection, trying to take as few shots as possible that aren't either at the rim or from behind the 3-point arc. In 2014–15, the Rockets set league records for both most 3-point attempts and makes, which helped fuel their league-leading (by a huge margin) 73.8 percent shot rate either from the restricted area encircling the rim or from 3-point range, per data collected from NBA.com. That shot strategy led Houston to have the best projected effective field goal percentage in the league, according to *Sports Analytics Blog.*

The team that was second on that combined restricted area/3-pointer percentage list? The 76ers.

For the 2014–15 season, the 76ers took 68.4 percent of their shots from those two zones on the floor. Additionally, they finished fifth in the NBA in free throw rate, a measure of how often you get to the free throw line. Visits to the "charity stripe" remain the sport's most efficient offensive trip, with a leaguewide average of around 1.5

points per possession (given two free throws and a 75 percent average conversion rate). The principal problem with the 76ers' offense wasn't the system. It was that the players they had couldn't actually make the shots they were taking. While on a normal team, you might criticize the coach for consistently creating shots his players couldn't convert, the idea was backwards with the 76ers. Brown wanted to create these decent shots, and then have his players (or new ones) learn to make them.

To wit, the 76ers only converted 56.4 percent of their restricted area shots, which was the league's fourth-worst rate in 2014–15, per NBA.com. They also shot a horrible 32.3 percent from 3-point range, including a truly terrible 34.2 percent combined from the left and right corners, which are the shortest 3-point shots and typically are more open because it's harder to rotate defensively into the far reaches of the court. Furthermore, they only attempted 407 corner threes all season (in comparison, the Rockets took 899), meaning nearly 81 percent of the 76ers' threes came from "above the break," where the shot is longer and defenders are more present. Finally, they were also the league's worst free throw shooting team, at 67.6 percent, which negated a lot of their above-average team free throw rate. All told, the 76ers scored 592.7 fewer points than they "should have" based on their overall shot selection, per expected effective field goal percentage calculations from Nylon Calculus' Seth Partnow. That's more than 7.2 points per game for a team that finished the season with a point differential of minus-9.0. Just a normal return on its shot attempts may have doubled the 76ers' win total.

The horrendous offensive production also masked the 76ers' above-average defense. They finished thirteenth in defensive efficiency, despite relying on a rookie rim protector in Noel and a team that hadn't played together long enough to not routinely blow some defensive rotations. To compensate, they forced a lot of turnovers and also played at one of the quickest paces in the league in order to take advantage of their length and athleticism. As Torre noted:

It remains scientifically impossible to develop arm length, an under-rated characteristic on defense. ("Sam is very studied in regards to that," Brown says.) But as Spurs wing Kawhi Leonard has verified, it is possible to grow a prospect's shooting ability over time. And Philly, forcing turnovers at a league-high 15.6 percent through the All-Star break but shooting a league-low 41 percent, is incentivized to wait on such a large-scale renovation.

So while there definitely were some rough edges to smooth out, Philadelphia was running a pretty decent system with bad offensive players, which is actually a good thing if you plan to improve the players. The 76ers plan to do so, eventually.

In that vein, the 76ers have been engaging in two other areas of asset accumulation (beyond the controversial lottery picks) that have yielded dividends and should continue going forward.

First, Philadelphia has frequently operated with a payroll well under the league salary cap floor. Since the penalty for being below the floor at the end of the season isn't really a penalty at all—the team would then simply be required to pay out the difference between the payroll and the floor as "bonus" payments to its current players—the suppressed payroll has allowed Hinkie and his staff to operate very strategically when money is involved, in both contracts and trades.

First-round draft pick contracts are guaranteed. They have a set rookie scale that dictates what the player has to be paid in the first two years of the deal, team option rights for years three and four, and the ability to match offers when the player is a restricted free agent after that fourth year if the team hasn't worked out a new contract with the player. Second-round picks, though, have open-contract structures, and teams can design contracts that best benefit them.

The 76ers have serially tried to collect and exploit second-rounders. On average, about 10 percent of second-round picks (or about three a season) will become solid NBA players, and Hinkie wants to place as many bets as possible to reap that potential yield.

The 76ers, famously, had six second-round selections in the 2014 draft and loaded up with five more in 2015 because Hinkie has been able to use the 76ers' financial freedom to nudge his way into trades as a facilitator, nabbing extra draft picks for his trouble. This has allowed them to stash several more players overseas to develop in addition to Saric. The ones who are intended for the current roster are then offered front-loaded deals that will reward the team heavily if the player develops well.

In 2014–15, the strategy worked with the signing of Robert Covington, a former NBA Development League MVP whose four-year contract was less than 25 percent guaranteed in total. He made himself into a valuable wing shooter and slasher, and now the team has control over his next three seasons at their discretion at an extremely low cost. Similarly, Jerami Grant, son of former NBA player Harvey Grant, also signed a four-year deal, with the last two years not fully guaranteed. The team tried the same tack with athletic guard K. J. McDaniel, but he balked and gambled on himself, signing just a one-year, nonguaranteed deal. Hinkie then traded him midseason to the Rockets for guard Isaiah Canaan and, you guessed it, a second-round pick.

Hinkie also used the team's copious cap space to his advantage. At the 2015 trade deadline, the 76ers agreed to take on JaVale McGee's onerous contract from the Denver Nuggets in order to receive yet another future first-round pick. Again, the team had to spend that money one way or another, either through player acquisition or as a distribution to their own players. Hinkie elected to use it to gain another valuable chip for down the road. The 76ers similarly exploited a cash-strapped team during the 2015 summer free agency period when they used the Sacramento Kings' need to create cap room to lure free agents against them. In exchange for taking on two contracts from the Kings, the 76ers received their 2014 lottery selection in shooting guard Nik Stauskas, as well as a future protected first-round pick, *and* the right to swap first-round picks in both the 2016 and 2017 drafts, should the Kings land the better pick. Sacramento is considered unlikely to dent the Western Conference playoffs in either of those seasons, so a lucky break with the lottery ping-pong balls has the potential to deliver another huge asset.

If a number of Hinkie's bets pan out, and the team can overcome its growing reputation of coldly treating players as fungible assets, the 76ers could be a very formidable team sooner than anyone thinks—and one that will have the cap space and assets in both players and future draft picks to work a mega-trade if that's determined to be the best path to becoming a contender. Of course, the bigger bets need to work out, and the Joel Embiid one may go bust on them, as the big man reinjured his foot and is expected to miss the entire 2015–16 season, as well.

Only Hinkie and team management know when the gambit will end and the gamble will begin, and he's still not talking about it. During a post-sessions happy hour at the 2015 Sloan Sports Analytics Conference, I introduced myself, offering up the double kiss of death that I was friendly with Pablo Torre though our time working together at *Sports Illustrated,* and that I was writing this book.

Hinkie cringed in mock horror, and pretended to start walking away.

Given the chance to comment on the record, Hinkie predictably declined, but he was happy to chat for a couple of minutes. He even chuckled when I compared the 76ers' rebuild to the famous Internet story "One Red Paperclip," where a guy started with said paperclip and kept bartering for something else that had slightly more value, ultimately ending up with a fully paid-for house.

After two seasons of designed losing, the 76ers had traded up from a paperclip to something akin to a toaster, but with Hinkie's moxie, the assets he has collected, and the patience of ownership that supports this controversial path, he may someday get that house. There's no guarantee it will have a roof or indoor plumbing, but whatever it ends up looking like, you can be sure that the neighbors will be talking about it.

The Houston Rockets and 3-Point Extremes

One of the major talking points during the 2014–15 preseason was the varying ways in which NBA teams viewed the 3-pointer. Even as the league as a whole continued to evolve away from dominant post play and toward the spacing/slashing/shooting mentality that fueled the recent Spurs and Heat championship teams, there remained considerable differences among the thirty franchises as to how to best utilize the shot.

The discussion came to a hysterical and almost comical peak when first-year Los Angeles Lakers head coach Byron Scott, likely in an effort to disassociate himself from the Mike D'Antoni era where 3-pointers were launched somewhat indiscriminately, openly talked about putting specific limits on the number of threes the Lakers took. In an interview detailed by the *Los Angeles Times,* Scott said curious and/or worrisome things like "I like the fact that we only shot 10 threes" (in the preseason opener against the Denver Nuggets), "If we shoot between 10 and 15, I think that's a good mixture of getting to that basket and shooting threes," and "I don't want us to be coming down, forcing up a bunch of threes."

Of course, no coach wants his team to force up shots of any vintage, but to seemingly put hard limits on one type of shot—especially one that, if used properly, has a much better points-per-shot yield than 2-point attempts, and creates much better spacing for the rest of your offense—raised many eyebrows in the media and analytics communities. It is extremely hard in today's NBA to succeed over the long run if you're constantly overmatched at the arc. The Memphis Grizzlies have been the most successful anti-establishment team, but they also have very specific personnel—potent bigs Zach Randolph and Marc Gasol inside, plus wing stopper Tony Allen and hard-nosed point guard Mike Conley—that cater to their defensive, grinding style.

The Lakers, even before losing rookie power forward Julius Randle for the season after he suffered a broken leg in the regular-season opener, did not have that type of personnel. What they did have was a large group of players that shot the three fairly well. All of Nick Young, Wayne Ellington, Wesley Johnson, Jeremy Lin, and Ryan Kelly had made at least 34 percent of their 3-point attempts in 2013–14, and with Kobe Bryant also returning from injury, there was yet another capable 3-point shooter in the starting lineup. Yet, in their second preseason game, against the high-tempo, 3-point-gunning Golden State Warriors, no less, the Lakers attempted only eleven threes. Then, in their third preseason game, this happened:

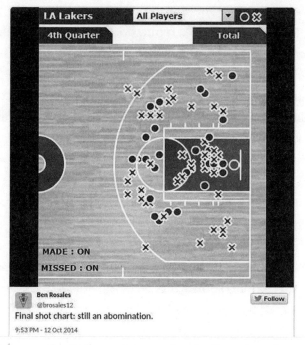

In that game, the Lakers attempted only *three* 3-pointers, including *zero* from either corner. That's almost impossible to do. And it's not like the Lakers didn't have players shooting from areas below the free throw line; they missed all six mid-range shots they attempted from the right baseline area, and took eight more of various lengths (making four) from the left side.

Instead of 3-point attempts, the Lakers took a hailstorm of shots from a couple steps inside the arc. They also fired away from deeper in the painted area, from the elbows on either side of the free throw line and, basically, from every place except around the rim and from behind the arc. It was a masterpiece of offensive inefficiency. Predictably, NBA Twitter howled. This was not how basketball was supposed to be played anymore, at least according to the wonks.

As mentioned in the 76ers' section above, the leader in the push toward eliminating mid-range shots has been the Houston Rockets, who have stretched the efficiency of offensive basketball toward its outer limits—as well as the discussion on how much is too much from an effectiveness standpoint.

Daryl Morey has a bit of a reputation as a media darling, and detractors of this style—or perhaps of Morey himself—point out that the 2014–15 Rockets had a fairly average offense (at 1.04 points per possession, twelfth out of the thirty NBA teams, per NBA.com's data), despite having one of the game's superstars in guard James Harden and also having (when healthy) one of the NBA's best traditional centers in Dwight Howard, both of whom get to the free throw line a ton. That's a great advantage for Harden, a very strong free throw shooter, but not as much for Howard, who struggles to make half of his attempts from the line.

The criticism about the offense's effectiveness has some fairness. The 2013–14 Rockets finished above 1.07 points per possession (albeit with different personnel that were much worse defensively than the 2014–15 version). The chart on page 69 maps offensive efficiency (in terms of points per one hundred possessions) against percentage of field goal attempts that come from 3-point range. While the trend is up as you increase your 3-point attempt rate, the Rockets drop back below the trend line, and there are several low-threes offenses that score more efficiently:

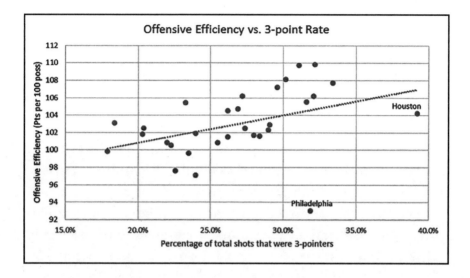

There has been significant discussion as to whether the Rockets, despite shot distribution that is more points-efficient than any other team in the league, have taken things too far. If so many of your shots are coming from two very specific areas on the court—at the rim and behind the arc—it might make you *too* predictable, which makes the job of the defense that much easier. The overall Moreyball philosophy, though, isn't validated or negated by what the team he runs is doing. Personnel (and health) makes a large difference in the execution of a plan, even if the plan is strategically sound, and this general approach to offensive basketball, mathematically, is sound.

Dr. Stephen Shea, a mathematician and the coauthor of *Basketball Analytics: Objective and Efficient Strategies for Understanding How Teams Win*, has noted that every team in the NBA would improve its effective field goal percentage if it adjusted its shot distribution closer to the Rockets' strategy. He also posted a blog entry in February 2015 that showed the distribution of all NBA teams over the past three seasons by what he terms their "Moreyball Efficiency"—a function of a team's percentages made and allowed in the restricted area and on 3-pointers—and suggested a very strong correlation between high positive figures and championship contention.

In that entry, he noted that the last two NBA champions—the 2014 San Antonio Spurs and the 2013 Miami Heat—led the league in those seasons in Moreyball Efficiency, which makes sense since they also led the paradigm shift toward the present "spacing and shooting" era. They also met each other in the Finals both seasons, so the runners-up each year also ranked very highly.

As the chart from that entry below shows, there was reason at the All-Star break to believe in teams like the Golden State Warriors, Atlanta Hawks, Portland Trail Blazers (who scored high in this metric despite having LaMarcus Aldridge, one of the world's best mid-range jump shooters) and, somewhat surprisingly, the Washington Wizards, who at midseason had the lowest "offensive Moreyball" percentage in the league, per the analytics blog *Nylon Calculus*. The Wizards were well known as a team that openly shunned threes, but they made a very high percentage of the ones they attempted, and they also had the frontcourt to make and prevent some easy twos, which helped them in this ratio calculation.

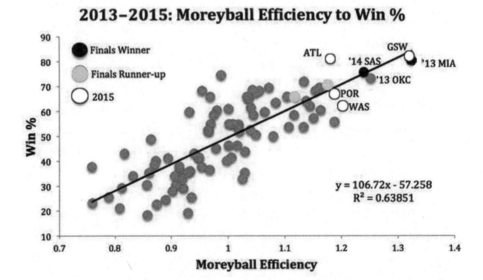

2013–2015: Moreyball Efficiency to Win %

$$y = 106.72x - 57.258$$
$$R^2 = 0.63851$$

There is a pretty strong data fit in this model, with the data suggesting that as you approach and then move beyond a 1:1 ratio on offense and defense, your winning percentage will see a significant boost. Below that Moreyball Efficiency of 1, most of the teams sit below the trend curve, or underachieve their projected win rate. At and above that point, that changes, and there are a good number more teams above the trend line that are overachieving.

At the extreme positive end lie both recent world champs, the losing team in each of those finals, and the aforementioned candidates from 2014–15 that looked like legitimate title contenders. (The data also re-emphasizes the disappointment that Russell Westbrook's injury in the 2013 playoffs was for Oklahoma City, when the Thunder very well could have ended up in the Finals and with a rematch against the Heat.) The blog entry concluded, presciently, by stating that the Warriors looked to be very significant favorites to win it all.

Still, Morey's concepts find themselves with a number of detractors, for varying reasons. Part of it is that Houston hadn't had much playoff success under Morey before the Rockets' run to the 2015 Western Conference Finals that included a stunning comeback from down three games to one against the Los Angeles Clippers. That was even though Morey had done a very commendable job refashioning the roster from the Tracy McGrady/Yao Ming days without having a significant drop-off in the standings.

Part is that the Rockets can be frustratingly dull to watch at times, with most variety drained out of their offensive attack in favor of a three-prong attack made up of an incredible number of threes, James Harden drives that end in fouls, and mostly inelegant Dwight Howard post ups. *Grantland*'s Jason Concepcion wrote well about this aspect in November 2014, likening the Rockets to some of the historically more successful practitioners of *catenaccio,* the infuriatingly boring and—in the hands of the right team—incredibly successful Italian defensive soccer strategy. There were similar comparisons to the left wing lock era New Jersey Devils of the NHL, when they were winning Stanley

Cups while playing a style that ultimately forced the league to enact rule changes to defuse it. The Rockets, despite Harden's individual brilliance, come off as boring and soulless in their approach, and grading out as an average offense increases this particular category of ire.

And part of it is, frankly, a number of people around the league dislike Morey, including some who are paid significant amounts of money to talk about basketball on TV. While the battle between "those who played" and "those who calculate" has raged on for years—with little in the way of viable conclusion, since the smartest analysts in the game look at advanced numbers and also watch copious amounts of games and film—the debate, as such, is rehashed every now and again, and flames are fanned with the vitriol. Accordingly, TNT's Charles Barkley made national headlines just before the All-Star break with a diatribe against Morey and the Rockets on the network's iconic *Inside the NBA* studio show that included Barkley claiming that recent NBA champions had won titles because they had great players, not because of advanced statistics.

Barkley's on-camera personality mix of former star player and honest everyman is designed to entertain more than inform, but even by those modest standards, his riff was woefully short on truth. There is ample documentation on how the Miami Heat used analytics to try to figure out how best to deploy LeBron James, Dwyane Wade, and Chris Bosh, specifically in relation to Bosh's usage, where he became a crucial pick-and-roll and perimeter-defending presence when the Heat reached their pinnacle. Likewise, the San Antonio Spurs are among the smartest teams in the league in every facet, and use heavy doses of analytics to their continuing advantage. The Rockets were also able to sniff out Harden's star potential through his performance levels as a sixth man with the Thunder. Barkley's riff also ignores that Synergy's Garrick Barr is a former NBA assistant coach, and other third-party analytics providers also have numerous former basketball players on their staffs.

Anyway, a funny thing happened to the Lakers on the way to being a leaguewide joke for their horrible shot selection: while they
ended up taking the most mid-range 2-point attempts in the league
while finishing a ghastly twenty-eighth in success rate from that
range, they actually ended up right on the league's 3-point trend line.
The Lakers took a below-average but not irregular number of threes
for the season and made a below-average but normal rate of them
(and then, somewhat surprisingly, moved advance scout Clay Moser
into a liaison role to try to better connect the team's analytics efforts
with the coaching staff that doesn't seem to care for them).

The outliers in terms of the number of 3-point attempts per game
versus the percentage made were the aforementioned 76ers, who
took a lot of threes and didn't make many; the Warriors, who led the
league at 39.8 percent and attempted 2,217 of them (fourth-most in
the league) and . . . the Rockets, who shattered league 3-point records
while shooting a mediocre-enough percentage to suggest that maybe
they should dial things back just a touch:

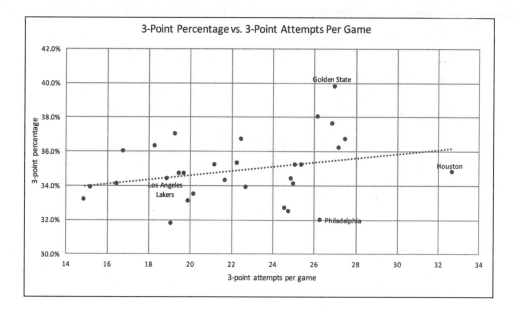

The only two good teams that were near the bottom of the league were the Grizzlies, who put a scare in the Warriors in the second round of the playoffs before getting figured out, and those curious Wizards, who actually went to a heavy dose of small ball once they got into the playoffs, shot a lot more threes, and had a good chance to make the Eastern Conference Finals had injuries not hindered them against the Atlanta Hawks. One other notable team in that grouping was the long, young, and interesting Milwaukee Bucks, who also have built a roster around disruption rather than marksmanship, but it's a bit too early to say that's their distinct style.

As January 2015 was the NBA's first month ever with more 3-point attempts than free throw attempts, this trend—and this debate on how many is enough—will continue to roll on. The league will never completely conform to one style, nor should it, but it's worth noting that the seven teams with the highest percentage of 3-point attempts at season's end all finished in the top nine in offensive efficiency, and the last five teams alive in the 2015 playoffs were the five most frequent 3-point shooting teams. In today's NBA, the 3-point shot, ever increasingly, is king, and if you don't shoot enough of them, you're going to need to do a heck of a lot of other things well in order to compete for the championship.

The Hunt for Future Perfected Players

There was only one thing I was trying to do—put numbers in front of our team to get them to understand that what we were doing is in their best interests, and that their efficiency numbers would be off the charts if they did this right . . . And that no one would be hurt by less minutes; you would be more efficient.

—John Calipari, head coach, University of Kentucky

When the University of Kentucky's men's basketball team is expected to be good, there's no bigger story in college basketball, and entering the 2014–15 season, the Wildcats were expected to be very, very good. Fueled by a superb freshman class led by multiskilled forward Karl-Anthony Towns, and a number of returnees from the season before, the biggest challenge for head coach John Calipari wasn't anyone on the team's schedule. It was that he had too much talent and depth on his roster, and needed to figure out a way to manage it all successfully. With as many as ten players who conceivably could start, and numerous prospects that looked like potential NBA lottery selections, he and his staff needed to get creative.

Calipari has been a master recruiter and self-promoter since his days at the University of Massachusetts a couple of decades ago. There, he built a national power around the skills of forwards Lou Roe and then Marcus Camby, whose shotblocking and athleticism in a 6-foot-11 frame ultimately made him the No. 2 overall pick in the 1996 NBA Draft. Calipari had a similar ramp-up at the University of Memphis in the middle of last decade, ultimately elevating that program back into national title contention when he had point guard Derrick Rose, who became the No. 1 overall pick in the 2008 NBA Draft and would win the league's MVP award three seasons later. The potent mixture of Kentucky basketball's platform and Calipari, though, lifted everything to another level.

Despite the school's basketball pedigree, the Wildcats program wasn't ready-made for Calipari when he arrived in the summer of 2009. Things had stagnated under former coach Tubby Smith, who had won a national title in 1998, his first season at the school, and then never got back to the Final Four. Kentucky then took a significant jolt from two tepid seasons under Billy Gillispie, who had led Texas A&M to unexpected heights but was overmatched in Lexington and also struggled with alcohol issues as the Wildcats sagged into national also-ran status.

The Wildcats weren't winning nearly enough, they weren't recruiting nearly well enough, and they didn't matter nearly as much as other elite programs like Kansas, which won the national title in 2008 (over Calipari's Memphis Tigers, in overtime in the final) and North Carolina, which rolled to the crown in 2009 behind four NBA lottery selections in that year's draft. But Kentucky was still *Kentucky,* the bluest of college bluebloods. It needed a coach—a CEO/evangelist, really—worthy of its grandeur, and no one was a better fit for that program at that moment than Calipari. It was the job, and the pulpit, he had been waiting for his whole career. Kentucky basketball is akin to religion in the Commonwealth, and Calipari can sell hoops faith like none other.

In his first season in Lexington, Calipari immediately made the Wildcats into one of the best teams in the nation behind the talents of John Wall (who would then be the NBA's No. 1 overall pick), DeMarcus "Boogie" Cousins (who went No. 5 overall in that same draft) and Eric Bledsoe (No. 18 overall). The following year, a less-talented version of the Wildcats unexpectedly clawed its way to the Final Four. The season after that, powered by the uber-talented frontcourt pair of Anthony Davis and Michael Kidd-Gilchrist, the Wildcats finished 38–2 and won the school's eighth national championship. Those two freshmen then went Nos. 1 and 2 overall in the 2012 NBA Draft. Two seasons later, in 2014, Kentucky was back in the national title game again after negotiating some in-season struggles.

Then, the unexpected happened. Kentucky, which under Calipari had been a program heavily fueled by "one-and-done" players who excelled as freshmen and then immediately jumped to the NBA, had a sizable number of players decide to return for the 2014–15 campaign. With yet another loaded class set to arrive, Calipari needed to find a way to manage everyone's minutes, win games on the floor, and set up as many players as possible for maximum NBA interest.

So, he hired a director of analytics to help him manage the whole process.

When the announcement of Joel Justus's hire was made, along with the subsequent proclamation that Kentucky would utilize a platoon system in which two distinct groups of five would come on and off the court together and effectively split up the two hundred total game minutes available, the reaction was that this was more of Calipari's marketing gimmicks. It wasn't a totally unfair assumption. There certainly was a sexy, promotional component to the role, which fit into the super-aggressive way Calipari has billed his program, which has generated five Elite Eight appearances, four Final Fours, a national title, and thirteen NBA lottery picks in his six seasons in charge. But Calipari insisted there was significant substance behind this particular sell, that platooning and having a dedicated analytics director was the best way to win now *and* get as many of his talented players to the NBA. In doing so, Kentucky became one of the more ambitious teams at the college level in trying to make targeted use of analytics to help its players and its performance.

"Well, the idea wasn't a marketing [one]. There was only one thing I was trying to do—put numbers in front of our team to get them to understand that what we were doing is in their best interests, and that their efficiency numbers would be off the charts if they did this right," Calipari said, as the experiment continued to unfold around him. "And that no one would be hurt by less minutes; you would be more efficient. And so that's why we did it.

"The numbers that Joel can come up with are better, just logical things that no one on the staff would just say. Every kind of rotation, every kind of combination, we keep score. So as much as we think this combination or that combination is doing well, you look and you say, 'Damn.' They look like they're doing better than they are. You know what I'm saying? They move the ball better, they space better, yeah. But the numbers don't foretell that—the other team may not look as good, but the spread is way bigger when they're in. So those are the kind of things that we're able to see and monitor and also let them know, to keep them [informed]."

Calipari's hard sell to his players was that NBA personnel care about percentages and rates more than gross numbers, and his players would have a huge opportunity to post impressive stat rates because they would only be playing for four- to five-minute spurts in a game, and not playing more than maybe twenty-three or twenty-four minutes most nights. He also relentlessly harped on his players' on-court effort as a key factor in their draft status.

"I told some of these guys, if you score twenty a game, but if you have no motor, you're done," Calipari said. "If you scored ten a game, but your motor's off the charts, you're going to be a top-ten pick. But, let me say this. [Having] the motor is way harder than scoring.

It's hard. And they break down. 'Can't I just shoot it more?' 'No, I'm sorry. Sorry, it doesn't work that way.' It's amazing. And when I stop them all the time at practice, and say [to an assistant], 'Now, why would he do it this way instead of the way we're talking?' 'Because it's easier.' 'No kidding.' Just whatever's the easiest route. But there is no easy route. It's not easy. The numbers show the hard workers, the aggressive, attacking players, are the guys they want, and those numbers show in all these stats. But the only way you get those stats is you just play harder."

The platoon system worked decently for a chunk of the nonconference schedule, but things changed a bit once forward Alex Poythress injured his knee and was lost for the season. There also was the dilemma in the backcourt, where often the shooting provided by Tyler Ulis and Devin Booker was more effective than what twins Andrew and Aaron Harrison were providing. Things eventually got blurrier as the season continued, certain games got tougher, and Kentucky kept winning (the Wildcats reeled off thirty-eight wins in a row before losing to Wisconsin in the national semifinals). Calipari pared his rotation a bit and went more often with eight players, with a more established hierarchy that blended his players from the two earlier fivesomes more often.

Still, the experiment was interesting and, in a way, Calipari had a unique opportunity because his team was so deep and so talented; the Wildcats ended up having six players selected in the 2015 NBA Draft. So, while Calipari had to win games, he and his staff also kept in constant contact with NBA personnel about what pro teams want to see from his players, and tried to put his players in the best position to compile the most impressive rates in categories that define them in the eyes of scouts. Calipari and his staff would distribute stat sheets after games, normalizing his players' rates projected over thirty-four minutes—a heavy starting player's load at the college level—but he wanted them to continue to focus particularly on the stats that helped them the most.

"Rebounding percentages. Like, in other words, there's ten or twelve rebounds, how many of them did you get? That percentage is huge for them. So we're able to monitor that," Calipari said. "The other thing that's huge for [scouts] is defensive playmaking. Defensive playmaking being your steals and blocks divided by your fouls. And all of sudden, you're like 'These numbers matter. We've got to put you in the position to be more of a defensive playmaker, be able to steal more balls, be able to . . . ,' you know, those kind of things."

Calipari seemed pleased enough with Justus's work that, after the season, he elevated him to the position of special assistant to the head coach. Justus will continue to provide analytics insights to Calipari and his staff, but also will be involved in opponent scouting and other special projects. As for the platoon system? That looks to be a one-off invention, in part because it took a crazy confluence of events to necessitate it, and also because competing schools started using the system against Kentucky in recruiting. The Wildcats missed out on several high-profile targets for the 2015–16 season, and Calipari was pretty clear in a blog entry on his personal website CoachCal.com that the days of the "white" and "blue" teams in Lexington were over.

"If you ask me if I'm ever going to platoon again, my answer is NO," Calipari wrote in May 2015. "Last season was an absolute outlier. It's just not the way I like to coach. I would rather play seven or eight guys because I believe that gives us the best chance to win. I think we wrote the book on platooning this year, but I hope we stick it on the shelf and never have to use it again."

⤙

Kentucky may be the pinnacle of college basketball talent procurement and draft placement, but future NBA players don't just appear ready-made at the college level. It takes years of cultivation and competition at the high school level to whittle down thousands of potential Division I players to the choice few that will be good enough to play for the college game's best programs.

And while, thanks to shoe-company money that fuels an ever-burgeoning grassroots basketball scene that allows the nation's best players to play with and against each other more often in a travel team setting, there's no real or consistent way for analytics as we strictly define them at the levels beyond that to have a huge impact on the development of elite high school prospects.

Box scores haven't been consistently available across the spectrum of different prep competitions, let alone there being the accuracy and the staff availability/competence to process anything more than the simplest of statistics. A company called Krossover is trying to bridge that gap, using Synergy-style human loggers to provide indexed video breakdowns and analysis services for modest (by college and pro standard) fees, but coaches still need to be sophisticated enough to use the output, and they have to have the budget to pay for it. And while top high schoolers may try to pattern their games to be more like top NBA players they admire—which in itself is an indirect form of analytics, since they're molding themselves into modern pros—according to Scout.com director of recruiting Evan Daniels, there really isn't that much chatter about advanced stats among the nation's elite teenagers.

"I'm not sure that they do. I'll be honest with you, I haven't heard many kids bring up analytics, if any," Daniels said. "I think once they get to college, they're more in tune with it, and it's hard to at the high-school level because up until this year—I guess Nike EYBL has done stats for a couple years—but not all the shoe-company events have done stats, so it's hard to get reliable stats for the kids, for the games. Now, this year, we can kind of look at more advanced stats than we have been able to in the past, so it's kind of a new thing, but to be honest with you, I haven't really heard any of them bring it up. And part of it is they aren't educated on that type of stuff. I think once they get to college, they open up to it a little more."

Perhaps the closest thing individual players have been able to adopt on the high school level is getting to work with a trainer able to develop aspects of their games that will make them more desirable to pro teams more quickly, should their college careers pan out. Daniels said that approach and mentality can differ from player to player, but he sees good examples of it in each high school graduating class.

"I think there's some kids that certainly take a professional mindset to getting better and working out," Daniels said. "I think Jayson Tatum is a perfect example; he's our No. 3 player in the '16 class [and committed to Duke University]. He's been working with Drew Hanlon really since he was a freshman in high school. I don't know how familiar you are with Drew Hanlon, but he works out pre-draft guys. He's worked out [Washington Wizards guard] Bradley Beal and [Boston Celtics forward] David Lee for years. He's a professional trainer and among the best I have seen. There's a reason Jayson Tatum has some of the best footwork I have seen in high school basketball. There's a reason for that. He's taken a professional outlook and aligned himself with someone who knows what he's doing. It's not just working out. It's working out with the right people who have information that can help you."

Daniels said that he thinks grassroots coaching continues to improve overall, and there have been numerous cases in the past few years of Amateur Athletic Union coaches getting hired for college jobs based on their performances, not solely for which players they can deliver to a college program. That's a good development, as is the ever-growing variety of tournaments and events that help put the best players on the floor together (and against each other) in more and more situations. Overall, though, the established high school level still isn't fully prepared to give elite players the refined attention they need to reach their ceilings. Enter USA Basketball, which in the last seven years has become another crucial development outlet for the best high schoolers, and one that is increasingly attuned to analytics as part of its overall mission.

Sean Ford has been the director of the US men's national basketball team since 2001. He and assistant director BJ Johnson (who is primarily tasked with overseeing the men's junior national team programs) are the two most responsible for keeping the USA Basketball talent pipeline full. At any one time, the pair of Villanova alums—Johnson played basketball for the Wildcats—may be managing up to five separate US national teams and their related qualification processes or actual championship competitions.

While USA Basketball doesn't use analytics in the same deep, complicated sense as many NBA teams, Ford and his staff still have a significant interest in using numbers to help them both define the style of play US national teams will feature on the court, and also the types of players the program is looking to bring in, from the youngest junior teams up to the Olympic and World Championship squads at the senior level.

Because USA Basketball doesn't have teams together for all that long—even including training camp practices along with the actual competitions—there isn't enough data to compile accurate assessments of individual player performance, but Ford and his staff do like to look at the team-level performances to try to ensure that the style they want to play at each level is being implemented. They also look at trends in terms of where players come from and where they end up matriculating in college, to see if there's any correlation to success or failure in their programs. There's still a good amount of eye test involved, too—especially as USA Basketball starts feeding the youngest age groups—because really up until the senior national team itself, physical talent will be ahead of actual basketball skill. In the interim, US athleticism is a sledgehammer.

"We like long, like everyone else—long and athletic players," Ford said. "We have the luxury of being able to pick or look at everyone in the United States. But we really like length, and [in the] international game, the style of play that we want to play, length carries a big part of that because the majority of [our kids are] not used to a twenty-four-second shot clock.

"And we want to play fast because our strength is we're more athletic than any other team. And the more possessions you have in a game, the more likelihood that the more talented team is going to win. And it's not very often that we step on the floor and are not the most talented team. It doesn't mean we will win every game, but talent does prevail . . . and if you play harder than your opponent, and you have more possessions, and you're more talented, it's a very strong likelihood that you'll win."

This type of analytic thinking also comes into play in actual roster construction, as witnessed with the final selections for the 2014 World Championships. Ford said the loose goal is to have a player or two who specifically plays the point guard spot, as well as one player who is a dedicated center. The United States may not need a back-to-the-basket player in every game in a tournament, but there are times when it's very useful to be able to dump the ball into the post and get a bucket or get fouled. Beyond that, USA Basketball is looking to cultivate a group of athletic, wing players who can move anywhere between the shooting guard and power forward positions.

At the senior team level, 3-point shooting is a significant consideration because of the elite skill level of the shooters. It's a shot that the United States can exploit. The younger national teams don't have that wealth or consistency of shooting, so Ford said their style of play focuses more on getting 2-point attempts in the paint and in transition, which also helps their offensive rebounding, and getting to the free throw line.

Overall, USA Basketball wants its teams to play in the neighborhood of ninety to ninety-five possessions in a forty-minute game, and to score at least one point per possession. The overall philosophy to punish teams closer to the rim also helps loosen up the 3-point arc, which helps the younger teams that may lack the deadeye shooters that the senior team often has in spades. Ford also hypothesized—although they don't track this statistic yet—that younger players may shoot the three better when their team is leading, which is more reason to attack early and try to establish a lead and/or foul trouble that will benefit the United States later, as their depth wears opponents down.

Whatever the offensive approach, USA Basketball wants a team that can impart its defensive style on opponents while getting the offense it needs on the other end.

"Everyone [besides the dedicated ones and fives] has a primary position, but also has a secondary position, which allows us to be very flexible in our offense and defense," Ford said. "We want to press—or at least press for the ball. We're not necessarily trying to just turn them over all the time when we press—and we do this primarily with our junior teams—[but] try to prevent them from running their offense too much. We want them to get into their offense with fifteen on the shot clock, sixteen on the shot clock.

"We can be taken advantage of by a good half-court offense team. That's where we struggle sometimes," he added. "And so if we can prevent a team from getting into their offense a second time, that's a good thing. So if we can use up the beginning of the clock with pressure and they get into their offense later, we don't have to play half-court defense as long. And the length comes in because it's deflecting a shot, the deflecting of passes, the angles that prevents good passing angles, but it also, when you do get into your offense, we always like to have the option of having a lineup that can switch on every screen, and that we're not hurt offensively or defensively."

Ford credits FIBA's decision in 2009 to eliminate its Under-21 World Championship, in part because many of the most promising young players were already with their nations' senior national teams at that point, and replacing it with an Under-17 World Championship, which included qualifying at the Under-16 level. That gave USA Basketball the opportunity to implement the same type of development strategy as program director Jerry Colangelo and head coach Mike Krzyzewski were putting in place for the senior team: they would build up pools of talent for that age group, hold training and tryout camps, select a twelve-man roster for a specific event, and then repeat the process with the next age-appropriate group while those who were in the program competed to stay in the mix for the next age cutoff and tournament.

Getting formal access to players as young as entering high school freshmen was a great opportunity for USA Basketball to lengthen the indoctrination process, getting players used to international play at much earlier levels. Because the new process is only seven years old, USA Basketball is just starting to see the yield of players from the very start of the talent development pipeline mature into senior national team players, but that's coming—and more and more high school standouts who end up as one-and-done college players will end up playing more games for USA Basketball at its various levels than at the collegiate level, further increasing USA Basketball's reach and impact on future NBA player development, as well as its own.

"Because of the success of the senior men's team and the resources developed as a result of Jerry Colangelo's leadership, especially the money to run good programs, our young programs—boys, girls, men, women—are outstanding," said Krzyzewski, who leads the US men's senior national team as well as Duke University. "These youngsters then get indoctrinated into a high level of play, what it means to play for their country, and develop relationships that then lead—for those who continue and are good enough to make the men's senior team—they get to know one another. There's familiarity, and that's what other countries have used against us: the continuity and familiarity of coaches and players doing things together."

Ford noted that entering the 2014–15 college season, expected standouts like Tyus Jones, Justise Winslow, Jahlil Okafor, and Stanley Johnson hadn't played a collegiate game yet, but had played for four years for USA Basketball and all had three gold medals from various age competitions.

"Even the guys that won in Spain [at the FIBA Basketball World Cup in 2014], all of those guys—[Mason] Plumlee played on an 18-and-under team, [Steph] Curry played on a 19-and-under team, Klay Thompson played on a 19-and-under team, Kyrie Irving played on an 18-and-under team. Those guys played on our younger teams. Rudy Gay played on a 21-and-under team, [and] he played in a Hoops Summit. [DeMarcus] Cousins played in a Hoops Summit," Ford said. "A lot of those guys played on our younger teams, but there wasn't the [Under-]16 and [Under-]17 available, so they didn't play on multiple teams where you got [situations like] Tyus Jones and Stanley Johnson. They've won three gold medals, they've played on multiple teams, they took ownership of USA Basketball while they were in high school.

"And that's where you're going to see. We've had kids that have played on the national team—our senior team—that have played on our junior team, but Andre Drummond was the only one, the first one, that played in the World Championship that was on a [Under-]16 and a [Under-]17. So now we're going to see that going forward and that culture, the USA Basketball culture, is not going to be new to them at the senior team because they were part of it at the junior team."

USA Basketball's improved development work isn't going unnoticed. Top-level college coaches like the enhanced atmosphere for elite recruits because they're getting better competition and coaching than they'd typically get at the high school and grassroots levels, along with the battle-hardening that comes with tournament competition where US teams are always favored. NBA teams aren't on the same level yet, as they don't immediately get their hands on these teenage prospects, but they like that they're able to see high schoolers more than they used to. Full-time high school scouts also see the difference in the way some of the nation's most-talented prospects handle themselves and improve their game.

"For the top tier guys, I think they're certainly making their mark," said Daniels, who is part of the junior national team selection committee. "USA Basketball, in my eyes, is the best place to evaluate a prospect. When I'm evaluating a guy, I want to see him in all settings, and with USA Basketball, it's structure, it's quality coaching, it's putting these kids through competitive drills and competitive situations. I'm not sure there's a higher honor than representing your country in high school basketball, so these kids compete there and they play hard. So it's certainly turned into the premier event, in my eyes.

"I think Sean and BJ have done a tremendous job of developing the brand with the younger generation. They're getting these kids early, and getting them in the program earlier and finding out about them earlier, so they're helping out with development. When a kid is able to go out to Colorado Springs for two weeks, and then go to Argentina and compete on a world stage, that's a big-time experience, but they're getting better in the process."

The current youth players won't make it to the senior level for a while—if they do at all—but Ford is excited that the new process has been in place long enough that some of their initial recruits for the Under-16 and Under-17 programs are now becoming more reasonable candidates for the senior national team.

Beyond the aforementioned Drummond, the initial youth roster in 2009 included Charlotte Hornets forward and defensive standout Michael Kidd-Gilchrist, Washington Wizards shooting guard Bradley Beal (who was in the mix for the 2014 World Cup team before breaking his wrist), Philadelphia 76ers combo guard Tony Wroten, and a handful of other new(ish) NBAers. The 2010 Under-17 roster included Milwaukee Bucks forward Jabari Parker (the No. 2 overall pick in 2014), Aaron Gordon of the Orlando Magic (No. 4 in that draft), along with Okafor, Jones, and Winslow, all lottery picks in 2015. We're moving closer and closer to the point where the pipeline will be fully connected, and a significant number of players on the senior national team will have started with USA Basketball at the very beginning of the current process.

"I think we're now just seeing the results of it, but I think the impact it could have on us is post-[2016]," Ford said. "A lot of the players that will be on the '16 [team] will still be the guys that were kind of raised through USA Basketball with Coach K, if you will. And then post-'16 and we head into the next [cycle], you're going to see players that first started to play for USA Basketball in our 16- and 17-and-under teams. That's where you'll see the Jabari Parkers, the Jahlil Okafors, even Marcus Smart, those types of guys."

⌒

Compared to high school, analytics are much more widely available and used at the college level. While longtime *Sports Illustrated* college basketball writer Luke Winn estimates that maybe a quarter of Division I programs have a staffer who is largely competent in advanced statistics and analysis, basically every program competing at that level has access to some type of analytics.

For starters, a subscription to Ken Pomeroy's KenPom.com site costs $19.99 a year and provides a wealth of information, starting with a team's four factors rankings and moving into more esoteric statistics like a team's relative height and contributions from its bench. Other web-based services like Basketball State provide even more granular stats and years of historic information, for a similar price point. Both of those service providers also have more expensive products tailored for college coaches to help them analyze their own team and to scout others. There are also independent consultants who work for individual programs, and basically every Division I program subscribes to Synergy, as well.

If you have extra cash and the ability to hire staff to process all of the data, though, SportVU is becoming a differentiator at the NCAA level, too. And whenever the system actually becomes more mainstream at that level, a few individual schools will already be well ahead of the curve.

During the 2014–15 season, there were four men's college basketball programs that used SportVU. Powerhouses Louisville and Duke—which had the highest and third-highest basketball budgets in the country in 2013–14, per data provided to the US Department of Education's Office of Postsecondary Education—were each on their second season with the system, as was Marquette, a perennial NCAA tournament team under former head coach Buzz Williams that now was under the command of former Duke point guard and assistant coach Steve Wojciechowski.

The fourth program, though, was a fairly unexpected one, coming not from the remaining pool of college bluebloods or even one of the nation's big-money conferences. It was from within the less-fancied Mountain West Conference, and even within that league, it wasn't nouveau power San Diego State or typical league heavyweight New Mexico or even glitzy University of Nevada-Las Vegas. The program that installed SportVU in its arena was Colorado State, located an hour north of Denver in bucolic Fort Collins, with a bigger basketball budget than either the Lobos or Rebels per that Department of Education data. The Rams elected to spend a modest chunk of it to gain an advantage.

Cutting-edge technology seems a funny fit for an old-school tactician like Colorado State head coach Larry Eustachy, who has won over five hundred games in his career despite coaching mostly at a series of out-of-the-way-and-spotlight locales. But the seeds for the idea were planted by the team's video coordinator, Willie Glover, who had worked with Eustachy both as a student assistant and assistant coach at Southern Mississippi and had connected with Brian Kopp at the 2014 NBA Summer League. Glover figured the spend would benefit the Rams as a recruiting tool, and also would enable the program to maximize the skills of the players they were able to bring in, as the Rams were much more likely to nab a one-year transfer than a one-and-done blue-chipper.

Glover got Eustachy to buy in, and he spent the 2014–15 season handling the interpretation and the reporting of the SportVU data for the coaching staff. Glover openly admitted that the first season was a work in progress, both in terms of the actual reports (which were delivered via e-mail, and after every four games to try to smooth out stats variance a bit) and in how messages were received and deliberated by the coaching staff. While a lot of what Glover sent along was fairly rudimentary, there were sometimes pieces of information that he flagged that would allow the team to more closely consider how it was deploying some of its personnel.

"If we want to look at assists, we can track Daniel [Bejarano] for example, and see on average . . . at home he touches it about eighty-four times a night," Glover said, showing off the SportVU product on his laptop as he sat in Eustachy's office. "As you can see, that's about roughly twenty times more than the next person, so what is he doing with those touches? His assist percentage is quite low considering the number of touches that he has. As compared to a JJ Avila, who touches the ball roughly twenty times less, but has a 3 percent higher assist percentage."

Of course, it's difficult to compare a guard (Bejarano) who is forced to be a primary ballhandler because of injuries and roster construction with a big man (Avila) who gets the ball in more favorable scoring positions (and also was a good passer from the post and off the bounce), and that is the kind of conversation Glover wanted to promote with his data e-mails to Eustachy and his assistants without making things too confrontational or complicated.

"That would be a good argument or discussion to have in the coaches meeting," Glover said about the Bejarano/Avila comparison. "Hey, how can we get the ball into JJ's hands more so we can be a more efficient offense. Daniel, for example, he has the ball in his hands a lot, but the percentages are not adding up for the touches he had. [Backup point guard] John Gillon, he was up there with JJ;

typically, when they have the ball, good things happen for our team compared to other guys, and that's something that I may put in a report because, again, I don't want to overwhelm him."

The 2014–15 Rams were an interesting test case for the introduction of SportVU because in certain ways, the way they played stepped well outside of Eustachy's long-established coaching footprint. Pomeroy's data goes back to the 2001–02 season and, prior to last season, a Eustachy team in his database had never taken more than 30 percent of its field goal attempts from behind the arc nor finished higher than 234th in the country in terms of the percentage of field goal attempts that were 3-pointers. That changed with the roster in question, as Colorado State took 36.6 percent of its shots from 3-point range and connected on a reasonable 34.8 percent of them. Four of their five primary 3-point shooters made at least 36 percent of their attempts, so the higher rate of shots from that distance, on the surface, made sense.

Things got more complicated for Eustachy because of what happened at the point guard position. Grambling University transfer Antwan Scott was presumed to be the starter at that position heading into the season, but he suffered an early foot injury, was never healthy, and ultimately played in just four games before missing the rest of the year. As noted earlier, sliding Bejarano over to the point had its limitations because he was not a great passer and also, relatively speaking, was a volume shooter who didn't shoot very well from inside the arc or get to the free throw line to bolster his decent 3-point marksmanship.

That left Eustachy with the option of Gillon, a transfer from the University of Arkansas-Little Rock. Gillon had a solid assist-to-turnover ratio, may have been the league's most effective penetrator off the dribble, shot 39 percent from the arc, and got to the free throw line a ton for a guy who only played around twenty minutes a game. Despite Gillon's seemingly solid offensive contributions, Eustachy—whose reputation centers around rugged defense and rebounding—had a hard time trusting the diminutive Gillon (who was six inches shorter than Bejarano, who was an excellent rebounder for a guard) on the defensive end of the floor. This was a great situation into which to introduce some of the SportVU data and create a discussion.

"As coaches, you tend to get things in your brain and you tend to see things, you see almost what your brain is telling you to see," said assistant coach Ross Hodge. "Like, John Gillon for example. We always had it in our head that he was a poor defender, he's a bad defender, but then you get into some of the SportVU stuff and some of the Synergy stuff, it's like 'He's grading out pretty well.' He may not be in a stance, jumping to the ball, closing out like crazy, but his man don't score. Or he gets over the ball screen. It may not be what you want, or how you want it [but it works]."

That said, the Rams' staff also had to figure out how and when was the best time to send information to Eustachy for his consideration.

"Coach is a timing guy, like most head coaches. Will will hit him with the stats. That's the best way to do it, we feel like, because usually it will give him a chance to be at home," Hodge added. "He can look at them, digest them a little bit, not feeling like it's an argument. Not coming in, feeling like 'I don't give a [expletive] what you all say, John Gillon can't guard.' And then you'll be like 'Well, coach . . . ' It just gives him some time to digest it. Sometimes, he'll come in and won't bring it up at all. Sometimes, we'll be in there watching film as a staff, and twenty minutes later, out of nowhere, he'll be like 'Yeah, I saw that on Will's stats.'"

Hodge said the new data they had at their disposal also helped the assistant coaches make a case to Eustachy for a different way to defend ball screens last season. Instead of having the handler's defender jam up and then go under the screen, or have the screener's defender hedge the screen to try to slow down the dribbler, they went to more of a soft drop from the screener's defender so they didn't end up allowing as much penetration and an easy kick for an open three.

They also were able to provide more context to some of Eustachy's preferred rebounding stats and tactics by showing that certain players were actually going hard for rebounds despite less-than-impressive rebounding numbers. They were collecting a high percentage of their realistic opportunities and/or the Rams were getting the rebound a large portion of the times a player was within a few feet of the rebound.

This is still a work in progress in Fort Collins, especially since Colorado State doesn't pay for SportVU use for practices, so the data set is limited to the Rams' home games, many of which come in non-conference play and can be somewhat lopsided affairs. But the Rams are bullish on what they were able to accomplish in their first year using the SportVU system; they say it has added just a little more clarity and insight to their staff discussions.

"If you didn't have the data, and it's just arguing what your account of events is, that's when it can get difficult," Hodge said. "When any person sees it one way, and you see it another way, basically you're just arguing what you both see, and you could both be seeing it right. And [SportVU clarifies] a little bit of the 'maybe this is happening. Or maybe this *isn't* happening. Maybe we're seeing it wrong.'"

⌐∾

Duke operates at a different level than Colorado State. The Blue Devils have the highest-paid college coach in the country in Mike Krzyzewski, one of the largest overall budgets in the country, and one of the most national presences of any college program in America. So when Duke was one of three schools to first dive in to SportVU in 2013, the Blue Devils also made sure it was installed in their practice facility. Through the end of the 2014–15 college season, they were the only team in the country with that privilege.

As noted in the Colorado State section above, sample size is one of the principal issues in effectiveness of data mining and analysis at the collegiate level. Even if you have the system, it's almost certain at this stage that your opponents will not, so teams that use SportVU for games are only able to collect data from their sixteen or seventeen home games a season. Since maybe half of those are against non-league competition, with a good percentage of those games being "guarantee games" against overmatched opponents grateful to receive a high five-figures check for playing, there is a lot of noise in the data provided, if you even have the proper staffing to analyze it.

By having the system also available for their practices, the Blue Devils are vastly increasing the number of times it can be utilized within a season, even if the primary purpose of the analysis then becomes self-scouting from practice sessions rather than understanding what has worked better against opponents. As the competition in practice may often be better than what a blueblood program will often face in nonconference play, there's additional merit to what's being analyzed from practices.

Krzyzewski was reluctant to discuss exactly how Duke is using SportVU and how the system has aided the Blue Devils, but his former assistant Wojciechowski was willing to provide a bit of detail on how the Blue Devils had started to explore its uses.

"It's one of those mechanisms that has tremendous potential to really take a look at the game from an analytical standpoint at the very highest level," he said. "And I think the challenge for us at Duke, and for anybody who uses that, [was] how do you use that data to generate things that are useful on a day-to-day basis to impacting the team? And I think that's the challenge of it. Again, it's in the infant stages, especially at the college level, of using it and figuring out, 'How do we take this slice of the pie, the analytics, and make it work for us in a positive and meaningful way?'"

Wojciechowski acknowledged that much of the value from the system came from breaking down the five-on-five sessions during practice, or self-scouting, since there are many more practices than games over the course of a season. The Blue Devils, per Wojciechowski, were able to use the SportVU data from practices for a variety of purposes.

"I think some of the things that you look for, or you want to kind of reinforce what your eyes see with data, are like rebound chances," he said. "How many times does a guy have a chance to rebound the ball? And then how many times they go after it, how many times do they get it? I think that's one thing. Shot selection. Where are guys actually an efficient and effective scorer and what type of shots do they produce and score them at a high percentage, and what type of shots do they shoot at a low percentage and what areas of the floor they are? Those I would say are two examples that we used [in 2013–14]."

A December 2014 column by Barry Jacobs in the *Charlotte Observer* noted that Duke was using SportVU data to break down the team's in-game perimeter shot selection as the Blue Devils were learning to play with gifted freshman low-post scorer Jahlil Okafor. Like many teams, Duke tries to limit the number of lower-success shots it takes, and having a post player as dominant as Okafor made that mandate even more important for the 2014-15 Blue Devils.

Per an *EdTech* article from March 2015, Duke ended up making 41 percent of 383 catch-and-shoot 3-point attempts during the 2014-15 regular season. Those shots generated 1.23 points per attempt, which was relatively close to the 1.33 points per attempt posted by Okafor (who made 279 of 420, or 66.4 percent, of his shots without attempting a 3-pointer). Add in the impact of floor spacing and optimizing Okafor's scoring load, and those are good shots to be taking. Conversely, according to the *EdTech* column, Duke only made 33 percent of its threes attempted off the dribble. That is not a good enough percentage to be taking those shots over giving Okafor low-post touches (or finding better catch-and-shoot looks), so those were shots Duke wanted to try to avoid as much as possible.

Per Wojciechowski (and numerous other college coaches), the ability not just to provide stats to the players, but to show specific breakdowns of where and how shots were coming from—paired with graphics or video to hammer home the point—is the best way to impact players.

"How you package the data, especially when you're dealing with college-aged kids, is important," he said. "For us [at Duke], it was more of a verbal [thing], talking about verbally what we saw, and then backing up with evidence of the data. Whether it's a 'You're not going to the boards enough' or 'You're taking low percentage shots,' it just gives another layer of proof that what you're saying is true and why you're saying those things to them. And I think in today's day and age with kids, it's why are you saying that and having as many layers as possible to kind of prove a point and to teach them."

Wojciechowski was more circumspect when asked about how he planned on using the Bradley Center access to enhance his Marquette program, but noted that because of last season's roster turnover from the year before, it was almost like starting fresh with a new set of data since the stuff from the season before wouldn't be particularly helpful. He also added that, as a newer coach taking over his first college program as a head coach, he would be more apt to revisit some of his decisions after being presented with the enhanced data SportVU can provide, in addition to using the output to back some of his predetermined thinking.

"In Coach [Krzyzewski]'s case, he's done it for so long. His feel and his eye for the game, when you have a guy that's at a master level of coaching, mostly it's used for validation," Wojciechowski said. "But mostly for younger coaches who are trying to establish a system and get know new personnel, I'll use it both ways. Hopefully, I'm validating the decisions I'm making, but I think there will be times more so than with Coach where you're taking a step back and asking yourself, 'Is this the right thing?'"

When asked, though, whether he recalled a specific instance where SportVU had altered his thinking, Wojciechowski demurred.

"Off the top of my head, from my experience with it, no, not to this point," he said with a laugh. "I assume that that day is coming."

A program doesn't even have to have SportVU, though, for it to have an analytics basis. And analytics don't just have to be about on-court performance for them to be very effective.

Buzz Williams is one of the more unique characters in the college head-coaching ranks. Williams himself is extremely comfortable with statistics and analysis, but he's also a master motivator and a voracious information hound. Williams is a huge fan of NFL coaches like Jon Gruden (who turned to a career as an analyst for ESPN's *Monday Night Football*) and Gus Bradley, the head coach of the NFL's Jacksonville Jaguars, for their creativity in thinking and motivating. Williams also says he has offered to pay reporters for their leftover interview notes from feature stories he finds interesting.

Williams, both at Marquette (where he did actually have a year of SportVU access through the Golden Eagles' games at the home of the Milwaukee Bucks) and now at Virginia Tech, also tends to cull from a different pool of recruits than many other top-tier coaches. He often dips into the junior college ranks to grab one- or two-year contributors to fill holes in his roster, believing (a) that the growing number of transfers each season in college basketball makes building around freshmen a bit riskier, and (b) that he's not going to get blue-chip recruits to come to Milwaukee or Blacksburg, Virginia, and needs to craft a team with a hard-nosed edge in order to compete, first in the old Big East and now the Atlantic Coast Conference.

Putting together rosters that way also shortens the time that Williams has to make things cohesive. He doesn't have the luxury of leaning on full recruiting classes that stay together for four seasons and increasingly understand what he wants from his team. Not that every year is a reboot, but there's a significant learning curve involved with playing for him, and Williams is aware that different handling is required of today's college players. Mostly gone are the days of coach as autonomy figure, so Williams needs to work harder to get his messages to sink in, and he likes using data and descriptive/visual presentation to help make his points.

"I think that the world's society, their attention span is much, much shorter than ever before," he said. "So I think when you're trying to teach, you have to do it with evidence. Because I think the way of how coaches from a generation above me once coached, I think that's over in some regards. In that, 'Well, the head coach said this, and that's it.' And everybody just takes it as if that's the gospel. Not saying that's completely gone—I think the position is still the position—but I think when you're talking to your staff, I think when you're talking to your team, there has to be some sort of evidence of why you're saying what you're saying.

"These kids can't listen to a diatribe for twelve minutes of 'Hey, this is how we do it.' You gotta explain why," he added. "And anything you can use from data—and I understand you can twist it and skew it however you want, but it's the best, in my opinion—it's one of the best ways to teach. Because it's something that kids can understand. It's something that you can hold them accountable to. And it's also something that not only can you get it as it relates to a stat, but you can you use video to show it, you can use stats to show it.

"And so, I'm always looking for ways to take opinions out of things and say 'These are facts. And from these facts, this is gonna determine how we should play, why we need to play this way, who we need to recruit, why we need to recruit them, etc., etc.'"

Williams loves to dive deep into advanced statistics, but understands that the meaning and usefulness of them can get lost in the message if it's not delivered in an accessible way. "I think in order to magnify something, you gotta simplify it," he said. And perhaps the most unique way that Williams shapes and simplifies his messages while building credibility with his players is through a weekly series of offseason chats he holds for his team. At Marquette, they were called Life Lessons. At Virginia Tech, they're called Tech Talks. Williams focuses each talk on a specific topic, which run the gamut from life skills like personal finance and understanding health insurance, to the more academic, like how different people's brains are wired differently.

One purpose of the talks is pretty straightforward. Williams wants to help his players understand each other better and also prepare them for life beyond the insular nature of college, whether they go on to professional basketball careers or out in the general workplace. The talks are also geared to have a significant side effect, though: Williams loads them with information and data, so when the players show they're starting to understand the Tech Talk lessons and show increased eagerness as each week brings a new one, Williams knows they are more likely to buy in during the season when he uses analytics to make his points about how he wants the team to play.

"If I have taught them things that they want to know, that utilize numbers, then their trust in me is, 'If coach is talking about numbers, [he] knows what he's talking about . . . ,'" Williams said. "You know what I'm saying? So, it's stuff that they need to learn, it's stuff that's healthy for their life, but it's also stuff that I build equity in what I'm teaching them, because when I get to December, there's never going to be, 'Well, Buzz is writing all those numbers up there. He don't know.' Because they're not going to view it like that."

Williams is well known for his obsession with "paint touches," or how often on offense his team can get the ball into the lane, or deny opponents those opportunities on the defensive end. He adjusts his philosophy on how best to get the ball there based on his personnel—his Elite Eight team at Marquette in 2012 was mostly undersized and more often got in the paint off the dribble than via the pass—but he harps on the overall concept so often that a Marquette basketball blog adopted *Paint Touches* as its name and Twitter handle while he was the coach there. Williams claims that field goal percentage is much higher on shots taken after the possession had a paint touch, even if the shot ultimately comes from outside the paint, than ones that don't.

So, in order to get his team playing in the style he wants, Williams concocts a variety of what he calls "whiteboard stats," because he (and only he) writes everything he wants his team to understand data-wise on a gigantic whiteboard in the locker room. Some of them he refers to as SID stats, or the more basic box score and aggregation stuff that gets disseminated to the media and is available on team websites. Other stuff is more complex, but ultimately the message is presented in a discrete format that makes it easy to understand and maintain during games.

"In all of the numbers that I study and all of the stuff I get into, I don't relate all of that to our team. I don't [even] relate all of that to our staff. But I do try to find ways to simplify what I think is most important as it relates to that particular team, or that particular kid," Williams said.

"I don't explain to them, 'You know when we do the shooting drills? Do you know how often somebody rebounds the ball, and then pitches it out to you to shoot it?" he added. "Like, they don't get that that's because the ball's coming from in to out . . . All they get is, 'Coach says our offense is red light, green light. The light is red until the ball touches the paint.'"

That's not to say that the talk topics are randomly selected. If the conversation is about taxes and other income deductions, Williams will use the context of salaries earned and tie them into a professional basketball context. Do you have an agent? Do you have a rep who landed you an endorsement deal? What are the different state tax rates or tax rates for Americans playing overseas? That helps teach his players that the same starting point ends up at decidedly different end points given the different paths you can choose.

He also uses the conversations on brain structure to help him understand his players as much as he wants the players to learn more about themselves. A huge part of coaching is teaching, and just like a classroom instructor, Williams needs to understand his students and their specific needs. The best ways to learn vary from person to person, and Williams wants to figure out as early as possible how each of his players are wired, so he can understand who is compatible with whom and also which groups will take best to various types of instruction.

"One of the Tech Talks is 'How do you think?' And I talk about left brain, right brain, and I do some things with them for them to understand which side are they," Williams said. "And how we all have to honor everybody's brain, because there's no right answer, there's no wrong answer, it's just how we're wired. And how you can be a great teammate, if you're a right-brain thinker, to a left-brain thinker. Because some guys need to hear it. Then I start talking about 'Are you a visual learner? Do you learn by hearing?' And so I explain to them, 'I can tell you what you guys are, but that's my responsibility because I pay attention to everything. So when I'm coaching you, I know which ones of you hear what I'm saying and can digest it, and which ones of you need to be on the floor and walk through it to learn it.'

"So, even when I say, 'Andy, Buzz, John, Dick, and Harry, on the court, we're walking through "23X,"' that may not be the starters. That may not be the maroon team, that may not be the white team. That's the team that I know needs to walk through 23X to absorb it. If you're not on the floor, that's because as I'm teaching and walking through 23X for these guys, I know you can listen and you can absorb it."

The absorbing is not just for the players, either. Williams makes sure he indoctrinates his staff in the language of utility for the Hokies, as well. Take assistant coach Jamie McNeilly, for example. He's been with Williams ever since he was a player at the University of New Orleans, when Williams was the head coach there. Since then, McNeilly has moved with Williams to Marquette and now to Virginia Tech, but 2014 was the first summer that McNeilly was out on the road recruiting for Williams's program.

Williams said he told McNeilly that, as part of his daily work, he had to keep a diary on the road that included every single thing that popped into his head, no matter whether it was before, during, or after a game that a potential recruit was in, or not even at one of the myriad gyms coaches traipse in and out of all summer long.

Williams would periodically connect with his newly blooded assistant on the road during that July period and would ask to examine the diary so he could see what McNeilly was thinking and also to make suggestions on what he should actually be observing. Late that summer, McNeilly was scouting wing Eli Wright, who ultimately committed to Mississippi State in August 2015, and noted in his Williams-provided old-school notepad that three of Wright's first four baskets in that game had come when he had been fouled in the process of scoring—an "and-1" in hoops parlance.

Williams latched onto that as a great example of how looking at things in a certain way, through an analytical lens, can benefit the staff, and in turn, benefit Virginia Tech's players.

"I'm like, 'See, Jamie, that translates to us.' Not, 'He's a good player,' not, 'He's left-handed and I like left-handed guards,'" Williams said. "Not all of that. You can see that immediately. But what is it underneath all of that that translates to us? Well, if three out of his first four shots were and-1s, obviously I would think—I would bet—that those were paint touch shots? 'Yes, sir, those were.' I go, 'But that's what I'm saying. Nobody is going to say that. They're going to say so-and-so recruited him, so-and-so offered him, this tweet that his team won, this tweet said something—none of that matters to us. It doesn't matter to me.'

"But, you take three out of his first four [baskets via and-1s], now all of a sudden when I have that conversation with the kid, I go, 'Hey, man, let me talk to you about your game.' And he's like, 'Wow, coach. I didn't even know you was looking like that.' I said, 'No, I want you to understand that that's how thin the line is, right? Because you have to [get to where] 25 percent of your points, if you're a real player, come from the free throw line. . . . If you do that throughout your college career, I promise you'll make more money than you've dreamed of.'

In Williams's first season in Blacksburg, Virginia Tech ended up finishing last again in the Atlantic Coast Conference, winning only two of eighteen games in the extremely competitive conference for the second straight season, but he isn't deterred. He's seen the benefits of his approach from his time at Marquette, where he inherited a successful program from Tom Crean, who moved to Indiana, and won at least twenty-two games in each of his first five seasons there. He is a true believer in stats, but an even bigger devotee to finding ever more creative ways in which to bridge his passion with his players' ability to process the information. Those ideas—and those talks—are the building blocks, and nothing good can happen during the season if they're not in place beforehand.

"I think that as I've matured, and maybe as I've evolved as a coach, you have to find ways—not using the game—to teach them the values of numbers," he said.

CHAPTER 5

Faster, Stronger, More Explosive

It's about faster, stronger, more explosive, all these types of things to optimize performance. We're not just trying to avoid injuries; we're trying to make them perform better on the court.

—Adam Hewitt, assistant general manager, P3

S anta Barbara, California, is one of the hidden gems of the West Coast, a tony, oceanfront community about ninety minutes northwest of Los Angeles up the Ventura Freeway. The drive through some of LA's northern suburbs is nice enough, but improves dramatically when the highway runs through Ventura and then starts winding its way up the coast, with the Pacific Ocean lapping at the shore as stunning companionship.

The city itself sits on the longest south-facing piece of shoreline on the entire West Coast, neatly tucked between the Santa Ynez Mountains and the water. Thanks to its moderate Mediterranean climate, its stunning location, and the number of major celebrities who own homes there, Santa Barbara has been referred to by the *New York Times* as "America's Riviera."

You wouldn't expect this vista to house one of the epicenters of cutting-edge professional sports diagnostics, but starting from

Stearns Wharf, the main commercial pier that juts out temptingly into the ocean, you're maybe half a mile from it by foot. Just walk several blocks down one of the nation's most aesthetically pleasing fitness paths, cross E. Cabrillo Boulevard, continue across a set of railroad tracks, wind through a small garden and a parking area, and spill out onto the southern end of modest Santa Barbara Street. There, at the base of a developing, trendy warehouse area filling up with more scene-appropriate businesses like art shops and wine bars, sits a mostly nondescript, mostly one-room building. Inside is P3—the Peak Performance Project—one of pro basketball's most important training and biometric testing facilities.

P3 is the brainchild of Dr. Marcus Elliott, a Harvard-trained physician who has spent the last seventeen years working with world-class athletes, sports organizations, and franchises to help them maximize athletic performance while minimizing injury risk. At various points in his career, he has worked with sportsmen and women who were training at the US Olympic Training Center, the Australian Institute of Sport, and the Sports Science Institute of South Africa. He also has served as a physiologist and injury prevention specialist for the NFL's New England Patriots, as the director of sports science for Major League Baseball's Seattle Mariners, and as an advisor to the NBA's Utah Jazz, among numerous other consulting positions. On P3's website, Mark McKown, the head strength and conditioning coach of the Jazz (the first NBA team to start sending its players to P3 in the middle of last decade), describes Elliott as "a true pioneer" who "has an eye and ability to pick up things and identify problems I've never seen anybody do."

The mission behind Elliott's enterprise is to help athletes—specifically in basketball and baseball, although they are also looking to move further into international soccer—refine their physical movements in order to maximize their explosiveness in the core motions specific to their sport while also making sure their bodies move in ways that significantly reduce injury risk. They accomplish this, in part, by designing workout programs that promote uniform muscle balance and a reduction of the torque on joints that can eventually lead to damage.

The inside of the facility is surprisingly normal looking given what happens there, at least on first glance. There's a set of steps up to a nice, wood-floored waiting area with a couple of couches and a greeting desk. A nicely marbled one-person bathroom complete with a shower is off to the right, and modest offices tucked into the front right corner of the space. There are three flat-screen TVs high up on the right-side wall toward the back of the room.

The main part of the training area is totally open aside from several floor-to-ceiling support beams running through the middle of it. There's a three-lane, straight-line running track that starts near where the front door opens and extends along the full length of the left wall. In several corners are standing weight racks and rubberized weight plates for squats and other leg exercises. There are rolling bins full of weight balls of different sizes and hefts, along with red metal stools of various heights to be used for step-ups or as devices to jump on or over.

Then you look a bit closer and see more sophisticated and unusual equipment. There are four-sided towers with various cables and other resistance bands. There are various angled and flat, laminated wood planks, designed for pushing off and sliding. Along the right side of the room toward the back, there is a cement brick wall to be used both for stretching and also to twist and hurl things into with significant force.

A few steps away from that wall is where P3 truly separates itself from a normal workout facility. Inset in the floor sit two large, parallel, metal "force plates," which essentially are sophisticated scales that can measure the amount of force and explosiveness created by athletes who jump on and off of them. Above the plates are numerous motion-sensing cameras that capture the movements as they happen, and feed the data into computers at a desk in the back right corner of the room. At that desk sit the company's biomechanists, who store, translate, and interpret the data, creating living profiles of an athlete's movements and performance. They also use the collective data to build trend profiles for various injuries and injury risk for each sport.

On this particular sunny Monday morning in November 2014, half an hour before the facility officially opened for business, lightly bearded assistant general manager Adam Hewitt already was waiting in the main greeting area. Hewitt is in charge of day-to-day operations at the facility, managing the relationships between P3 and its clients, and also handling the company's brand awareness. As the rest of the staff was busily prepping for the arrival of an NBA player and his team's trainer at 9 a.m., Hewitt walked through the company's philosophy and how P3 works with their range of clients at both the individual and team levels.

"Everything is so tailored to the individual," Hewitt said. "Our training programs, we definitely have a formula we like to follow, and there's definitely a rationale for putting different types of movements together, and there are certain ways we like to progress things, but the heart of it is just finding exactly what each athlete needs, and giving them an exact prescription. Ultimately, nothing is generalized. Obviously, we're not inventing new exercises for each guy—it's stuff that's been done before—but prescribe it.

"If the guy is unbelievably sound and has great mechanics, it's about optimizing power development and the movements of the sport," he continued. "It's about faster, stronger, more explosive, all these types of things to optimize performance. We're not just trying to avoid injuries; we're trying to make them perform better on the court. Jump a little higher, run a little quicker, accelerate a little faster, change direction more efficiently. And it goes hand in hand. The guys with the best mechanics tend to move a little more quickly, but there are some guys with horrible mechanics that are able to figure it out on the court because they are special athletes and they have an unbelievable nervous system and all these fast-twitch muscles. But at the same time, one little glitch can throw everything off."

Hewitt explained that athletes and team strength coaches will spend time at P3 conducting initial workout assessments, and then P3 will put together summaries for the teams that highlight the athletes' biggest primary needs. Those summaries include the testing results and specific rationale as to why particular issues were flagged, and what could happen if they're not fixed. Then P3 plies the strength coaches with corrective strategies and specific exercises the athlete needs to train themselves out of the current harmful pattern.

On this morning, the NBA player (who is recovering from an injury) was coming in for a follow-up assessment, so we headed back to the biometric testing area, where two of the company's biomechanists were preparing. One of them was Stanford-educated Eric Leidersdorf, who was helping lead P3's efforts in data analysis and bigger-picture trend identification. As P3's player database continues to grow, the company can get more accurate interpretations of risk ranges and what types of muscle imbalances lead to what kinds of injuries with what kind of frequency.

For the force plate testing, Leidersdorf explained that the technicians place around two dozen reflective dots, or "markers," on various anatomical landmarks on the athlete's body. These dots reflect light back to the cameras, which then feed that motion data into the computer. The technicians then go back and identify each segment of data and link it to a specific body part—left knee, right ankle, and so forth—and from that can generate a skeleton on screen that displays the movements of the athlete as well as the various levels of force generated and the discrepancies between the player's left and right sides.

"We can replicate exactly what their bodies are doing when they go through these movements," Leidersdorf said. "What the force plates allow us to do is look at things beyond how high a guy jumps.

[Vertical leap has] been done at the [NBA Draft] Combine for however long they've done it, but what this allows us to look at is rates of force development."

As an example, he pulled up an anonymous NBA player's file on the computer monitor and showed the skeleton going through the movements of when the player did a "drop jump"—a drill where the player starts on an eighteen-inch-high box, drops onto the force plates, and then immediately jumps as high as he can vertically. The drill is somewhat akin to the experience of making a second jump for a rebound, and tries to isolate the kind of dynamic muscle systems that would be used in basketball games.

Leidersdorf then pointed to two colored lines on the screen, which corresponded to the data being fed back from the cameras. In this particular player's case, there was roughly a 20 percent discrepancy between the force generated by his left and right legs during that test drill. That was almost double the average differential that P3 sees in athletes in this drill, and was an initial sign that there may be a problem brewing.

"This asymmetry is our first window into some sort of injury, whether or not it's compensation, or otherwise," Leidersdorf said. "It could be something where, in this guy's case, where he has some injury and develops a compensation pattern and is moving away from it, or this could be the calm before the storm. And you can't tell this with the naked eye when he jumps that you have 20 percent more force in one of your legs. And if you use that over the course of a couple of years, there goes the meniscus."

Next Leidersdorf went back to the on-screen skeleton and, as it was simulating the jump, he pointed to its right leg.

"Now, when he goes through the movement, you see his right knee start to dive in a little bit," he said. "When he contacts the ground, his right knee sinks inwards. That's called a valgus maneuver, or knock-kneed—a medical term. It's closely linked to a number of knee injuries: ACL, MCL, meniscus, all the things that are associated with this movement pattern."

As the skeleton continued its movement, Leidersdorf pointed out another red flag.

"So, beyond going into this aggressive valgus motion, at the end of the movement, you see this [extra] rotation, so this knee swings in-to-out pretty aggressively compared to everyone else we have tested. So this is a combination of a couple of factors. He's overloading this right side, and he also has this aggressive twist in and twist out, so there's something going on there which is a little scary."

Leidersdorf then noted that this player also has a significant differential in his ankle flexibility, which is an additional piece of concerning information.

"All these things together say 'We're worried about your right side, but specifically, that right knee is not going to hold up if this keeps happening,'" he said.

As it turns out, this particular player had a foot issue in college, and his current jumping motion was leftover compensation from when he was feeling pain in that foot. More crucially, the player had recently disclosed that he had been experiencing some burning in that right knee. Luckily, he was only suffering from some swelling, and P3 helped diagnose his muscle imbalances and movement deficiencies before any major damage to ligaments was done. P3 prescribed a set of transformational exercises for the player to the team's strength coach, and the team installed a set of force plates at its own training facility. The player comes back periodically for a follow-up exam of sorts, so the P3 staff can see his development and how closely his adjusted movements are staying to what is optimal. Through the end of the 2014–15 season, the player had remained healthy.

As Leidersdorf wrapped up his explanation with the visuals, Elliott wandered over from where he'd been chatting with the NBA team's strength coach. His floppy hair and relaxed demeanor suggest someone who may have seen a surfboard or two in his time, but he was anything but laissez-faire about his enterprise and its potential growth.

From its humble start where former Utah Jazz players Paul Millsap and Ronnie Brewer were among the first to buy into the testing, P3 has made significant headway with a large number of NBA teams. One drawback of the business, though—at least until 2014—was that P3 was working exclusively with athletes who already had made it to the NBA, which meant any testing started with advanced medical baselines and, in most cases, somewhat incomplete data sets. In essence, P3 was exploring players who already had established physical habits or may already have been injured significantly, so it was harder to know exactly what was possible or how a player used to perform before the injury.

Ahead of the 2014 NBA Draft, though, the league quietly invited P3 in to do some testing of prospects at the Combine. Elliott and his staff were able to get force plate baselines established in the normal vertical leap (stand on the plates and jump as high as you can), the drop jump (as described above) and the lateral skater test (where you push off one leg and stride as far as you can to one side or the other). Additionally, Adidas reached out to P3 to do similar baseline testing for high school and college prospects at its high-profile Adidas Nations camp.

"Seven or eight years ago, we decided to stake out this claim and do this objectively. And originally, the data was interesting, but we had no context for it," Elliott said after that year's testing had been done. "We tested a player, and he had a difference in impact spike of like 15 percent, and we'd say 'OK, this is a problem. We need to balance this out, make this side stronger, to absorb more of the force.' But now we have a database of, oh, I don't know, 160 NBA players and we know that the mean delta in spikes on impact in an NBA player is 16 percent. We know this now. We know how they move.

And we can't generalize and study a population walking around the street and compare them to NBA players. It doesn't work.

"The last couple of years, [the business is] starting to really sing," Elliott continued. "And it's just going to do this [pointing upward on a diagonal with his hand] right now because of how much data flow we have coming in. From the best teams in the league sending players to us to the players coming back to getting guys at the Combine and Adidas Nations, it's just going to be ridiculous."

Starting to build a data set of teenage athletes was a very important development for P3 (and companies like it). Not only will getting the data earlier provide them with additional insights in terms of their overall strategies and data ranges, but they will get a first look at an athlete when he's still relatively formative, which means they will have the cleanest baseline information possible to use as a reference for the rest of that player's career. This is all highly desirable information when potential NBA players are such a limited resource to begin with.

"These guys get talent ID'd at twelve [years old], and it's a pretty small cohort. It's not like baseball. There aren't that many of them, and very few are going to be the next thing," Elliott said. "We have the potential to have some of the best guys in the league serially tested from when they're like sixteen, maybe four or five times before teams even have them. We'll know what their development curve looks like, what some of these propensities for injuries look like, if they've had some radical change in their biomechanics, if that ankle they sprained changed everything about how they move and now they're wearing out their right knee. It could be crazy valuable."

⮎

P3 isn't the only enterprise trying to unlock the promise (and profits) from merging technology and kinesiological improvements. One of the other leaders in this industry is Dr. Michael Clark, who is the founder of Fusionetics, which has developed a technology platform that helps design and track training programs for everyone from middle-aged gym members to world-class athletes. Initial testing on the client yields data that is interpreted into thousands of variables in the Fusionetics system, and then the platform creates a workout plan designed to fix whatever flaws registered.

Clark, though, is much more widely known as the visionary behind the training program for the Phoenix Suns, who long have been considered the NBA's most successful team in terms of helping their players avoid and recover from injuries. Clark has worked since 2000 with Suns head trainer Aaron Nelson, first creating and then sophisticating an all-inclusive program that has regularly placed the Suns among the NBA's league leaders in fewest player games missed, and has resurrected the injury-affected careers of stars like Grant Hill and Shaquille O'Neal.

"What we wanted to build is a comprehensive athletic performance system that focuses on three pieces: injury prevention, performance, and recovery. And so what we did is change the whole structure [in Phoenix]," Clark said. "We tested every single athlete's movement efficiency, their performance, and then we implemented manual therapy two to three days a week on all of the starters. Then they would get something called DMS, which is deep muscle stimulation and vibration in the muscle, followed by stretching.

"So every other day, they'd get manual therapy, so soft tissue and joint work. And the next day they'd get vibration and stretching, and then after either of those sessions, they would go through very specific corrective exercises and then we implemented very specific functional training programs that we actually published, and we showed that the functional training approach was anywhere between 50 and 200 percent better than traditional lifting.

"And then after that, we had a very specific recovery process where again, every guy had to either wrap ice on their knees, ankles, and shoulders, or they had to get into the ice tub. Now, we have the cryosauna; back then, we didn't. And then they either had to go home and stretch themselves, or we would put them on the table and stretch them back out. Every athlete had that."

Clark went on to say that while technology has improved in the sixteen years since he started with the Suns, his overall approach has remained the same, with stretching, muscle balance, and proper movement being huge keys to the equation. He estimates that an NBA player's flexibility is reduced by 25 percent after they have played a game, and the muscle tightening can increase a further 12 percent if the player then has to get on a plane to head to the next road destination. His staff and the recovery program are designed to minimize that impact as much as possible.

So, Clark and his team have overseen ongoing improvements in player nutrition, vitamins, and supplement intake. They pay attention to the amount and quality of sleep players get. They now use boots and other compression gear to help in recovery after muscle stress. Instead of ice baths, they now have a cryochamber that helps cool the athletes' muscles and creates what Clark called "a significant, total body effect."

Clark believes his focus on overall movement rather than issues at the point of a problem is what has separated his program from most others' to this point. Traditional NBA strength and recovery programs tended to be what Clark termed patho-anatomical, or "bad structure" oriented. Clark's plan is patho-kinesiological, or focused on fixing bad motion in a player's movement.

In listening to Clark talk about the three-pronged basis of his plan, he makes things sound very simple, but even after his long-term involvement with an NBA team, very few other franchises have approached the Suns' level of success in terms of player health. While entities like P3 are helping place more and more trainers at NBA teams themselves, there's still a vast range of training and recovery capabilities across the league. Technology is a great equalizer in that every team can pay to have data on their players collected, but you still need to be able to properly interpret that data, and also have a comprehensive plan in place that knows what to do with it.

"Aaron and I have, so many times, just scratched our heads and said, 'Why are people making this so difficult?'" Clark said. "It's not rocket science. Guys have to be able to bend their ankles, rotate their hips, extend their hips, because they have to be able to jump and run, and so there's a few things that you do to make that work."

A good example of this was the Suns' work with Hill, who had been a star in his six seasons with the Detroit Pistons after being drafted No. 3 overall in the 1994 draft. Hill then moved to the Orlando Magic in a sign-and-trade deal in the summer of 2000, and suffered through a brutal stretch of ankle-related injuries there. Hill only played in four games his first season with the Magic, and only managed to compete in a total of forty-seven games in his first three seasons in Orlando.

Hill's ankle issues were so bad, he underwent surgery in March 2003 where his ankle was rebroken and realigned with his leg. That surgery resulted in his contracting a MRSA infection, and he ended up missing the entirety of the 2003–04 season, as well. Hill managed to play in sixty-seven games the following year and averaged almost twenty points a game, but then a sports hernia—thought to be caused by his compensation for his ankle issues—cost him most of the 2005–06 campaign. By the time he signed with Phoenix in the summer of 2007, there was considerable talk of Hill retiring, as he was a shell of the player he once had been.

"When he came to us at Phoenix, he had had seven surgeries on his ankle. That's all published data," Clark said. "But the biggest thing for him is that his ankle didn't bend. Obviously, he needed surgery, but still, nobody really worked on it, and the big thing for him is his hip didn't rotate. So he played with Detroit against Chicago, went up for a dunk on the left-hand side of the rim, dunked, landed on his hip, and pushed his hip out of position. It changed his leg length, and as his leg length changed, it forced his foot to turn out and his leg to compensate.

"Over a little bit of time, he started to get pain in his Achilles, his foot, and the next thing you know, seven surgeries later, everyone's still focusing on his foot. They're doing all this laser therapy, everything you can imagine on his foot. But when he came to us, his problem was his hip. We loosened his hip, then loosened up his ankle, and his ankle could stay loose because his hip could bend. Then, in three weeks, the guy was back, and he played I don't know how many seasons for us, only missing a couple of games because of his appendix and once he was sick."

Hill played five seasons in Phoenix (and one more after that with the Los Angeles Clippers), including the 2008–09 season when Hill appeared in all eighty-two games for the first time in his career.

O'Neal's story was fairly similar, where it actually was a toe problem on his opposite foot that was causing him hip issues. In Shaq's autobiography, written with longtime *Boston Globe* and ESPN NBA writer Jackie MacMullen, he credited the Suns' training staff with prolonging his career.

Just like Elliott's team at P3, Clark's group also has been doing evaluations at the NBA Draft Combine to test the incoming prospects, and the two groups came to a similar conclusion: There were a lot of players in the 2014 rookie class who were in danger of significant injury based on the way they moved and the muscle imbalances they measured. Months later, that class did indeed suffer a number of season-ending and significant injuries, which piqued the league's attention.

"They're trying to wrap their head around it, to be honest with you," Clark said. "They're trying to figure out what is this. This is kind of an epidemic, and these numbers are bad. Red [the color-coded danger area for Clark's measurements] is bad.

"Sometimes, when you're just measuring movement or performance with gravity, what happens is you'll see compensation," Clark continued. "What we do is, we lay the person down on the table, take gravity away and we measure every joint. Their big toe, their ankle, the back of the knee, their hip rotation and hip extension. And those things, there's very, very specific range of motion of every one of those joints that's very well documented.

"And what we can identify is your knee might be caving in on the right, but it could be coming from your left ankle, it could be coming from your left knee, or left hip, or thigh joint. So we can precisely identify it, then we score that. And then our two scores—the movement score and the mobility score—come together, and from that, you literally predict what stresses an athlete's going to be under. And most importantly, you can fix it. It's really easy to fix."

In Clark's opinion, the young players he has seen in the past five to ten years are showing worse and worse movement. Today's budding basketball talents are building more strength and weight earlier in their growing process while also working on their basketball-specific skills, but Clark believes they are not doing enough proper stretching or figuring out the efficient way to move or jump. P3's Hewitt agrees, noting that among the most surprising things they see in their data capture is "how untrained" the major-college players are when they are tested. Their muscles are not developed symmetrically and they have dangerous movements that are putting strain on their joints and ligaments. According to Clark, every ten degrees of inward bend of a knee when jumping or running puts 50 percent more torque on a player's anterior cruciate ligament. He also said that he believes 75 percent of all muscle-related injuries are preventable through proper training, monitoring, and treatment.

⌒

This kind of off-court movement training has become an increasingly large part of what is an increasingly sophisticated data puzzle for NBA teams, with the so-called Holy Grail of athlete injury prevention and performance improvement expertly connecting in-game tracking data, practice tracking data, and so-called off-site biometric data culled from tracking sleep, monitoring diets, and taking periodic bloodwork to check players' vital levels. Unfortunately, all of this data continues to come from disparate sources, with different levels of exactness, and all of it is complicated by the National Basketball Players Association (NBPA)'s collective bargaining agreement with the league, which prevents certain current measures, while others—namely, possible invasions of privacy like blood samples—will be a major talking point for the next agreement that could come as early as 2017 should either the owners or players opt out of the existing deal. That seems likely in light of the new $2.6 billion national TV contract the league struck late in 2014, which creates a huge new pot of money for the franchises and players to haggle over.

The current agreement allows players to wear biometric tracking devices that keep constant track of players' vital signs and workloads in practices, but not in games. According to a CBSSports.com column by Ken Berger during the 2015 NBA Finals, twelve NBA teams used Catapult devices during the 2014–15 season. They included the usual analytics suspects like the Dallas Mavericks, Golden State Warriors, Houston Rockets, Philadelphia 76ers, and Toronto Raptors, as well as the Memphis Grizzlies, New York Knicks, Orlando Magic, Sacramento Kings, and San Antonio Spurs. Zephyr Technology Corporation is a competing firm that makes wearable harnesses that monitor things like core temperature, heart rate, and other body data. Zephyr clients include the Phoenix Suns, the Oklahoma City Thunder, and (of course) the Houston Rockets.

Because of the limitation of such devices to practice, though, in-game data has to come from the three-dimensional player tracking provided by SportVU, which is still a fairly rough interpretive cut of player workload. An additional issue with the value of practice data is that NBA team schedules are very compact, so teams tend to practice less and less as the season wears on. If they do practice at all, the effort levels in those sessions usually are well below the standards needed in games, so even if the players are being monitored, there is a question as to the value of the data being collected. Getting data established at the beginning of a season, when players are going harder in practice, is valuable—especially as a baseline if a player is injured and you need to gauge their recovery—but in-season data can start to lose value pretty quickly in terms of real-time monitoring of player loads.

All this said, bargaining issues will work themselves out. In Berger's column, NBPA executive director Michele Roberts said, "To the extent that the team and the player could come up with a better advantage based on the information, who's got a problem with that?" The technologies also will continue to improve, and there will be a huge amount of value (and money) for the teams (and companies) that figure out the best ways to tie all of this data together into a comprehensive monitoring plan for players.

A key figure in all of this is Kopp, who built up SportVU before joining Catapult in 2013. Early in his tenure at STATS, he hired Paul Robbins as the company's director of elite performance. According to Kopp, it was Robbins who came to him early on during the SportVU experiment and convinced him that SportVU's on-court data would be the primary source of load-measuring during games, and that that feature would be a big selling point to potential clients.

"What he basically told me was, 'I do all of the stuff in training,'—so kind of like P3 and Marcus Elliott. You mentioned those guys, they do amazing work in a lab," Kopp said. "And there's other things, like Catapult and others that you can do in practice, but the missing piece was anything in games. You do all the stuff in labs, you do all the stuff in practice, [then] you go to a game, and there's nothing. So he convinced me this could be the game part of that equation, but as part of that, not only do we want to create things like speed and distance, but being able to approximate player load using x, y data. [That] isn't true player load, but in a sense, the way we sold it was, 'Well, currently there's nothing. It's better than nothing,' which isn't the best sales pitch, but it worked there for a while."

Kopp understands the current critiques about the usefulness of Catapult's data. He hopes the players' union will relent in the next series of labor negotiations because, unlike sleep monitoring devices and blood samples, Kopp reiterates that Catapult devices are to be used "in a workplace setting." He then used an example from a sports league in Catapult's home country to make a point that significant advancements could come to the NBA once the devices are approved for game use.

"The best example we have—it's really the only example in the world that you can point to—is what happens in Australia with Aussie Rules football," Kopp said. "They use these devices in games . . . on the sidelines, and they actually—it's kind of like hockey with its dynamic substitutions—they make substitution patterns based on what they see in the data. And they use it in practice in terms of monitoring guys and how hard they push.

"And they also use it in the Combine for guys that are coming up through the system, and what they found is, it's actually eliminated injuries in the Combine—because they used to have all these injury problems with guys coming to the Combine and pushing themselves too hard and they get hurt.

"It eliminated those injuries and they use it in a way to create that baseline for players. And it's all viewed as a positive. It's not viewed as a negative. It's not viewed as something where we're going to make a decision based on, 'Oh, hey, you're not trying hard enough.' The fact of that matter is, can you use it to say someone's not trying hard enough? I guess, but is that a bad thing?"

In the interim, SportVU data remains the most useful on-court load tracking data available, and Robbins is a key figure in its interpretation. As of early 2015, he said he was working as a consultant to seventeen different NBA teams to help them review performance data to aid their maintenance programs. According to Robbins, five NBA teams were already working with a Canadian company called

Kinduct, which provides a technology platform designed to tie all of these different data sources together, but the quantity and preciseness of data simply isn't there yet to properly piece everything together.

Robbins, who comes from an exercise science background and was a strength coach for many years, works directly with the strength coaches and trainers for the teams that engage STATS for this service, which is an interesting intersection with the on-court analytic data provided by SportVU. He provides weekly reports to his clients that help them consider issues regarding their players' physical workloads.

"I will start by giving some predictions on basically what kind of workload a player might have this upcoming week, and that's based off of how did that guy play against whom he's matched up coming up this week, so [at first] I'm using last year's data just to give me a feel of what a player might be going through," Robbins said. "Later in the season, I'll be able to use more of this year's data, obviously, in comparing players.

"So I'm looking at predictions. What happens to a player, who's covering Kobe Bryant, how much load is that player getting, what does Kobe typically do to a player? And I'll do that for all the teams, and basically the top five, six players on the teams. So I'll give them prediction of the load—that's the first thing I'll do for everybody in the week.

"And the second thing, I'll review last week or the trends that are going on in players right now. If it looks like their intensities are dropping—it could be because of fatigue, a minor injury, it could be just the matchup he's playing against—I will highlight anything I think is interesting to look into.

"And again, somebody could come back and say, 'Oh, it's just a matchup, no big deal,' or, 'we blew those guys out by twenty points, it really doesn't mean anything,' but what I'm really trying to do when I send out these reports and I'll go through each player, and anyone

I'm concerned with, it's to engage the strength coaches and the athletic trainers, and if there's something that they're like, 'Well, I'm not sure why the intensity's dropped in this guy. Paul, can you go and look deeper?' And that's when I go into the data. So what I'm trying to do is bring up red flags and question them, 'What do you need me to look into?'"

In 2015, Robbins estimates that SportVU's on-court cameras are only providing him with maybe 30 to 40 percent of the data he would ideally need to track player loads. He assumes at some point, the league will allow on-court tracking monitors during games, which will close that data gap. Until then, there's no issue with him providing consulting advice to more than half of the league, because Robbins says there's a surprising amount of information sharing going on between training staffs at the team level. A lot of new team trainers and strength coaches are coming from the same placement sources, and a good number of them know each other. According to Robbins, there were two teams in the league that absolutely will not share data or any findings or techniques with other teams, but he guesses that as many as two-thirds of the strength coaches in the league are friendly enough to trade some basic tips.

While advancements continue to be made across the board, the ability to truly know what the game-to-game loads are for players, and to track those trends against the off-court training, diet, and sleep data, would lift this discipline to an entirely new level.

"The whole thing is managing loads for a player," Robbins said. "Just make up some numbers here, but a player may have a load of '5,000' in a week. That's what he could do. I've got to manage that load. Is 3,000 of that load coming from games? Well, that means he only has 2,000 on all the other things going on. Now can they get some points back if they sleep well? Can they lose more points if they don't sleep well? And the same thing with eating. They eat poorly, maybe it's not 5,000, now it's only 4,500. So I can manage that. And then the players start understanding the big picture.

"So that's where we're really going. And then that will then help start connecting that with injuries because there's a lot of injuries due to overuse. And that's the load—if you have too high of a load, then that's overuse, and there's going to be injuries. So if I can manage those injuries . . . There's other injuries that I'll never be able to manage, but if I can manage overuse injuries? That's the ultimate goal. But we're nowhere near that yet."

⌒

Nine months later, back in Santa Barbara, P3's business is booming. Just during the summer of 2015 alone, Elliott estimates that they did one hundred new or continuing assessments of NBA players. The company's Twitter feed periodically posts photos of the players who do training there, and the 2015 batch included Detroit Pistons center Andre Drummond, Memphis Grizzlies wing defensive specialist Tony Allen, Charlotte Hornets big man Al Jefferson, Chicago Bulls center Joakim Noah, Atlanta Hawks center Al Horford, and many other well-known NBA veterans. The company also did a lot of pre-draft work for incoming rookies, with players like Jahlil Okafor (the No. 3 overall pick to the Philadelphia 76ers) and Emmanuel Mudiay (No. 7 to the Denver Nuggets) also training there.

Word of mouth clearly is driving the expansion of P3's business, but it's not specious to also draw a connection between the burgeoning client list and the testing the company did at the 2014 NBA Draft Combine. After P3's technicians analyzed the results of that testing, the company provided the NBA with a list of fifty-eight to sixty players in order of their likelihood of getting seriously injured. Then the 2014–15 season unfolded, and as noted earlier, a huge number of high-profile rookies suffered serious injuries. Like Mike Clark, Elliott is not at liberty to divulge exactly what risks were assigned to which players, but he did say, "We didn't just say who was likely to be injured, but we said *where* they would be injured. And it ended up being very predictive."

The accuracy of scale and specificity of injury really spooked the NBA, which ran the 2014 exercise as a closed test, but invited Elliott and Clark back to the 2015 Combine, where Elliott says P3 examined all but about four or five of the attendees, even though they were an opt-in process and not required. And the NBA subsequently changed its stance about allowing P3 to share its prognosis projections with the players.

"This is going to be a great project with the NBA," Elliott said about his company's now-annual involvement at the Combine. "There is going to be so much value that comes out of this. This is the first time a league has taken something like this on. We collect thousands of data points on each one of these guys, and we make predictions about them, and then we get to see what happens."

This new disclosure created a much bigger talking point than the actual test results, though, which relates back to the collective bargaining agreement and the players' union's stance on biometric data: Who owns the data that companies like P3 are collecting?

The league has engaged P3 to come to the Draft Combine. The players are being tested, and it's their bodies being diagnosed. The teams are the employers of these players and are investing significant amounts of money in them. It's a very difficult and nuanced question that raises some of the same issues as blood-testing and sleep-tracking data, as some players will greatly be helped by early diagnosis of structural issues while others could suffer economic consequences from the leak of such data. As Elliott notes, there's even debate as to what category of data this analysis falls under: Is it more akin to the bench press at the Draft Combine (which is released publicly) or like an MRI, which has much more distribution protection on it?

"Originally, [the NBA] planned to give the data to the team, and they've come around to which is what I think is our position—well, I know it's our position—that the data should rest with the players," Elliott said. "The players control it, it's their bodies, and they should have control of this information. And we're going to encourage the players—especially those who have significant pathologies—to share the data with the teams, but there won't be a mandate. The teams will only get this information if the players requested to share a copy with them.

"This is about protecting the players, this rare resource that these guys are, and they didn't have access to this before," he added. "They just waited until their bodies broke. Now they have access and they can cut off some of these [injuries] and it's amazing for the players. If the Players Association is going to rebel against this, it kind of undercuts the whole project."

As all of this develops, teams are getting increasingly interested in working more in concert with P3, which is focusing more on the collection and analysis of the data, and less on having physical training actually at their own gym. The corrective work, with the proper oversight and equipment, can occur anywhere, and as the salaries paid to individual players continue to rise rapidly thanks to the league's new TV rights deal, teams are more and more concerned about protecting their investments to the best extent possible. Players and their agents are increasingly interested in this, as well, as tens of millions of dollars can be at stake on their side, too—even as everyone continues to try to figure out what it all means, and who exactly should know what about whom.

"Just the idea of trying to perfect athletes in the NBA, it's so timely right now," Elliott said. "It's unlike any of the other sports, and it's changing so fast. Honestly, I think it's the biggest sort of imperfect market that there is in basketball still, this piece that hasn't been optimized yet. They went from having no real training culture to saying this is maybe the most important piece that we have. They've gone from zero to sixty in like three seconds."

CHAPTER 6

The Tricky Art and Science of Turning Data into Wins

It really starts with leadership's appetite for that kind of information . . . the owner, the head of team operations . . . the head coach. . . . If anyone of those, particularly the head coach, is . . . not open to this, it's useless. It really comes down to where the rubber meets the road and where the decision makers are willing to legitimately give this stuff weight.

—**Tom Penn, ESPN basketball analyst**

An hour or so before a mid-November 2014 home date with the New Orleans Pelicans, Sacramento Kings general manager Pete D'Alessandro was standing against a wall just off the tunnel that leads from the home team's locker room to the court at Sleep Train Arena. At the time, D'Alessandro was in the early stages of his second season with the Kings after coming over from Denver, where he was an assistant to Masai Ujiri (who then became the general manager of the Toronto Raptors), and things were going unexpectedly well for his team.

Six months earlier, the Kings had been the talk of the league for off-court reasons when they openly engaged in a crowdsourcing analysis exercise ahead of the 2014 NBA Draft, in which they held the No. 8 overall pick. The Kings were open-minded to all sorts of analysis and ideas that came from outside their management team, and entertained numerous strategies about which player to take with the pick or whether they should try to trade up or down in the first round.

Eventually, ESPN's *Grantland* site documented the team's experiment in a short film, which showed a variety of interesting and awkward interactions among Kings officials. For basketball fans, the juiciest part of the film was the disclosure that Sacramento was very much considering Louisiana-Lafayette point guard Elfrid Payton against their eventual selection, Michigan shooting guard Nik Stauskas, but ultimately decided they needed more quality shooting to help space the floor around blossoming star center DeMarcus Cousins.

By November, though, the Kings were making news on the court, where they were one of the early surprises of the season. They had compiled a 6–4 record against a very difficult schedule, and were coming off a home win over the defending champion San Antonio Spurs, during which Cousins had his way with all-time great Tim Duncan down the stretch. Furthermore, a widely questioned pair of summer moves—when the club allowed diminutive scoring point guard Isaiah Thomas to leave via free agency, and then signed the older, less dynamic Darren Collison for similar money—was paying early dividends. Collison was bringing much more stability and defense to the point guard position, in addition to a better understanding of Cousins's role as the team's star, rather than needing the ball in his hands as Thomas did to be effective.

The day before this particular encounter, news had surfaced that another Kings' gamble had paid off. Eleven months earlier, the team had traded for small forward Rudy Gay, whose low-efficiency offensive game made him one of the analytics community's poster children for how you *didn't* want to play. Gay was on his third team in a year after moving from the Memphis Grizzlies to Toronto in a previous trade, and was more or less considered to be an albatross, on a contract that was paying him over $17 million a season. The conventional thought process was Gay was being paid far too much money for what he was producing in a league where salary caps and luxury taxes have significant effects on both team-building and roster preservation, if things are going well.

Gay, though, was evolving his offensive game under second-year head coach Michael Malone, who had been brought in a few weeks before D'Alessandro by owner Vivek Ranadive in the summer of 2013. Malone was utilizing Gay a lot more in the post and deriving excellent early results. Gay was shooting the ball more efficiently, getting to the free throw line more than he historically did, and providing the Kings with some late-game mismatch advantages, as Gay often found himself posting up a smaller forward.

The Kings moved quickly and got Gay to accept a three-year extension for about $40 million, which was much more appropriate market value for him, given his improved performance and the pending increase in the NBA's national TV deals, which will see the cap increase from around $70 million for the 2015–16 season to perhaps $110 million for the 2017–18 season. Under the new financial structure for the league, Gay's new deal approximates a deal worth $9 million or so in the 2014–15 environment, and even analytics folks are more than OK with that value.

All of these types of decisions—the hiring of a coach and general manager, free-agency decisions, trade choices—are very complicated and have to be made in concert across an organization. When done correctly, with the Spurs being the most widely held example, they can produce symbiotic beauty and extended excellence, but in the wrong setting, conflicting egos and agendas can quickly rip a franchise apart. As D'Alessandro noted before this Pelicans game, the educated risks the Kings took over his first eighteen months are the type a franchise like Sacramento—far from a premier free-agent destination—needs to pull itself out of a decade-long mire after nearly winning the NBA title in the early 2000s.

"Look, if Rudy Gay is playing in Toronto right now and is a free agent next year, what chance do we have to sign him to a three-year deal, like we just did? We don't have a chance to do that. We don't," D'Alessandro said.

Throw in the club's decision to offer Cousins—who had struggled with maturity and frustration issues even as he began to emerge as the most gifted center in the league—a five-year maximum extension the year before, and the Kings were running very hot on roster-building gambles. The team's philosophy on Cousins was simple: you don't get your hands on talents like him very often, and once management decided to make him the centerpiece of the organization, they had to treat him as such financially instead of asking him to wait and prove he could live up to that kind of deal.

There was risk involved in investing so much money in a young player who had made some mistakes in comportment, but it was a reasonable risk given the potential upside.

"We're not a big market," D'Alessandro said about Sacramento's standing in a league with franchises in Los Angeles, New York, Chicago, Miami, and many other large, desirable cities. "So, [we need to] be willing to seem stupid, because you have to do things that maybe are on the fringe of what other teams can do. And you do them with the idea that [only] some are going to work. Even in the deals I've done so far, some have worked, some haven't.

"As a GM here, I have to be much more willing to say, 'Don't be wedded to your ideas.' [Owner] Vivek [Ranadive] has a saying like, 'Do you want to be right, or do you want to be successful?' So be willing to acknowledge that, hey—and I think here, especially, in small markets—you need to be able to work those edges and be willing to be wrong and put yourself out there and say, 'It's OK, because the next one, I might be right and it might be a bigger thing.'"

After Ujiri left Denver for a return home to Toronto (and a much bigger paycheck), it was expected by many that D'Alessandro would inherit the general manager role in Denver to carry on the

Nuggets' success. That was even after ownership—which had officially transitioned from Stan Kroenke to his son, Josh, to satisfy NFL cross-ownership requirements involving Kroenke's St. Louis Rams—had dismissed NBA coach of the year George Karl after a 57-win 2012–13 season that ended prematurely in a first-round playoff loss to the Golden State Warriors.

D'Alessandro admits he was deep in the process to finalize an agreement with the Nuggets, but a deal still hadn't been reached when Ranadive, who bought the Kings in 2013, repeatedly called to offer D'Alessandro an interview for the open Kings position. Sacramento had been searching for a general manager for a number of weeks, so D'Alessandro didn't expect the interview to be much more than a chance to continue to grow his own experience set.

In fact, the possible alliance got off to an awkward start when D'Alessandro, who had just finished putting his presentation together around midnight the night before he was set to fly to Sacramento the next morning, got an e-mail from Ranadive detailing what the owner wanted to discuss in the sit-down. D'Alessandro says he pulled an all-nighter to assemble the new materials, got an hour of sleep, and flew out to meet with Ranadive, where the two had a very open exchange of ideas and questions about how to rebuild the Kings. D'Alessandro walked out of the meeting feeling like he wasn't going to get the job, since Sacramento was so far along in its own process, but that he told his wife that he "had a friend here. I know that, because the guy's a great dude."

Soon after, D'Alessandro was hired to help lead the Kings' revolution, which continues to include unique and sometimes offbeat concepts about how to improve the team. The example that got the most media attention (and ridicule) during 2014–15 was Ranadive's public admission that he wanted the team to consider a four-on-five defensive strategy with a basket-hanger who would remain at the offensive end of the floor. Most NBA observers believe this approach would get shredded in the long run as teams countered defensively *and* exploited the greater space of four-on-four basketball at their offensive end, but to D'Alessandro, the ideas weren't the thing in Sacramento. It was the process of discovering them.

"I think Vivek has had a really open approach, an approach that—and I do this in my office, too—anyone in the office, all the young guys running around, can walk in my door and say, 'I have an idea' and throw it at me," he said. "Anytime. I don't care if you work at the front desk. And everyone knows that. It's funny to me, you find that personalities start to shine that way. I find that you start to see things in people that maybe you didn't envision before.

"Because ideas are where it all starts, and so I think Vivek is an incredible ideas guy," D'Alessandro added. "He comes up with these ideas, and they blow me away every time. We're just having a meeting, and Vivek's going to come in, we're going to be doing some stuff that we're going to send to the league, and I told someone, 'Have a notepad, write down everything he says,' because when he says it, sometimes, I'm like, 'Oh c'mon.' And then I'll go back and think about some of the stuff he said and like, you know, there's a germ of an idea that you can turn into something big."

The Kings continued to push resources into better and more creative decision making with the fall 2014 hiring of Dean Oliver, the father of the modern analytics movement, from his role as director of production analytics at ESPN. Ranadive, like a number of new NBA owners, made his fortune in technology, so the work of Oliver and his charges were to be a rapidly increasing portion of what the Kings considered as they weighed their next risk/reward decisions, and the whole management team, including more-traditional advisors like former NBA star Chris Mullin, were to become more aligned philosophically.

"We're in our infancy, we're in year one, we can't have it all done, and Dean just came on," D'Alessandro said at the time. "I think we'll have a fast infancy because I think we have really qualified people, and

I think we have an incredible support cast in our ownership group. So in that regard, I feel really good about where we're positioned.

"But, in the way I'm looking at it, there's so much of it that we have already, the question is: How do you use it? And how does each area use it? And I think, as the general manager, I'm trying to figure out how to create the most flexible way of having [the data] tell its story."

Unfortunately for D'Alessandro, and perhaps the Kings, the story would quickly take a very different turn.

What seemed like a solid plan that was being implemented well started to unravel a couple of weeks after this conversation. What exactly went down over the next six months isn't 100 percent known, but the craziness started when the team elected to dismiss Malone in late November, during a period when Cousins was out of the lineup with viral meningitis. There was much debate at the time about whether management favored a faster tempo than what Malone was playing with a roster designed for more of a halfcourt approach, and local and national media differed on whether D'Alessandro or Ranadive himself was responsible for the move.

Subsequently, the Kings promoted assistant coach Ty Corbin to interim head coach, may or may not have asked Mullin to take over as coach, elected to make Corbin the coach for the rest of the season, kept losing games and looked terrible in the process, were forced to remove Corbin from the job, and eventually hired Karl, with whom D'Alessandro had worked in Denver.

None of it really made any sense, and it all became more confusing when Ranadive brought back former Kings center Vlade Divac in a front-office role and then quickly handed the basketball operations over to him without telling anyone else. Mullin quickly left the Kings to take the head coaching job at St. John's, his alma mater, and D'Alessandro, having been neutered, quietly returned to Denver after the season to take a business and team operations role under owner Josh Kroenke. In late July 2015, it was reported that the Kings would be releasing Oliver, while also looking for a new analytics person to replace him. They did well to land Roland Beech, but it still was very curious.

The whole Kings saga is a cautionary tale of mismanagement, but there was a lot going into the buildup of the analytics approach that was worthwhile. All of the decisions they made—swapping out Thomas for Collison, gambling on Gay, maxing out Cousins, the debate over tempo, and so forth—were rooted in analytics as part of a team-building plan. Maybe Divac and his staff will find a method that works—and they need to quickly, because they (perhaps recklessly) invested a lot of the Kings' future in some third-tier free agents for the 2015–16 season—but there clearly was a breakdown in the process with the old regime.

Sacramento's journey to wonk and back is illustrative in an exploration of how analytics move through an organization, and how many things can derail them. The next section provides some additional perspectives, from different layers involved in this kind of decision making and implementation.

With the deluge of on- and off-court data now available, basketball data analysis is rapidly becoming, as Daryl Morey has suggested at the Sloan Sports Analytics Conference he co-chairs, "only constricted by money, time, and the questions you ask." The bigger challenge for every NBA team lies in how to value, disseminate, and use the information they can generate.

Information-gathering and -sharing structures for NBA teams differ wildly, but at a baseline, the operations are very complicated and nuanced. The possible data pieces a team can gather include in-game data from SportVU, in-game proprietary data being tracked by staffers, in-game/trend data from Synergy, practice data coming from Catapult or other wearable technology devices, practice data being tracked by staffers (the 76ers, notably, track every shot, including free throws, taken in practices), medical data, sleep data, salary and cap data, college and international scouting data, NBA pro personnel data, and advance scouting data.

All of that different data can be parsed in an enormous number of ways, and there are different constituents for each kind of data, all of whom consume and subsequently communicate findings to other constituents in very different ways. Sometimes, a report immediately finds its end user. Sometimes, the initial reader is a conduit to the eventual end users. Some people want very complicated, nuanced answers. Some need very simple ones. The possibilities of how and what to do with the data being collected by NBA teams are effectively endless, and the communication network has to be tailored to the wants and capacities of the target users. To make it more complex, team management often is hiring data staffers whose expertise stretch well beyond the hirers', making ongoing evaluation of the data team's work all that much more difficult.

As a quick example of how complicated one single decision can be, take an instance of the work of Ben Alamar. Alamar is a former professor of sports management at Menlo College in California who rose to prominence in the sports analytics world thanks to seven years of NBA work, first as the director of analytics with the Seattle SuperSonics/Oklahoma City Thunder and then later as a consultant with the Cleveland Cavaliers. In his 2013 book *Sports Analytics: A Guide for Coaches, Managers and Other Decision Makers,* Alamar discusses the process he undertook in 2008 to try to help the Super-Sonics (who were moving to Oklahoma City that summer) evaluate UCLA guard prospect Russell Westbrook, who was entering the draft after two seasons of college ball.

Westbrook was a tricky draft case because he mostly played shooting guard at UCLA (with the Kings' Collison playing the point for those Bruins teams), but the Thunder wanted a point guard with their No. 4 overall pick to go with star-in-the-making Kevin Durant, who had just finished his rookie season. The team loved Westbrook's physical attributes and mental makeup, but wasn't sure he would transition to the NBA level as a primary ballhandler or distributor.

As such, the team needed a way to try to measure Westbrook's passing acumen in college, and then project that to the NBA level. Standard statistics (like assists) were not going to provide the team with enough information to judge Westbrook's decision making, so they needed to do some proprietary work to evaluate him more appropriately.

Alamar, through extensive film work, created a metric that looked at UCLA's shooting percentages when Westbrook passed a teammate the ball versus shots that came unassisted or when other teammates made the pass that led to a shot. Alamar found that Westbrook's impact on UCLA's shooting was greater than the team's point guard, Collison (who would be picked twenty-first overall in the 2009 NBA Draft), and stacked up favorably against both the performance of other prospects in the 2008 draft and a pool of established NBA point guards.

Once Alamar had data he was comfortable with, the challenge became communicating this new metric and what it meant to the decision makers in charge of the draft. It was enormously helpful to be able to show that Westbrook's impact at UCLA was comparable (adjusted for context) to that of elite NBA point guards, as well as a projected elite point guard (University of Memphis' Derrick Rose, who would be the number one overall pick in 2008). Also, being able to show that lesser NBA point guards scored worse on this metric than both the best NBA point guards and Westbrook also helped slot Westbrook higher in the minds of the brass.

Alamar wasn't even in the team's draft war room when they selected Westbrook, and Alamar's analysis wasn't (by a long shot) the only factor that encouraged the team to select him, but that didn't stop a team official from emerging from the room after the pick had been made and yelling at Alamar, "You got your guy!" The pick has worked out brilliantly for the Thunder. Westbrook turned into an

All-Star by his third season in the league, and made second-team All-NBA in the 2014–15 season. He's not a conventional point guard by any means, but while being one of the most physically dominant and destructive perimeter players in the world, he also led the NBA in 2014–15 in percentage of teammates' baskets assisted while he's on the floor at an astounding 47 percent.

The above described one part of the work that went into the evaluation of one potential draft prospect, so you can see how expansive this can get. An analytics team needs to find the right balance between pushing information to the different end users, pulling information requested by those users, and communicating it in varying ways such that each end user will be as receptive as possible to the conclusions drawn.

"I think analytics is best when it works in concert with everybody," said Alamar, who now is ESPN's director of production analytics, having taken over the job from Oliver. "And we ask a lot of questions to find out what people are really interested in. And when people are actually asking us questions, that's great because that provides us ways to demonstrate the value and know that our audience is going to be listening when we deliver something. What is difficult is when we know the answer that they're looking for, and the answer that we come up with is different. That can be challenging. But in general, I think a process that works with and in conjunction with all our audiences—as opposed to us just doling out the data—is a better, more effective model."

Per Alamar, the two main goals of an analytics group are to provide new and/or actionable information, and to save time for decision makers. As good as a data team can be in managing and exploring data to solve team questions, though, the effectiveness of the operation is judged heavily by its ability to communicate the findings to audiences that will range from completely open-minded to those looking for validation of their gut. Alamar provides a simple but fairly common example in today's NBA.

"Well, when a coach comes to you and says, 'I think our problem is X, can you show me data that supports that, so I can show it to the player?' It's tough, particularly when that coach is new and you've worked with him for a couple of weeks, to come back and say, 'Coach, no, actually you're wrong,' Alamar said. "If it's not delivered well and it's not delivered carefully, that's a message that, 'Oh, this guy doesn't know what he's talking about. I've been in the league for twenty years, I know that this is the problem. He's just either dumb or he's not very good at his job or he couldn't deliver what I wanted.' And so that's a problem. Now, for the analytics person to find a way to support the coach's answer, you don't want to do that either because then you're giving people the wrong information. So in the end, what you have to do is be really careful about how you present the information."

Some current team analytics staffers echo Alamar's sentiments. Alex Rucker started leading analytics for the Toronto Raptors in 2009, and his group developed one of the seminal analytics concepts that has made it to the public realm. In 2013, *Grantland*'s Zach Lowe detailed the group's "ghost defenders" visual model which showed, in animated form, where Raptors defenders ideally would be on a play as the actual offensive and defensive players (and the ball) were shown moving around the court. While the model may have been more high-concept art than something that was highly implementable for human players, there were some interesting takeaways from the computer-generated data, including the suggestion that defending teams should double-team the ball way more often and more aggressively than they currently do.

Like every other analytics staffer contacted, Rucker is not permitted to discuss specifics about his team or any of their players, but he faces many of the same challenges detailed above in terms of trying to find the right balance in the questions his group is trying to solve, and then how to disseminate that information in the most optimal way.

"On the one hand, I think the analytics—the technical guys—they have a push responsibility to go through the data and find out . . . for themselves, to use their basketball knowledge, use the data set to gain some insights to some aspect of the game, and then hopefully push that to whoever is their more immediate consumer, which is usually the front office, the executive management level," he said.

"But, at the other end, you do have kind of an end user, you do have a consumer, you do have somebody who is wanting something from this analytics thing, if you will. . . . [T]hey're the ones paying for it, they're the ones asking for things, and quite honestly, they do ask for specific things. 'I want to know this.' So, on our level, can we give you an answer to that, and if so, go about doing it? And at some level, it's prioritizing between what they want to know and what you think is important to push, and just kind of finding a balance between those two things."

Dean Oliver adds: "Any place I've been, I've tried to make sure that the communication, the translation between the words and the numbers—the basketball language—is clear, because you can do the greatest analysis behind the scenes, and if you can't put it into basketball language, then it's not going to get implemented right, even if they want to understand."

But even when you do have end product that is framed in a way that can be used by the basketball side of the operation, that doesn't mean that the information will be used. There are tons of limitations—even in the current data-intensive world of basketball—in the output an analytics team can generate on a regular basis. When you then factor in that merely a small percentage of that work likely even gets fully considered, let alone implemented, it's difficult to pinpoint the specific value of analytics operations, even though every NBA team is investing in them to some degree.

As Rucker notes, there's a difficult balance between maintaining the academic rigor of statistical exercises—which includes understanding and accepting the inherent uncertainty in most calculations involving such a dynamic sport played by humans with imperfect decision making—and expressing enough confidence and certainty in your conclusions that they will be taken seriously by the basketball part of the operation.

"That's an extraordinarily difficult balance to strike between being intellectually honest and truthful, which is saying, 'Hey, this stuff I'm talking about has all sorts of limitations and disclaimers and caveats'—the academic side, if you will." Rucker said. "As a data scientist, if I'm going to be any good, [I have to be] astutely aware of the limitations in my data and the errors that come with anything I create.

"But you're dealing with people that don't function in academia, that don't live in that world, so you can't very well offer everything with error terms and uncertainties and risk. I think that you have to—to me, I guess the right balance is to continuously openly acknowledge that there are limitations. This is not gospel, this is not truth, this is hopefully we're turning a flashlight onto a part of the table that we haven't looked at before, and hopefully offering some insight, but that might not be, we might not be seeing what we think we're seeing."

And even when the information is good, and is presented well, and is well received by the decision makers, that's far from the only information being considered when a team makes any choice, whether it be on game strategy, pro player evaluation, the college draft, or trades.

"It's really up to the coach or the general manager to distill all the information, because they're getting information from all different sides, all different types of information," Alamar said. "They have the really, really hard job of figuring out what's the best set of information to use and how to utilize it. And so that's difficult, because we're right more than we're wrong, but we're wrong sometimes, and if a coach or general manager is really good at what they do, and is honestly weighing all of the information and working through it, they may choose not to do it.

"Not because there's a breakdown, but because they see other information that is counter to what we see as more compelling to them. The trick is to make sure that they're honestly weighing all the information. And you get them to a place where they will take what you're saying seriously and think about it carefully. As long as they're doing that, then that's all in basketball I think you can honestly ask for."

And then, again, there is the human element in all of this. It's entirely possible that a coaching strategy choice is correct, but a player blows an assignment and the play unravels. It's possible that you can make the proper pick in the draft, but a series of external factors influence the player in a way that was unpredictable at the time. Rucker takes that uncertainty one step further, noting that it's often difficult to isolate when analytics are even being applied by coaches, management, and players.

"If I give my wife a recommendation for a car, she goes to the car lot and inspects a bunch of different cars, and buys the one I recommended—I have no idea why she bought it," Rucker said. "I can ask, but until that conversation takes place, I have no clue what kind of decision chain occurred there. Whether it's my commanding and compelling recommendation, or whether . . . she did her own investigation, talked to some people, looked online, test drove the model, and it was the best one for her, it turns out.

"I guess it's a similar decision for us . . . on the basketball court. Like, I know all the things I recommended, but when they occur on the court, does that mean [it was] because of me? I seriously doubt it. I think that it was a small piece, and maybe a helpful piece, but I also don't know . . . in the absence of that recommendation, does it happen anyway? Possibly."

⇜

Five years ago, Brad Stevens was the boy wonder of college basketball head coaches, having led unfancied Butler University to the national title game in both 2010 and 2011 while not looking very much older than any of his Bulldogs players. Stevens had long been rumored as the possible savior at Indiana University, his home state's flagship program, and there even were some rumblings about him being a possible candidate to replace Hall of Famer Mike Krzyzewski at Duke whenever he finished there, so it wasn't totally shocking when the Boston Celtics poached him in the summer of 2013 to lead their rebuilding process. Former head coach Doc Rivers had pushed his way to the Los Angeles Clippers in the wake of multiple trades that left the Celtics' roster short on talent but long on future draft picks and cap flexibility, and the Celtics were excited about how much the young and extremely bright Stevens could bring to the table coaching a young and transitioning team.

It's hard to overstate how well Stevens did at Butler, even after taking over a successful program that had grown under the command of Thad Matta (now the highly successful coach at Ohio State) and then Todd Lickliter (who left for Iowa, but didn't last long there). In his six seasons in charge of the Bulldogs, Stevens went 166–49, never won fewer than twenty-two games in a season, and made five NCAA tournament trips, including the shocking back-to-back title-game trips with squads led by Gordon Hayward (now a blossoming star with the Utah Jazz, who was a lottery pick after leading the 2010 team) and Shelvin Mack (a guard with the Atlanta Hawks).

While Stevens's coaching reputation blossomed thanks to all of the success he had at Butler, he also was one of the earliest adopters of advanced stats on the college level. While at the school, he hired Drew Cannon, a former intern of Dave Telep (now the scouting director for the San Antonio Spurs after being a long-time scouting analyst for high school players), who had been combining traditional scouting with analytical slant in written work. The move was the first strictly analytics hire at the Division I level, and helped cement Stevens's reputation as a creative thinker in addition to being an excellent strategist and program CEO.

When Stevens was hired by Boston, he elected to bring along Cannon, who was just a year removed from graduating from Duke University. When the move was announced, Stevens told the *Boston Globe* that "what Drew has a great ability to do is not only to analyze but communicate it. He can break things down into the simplest terms. He's got a sense for the basketball side of things and he's a good communicator to me with it." Since then, the two have combined with general manager Danny Ainge, vice president Mike Zarren, and director of basketball analytics David Sparks to form one of the most respected and cohesive analytics staffs in the NBA.

With Stevens still working through the transition into the pro game and the Celtics being both long on smart thinking and short on roster talent and stability, how Stevens thinks about the use of analytics across the Celtics' operation is pretty unique and informative. While his depiction of what his staff gets in terms of pre-game prep doesn't seem particularly unusual, his own utility from the stats and the way his staff communicates info to the players foots with the very practical, mature approach that he carried with him from the college level.

"They're really receptive," Stevens said about the Celtics' players, who receive their scouting information and analytics breakdowns only via iPad. "I don't think they need [too much]. This is a great balance, because it's a beautiful game played with great pace without really any breaks when it's played really well, other than the timeouts that are allotted to each team. And so you have to make decisions on the fly, and you have to be able to apply what you know on the fly. So what you know has to be limited to what's important. And if you present what's important, then the guys really like that. If you over-present, then you can de-simplify the game, and that's not what you need to do. Or that's not what I think is best."

In discussing his approach to communication, Stevens semi-jokingly made reference to the famous quote from seventeenth-century

French philosopher and mathematician Blaise Pascal, who loosely wrote, "I would have written a shorter letter, but I didn't have the time." From the coaches' meetings on down to interactions with the players, Stevens feels it's his and his staff's responsibility to boil down the most important information they receive into the shortest, most concise and implementable base points, while leaving the time and flexibility to adjust as needed.

Stevens noted that as a still-learning NBA coach in just his second year at the pro level at the time of our conversation, he had to spend some extra time on opposition scouting so he could continue to get comfortable with opposing personnel. He also said he spends more time on his own team's planning and preparation than he typically did at Butler, where the time available between games in a college schedule lends itself much more to game plans designed to defuse what an opponent does well. During the eighty-two-game regular season, with many back-to-backs and all of the travel between games, many teams mostly focus on their own execution. (That changes during the postseason, when teams have a specific opponent for a series of games and more consistent time between games.)

Stevens's focus is helped by both his own affinity for advanced stats and the team the Celtics have put together. Stevens said that so far in his tenure, there have been very few things that Cannon, Sparks, and their staff haven't been able to provide for him in fairly short order. That said, Stevens is still a coach first and foremost, and coaches not only have innate instincts for ideas, but also like the visual benefit of video beyond what numerical reports can suggest.

"So I get the data, [and] the data reaffirms or argues against what I already think," Stevens said. "And 99.9 percent of the time, it just affirms it. So what it is, is a validation, rather than a . . . I don't take any data without film, nor do I take any film without data. But if I had to throw one out, I'd probably throw the data out because film is so . . . I think film is such an important learning part of how teams play and how teams like to play, who affects you, how does it affect you, how do people match up when certain guys are in the lineup, or out of the lineup. All that other stuff, you just can't get as much from the data. Now, the data is really important because it can help put you over the top, it can give you a small edge as you're defending, or a small edge as you're attacking, whatever the case may be, but I am not of the belief that it's more important than film."

One of the biggest challenges of Stevens's second season was what to do with point guard Rajon Rondo, whose overall skills had eroded some after a serious knee injury in January 2013 and whose lack of shooting ability, whether it was from the perimeter or the free throw line, made spacing and scoring very challenging for a roster that didn't have much quality shooting.

When asked about how the team's data helped him find an approach that worked for Rondo, a gifted passer when he was right (along with a markedly mercurial temperament), Stevens took a positive and diplomatic approach.

"Who best complements him, right? [There's] guys in this league for a reason, [and] those reasons are all different depending on the guy," Stevens said. "And I think that every one of them has incredible strengths and incredible ability that makes them amongst the 450 best players available, and I think that you try to find—if somebody has something that's outstanding—you try to find a complement for that, and that's what I see in trying to piece a team together.

"I've kind of always looked at teams that way because there's only so many of the Kevin Durants or the LeBron Jameses around. There's only so many guys who can do every little thing well, and there's guys that can challenge them on a given night, but it's hard for anybody to do it for eighty-two games."

Rondo's welcome eventually wore out in Boston, and he was traded to the Dallas Mavericks, where he continued to struggle and ultimately was booted from the team during the Mavericks' first-round playoff series with the Rockets. He ended up as one of the Kings' summer signings on a one-year, $10 million "show me" deal.

Somewhat surprisingly, Stevens's views foot fairly closely with the aforementioned Stan Van Gundy, he of the animated analytics diatribe. While standing courtside at a morning shootaround before a game in Denver, Van Gundy laughed about the perception of that Sloan appearance before saying, "No, I like the analytics. I think the analytics are very helpful. I think there are some people who think the analytics are everything. I don't think that. I think it's a big part of the puzzle, I think you have to give a lot of credence to what the analytics say, but it can't be the only thing you have. I think there are a lot of intangible factors, putting the team together, chemistry."

Van Gundy's setup in Detroit at the outset of his debut season there had analytics information being filtered to him through assistant coach Charles Klask, about whom Van Gundy said "still tends to give me a little too much information. What I really want is him to distill that information down to the stuff he thinks is important and that I can use. . . . Both in terms of coaching and player personnel, I think the biggest challenge in analytics right now is to figure out what is really important."

Van Gundy and his staff also entered the 2014–15 season with a significant roster challenge: figuring out how to play low-post-focused bigs Andre Drummond and Greg Monroe, as well as Josh Smith, who was much better suited for the power forward spot than small forward alongside those two guys, for spacing and shot selection reasons. The Pistons quickly "solved" part of that issue by cutting Smith from the team, causing a charge of over $5 million to hit their cap in each of the next five seasons for a player they no longer had. They then rode out the rest of an uneven season with Drummond and Monroe before the latter left for Milwaukee in free agency.

As Van Gundy noted in his Sloan discussion, much of his concern with analytics is the integrity and sourcing of the data, and that extends to the current trend in the league with how player workloads are being measured and reduced in order to improve effectiveness. Van Gundy notes that Michael Jordan was playing "thirty-eight minutes a night and eighty-two games a year" during his final three championship seasons in the late 1990s, and now we have better conditioning and awareness about how bodies work, and practically no players are able or asked to play that amount. There's also a practical sidebar to Van Gundy's questions about workload versus rest, and how critique of a coach like Tom Thibodeau, who had significant success with the Chicago Bulls before being let go after the 2014–15 season and was known to play his starters very heavy minutes, bothers him.

"In 1983, I was coaching Division III basketball in Vermont and there was an exercise physiologist in the [physical education] department, and I was twenty-four years old. He said, 'Can I talk to you?' and I said 'Sure.' He was a really nice guy and he showed me like four or five studies, because he thought I practiced too hard. It was about going hard day, easy day, hard day, easy day . . . and there were studies with track and swimmers and they were better and the whole thing.

"I got it. I understand all that. But our game isn't just who runs fastest or who jumps the highest. You've also got to be able to execute offensive and defensive schemes. I can't do that without practice time. Swimming and running are just the physical part.

"I think it's one of things that, when people get on a guy like Tom Thibodeau about overplaying people, the part they're missing out is that they're assuming that if those guys did less, they would still execute at both ends the same way, and I don't buy that. One of the reasons they are as good as they are and execute the way they are is they spent more time at it than other people."

↩

Tom Penn spent eleven years as an NBA executive, the first seven with the Vancouver/Memphis Grizzlies as assistant general manager/legal counsel, and then four with the Portland Trail Blazers, first as assistant general manager and then as vice president of basketball operations. Since 2010, he has been a basketball analyst for ESPN, specializing in salary cap, team-building, and draft discussions on *SportsCenter* and other programs.

Penn was part of the management team that helped build the Grizzlies from a league doormat into a team that made the first three playoff appearances in franchise history, despite the franchise not getting anything from the No. 2 overall pick in 2003. That year, they were pipped for No. 1 overall by the Cleveland Cavaliers (in the LeBron James draft) and then had to confer their (only top-1-protected) pick to the Detroit Pistons because of a 1997 trade for Otis Thorpe, missing out on potential stars like Carmelo Anthony, Chris Bosh, and Dwyane Wade (or taking Darko Milicic, like Detroit did). While in Portland, Penn helped orchestrate the progression from the infamous "Jail Blazers" era, peaking with a fifty-four-win campaign in 2008–09.

As someone who remains very much plugged into the league (and also is co-owner and president of the new MLS soccer team launching in Los Angeles as early as 2017) but isn't a part of a franchise, Penn spoke openly on the importance of information transfer and value inside an NBA front office.

"It really starts first with leadership's appetite for that kind of information," Penn said. "And when I say leadership, you've got the owner, the head of team operations—whatever title you're going to call that—and then you got the head coach. And if any one of those, particularly the head coach, is a roadblock, or is not open to this, it's useless. It really comes down to where the rubber meets the road and where the decision makers are willing to legitimately give this stuff weight.

"Every team over the last fifteen years—doesn't matter whether they believe in it or not—they do this in order to cover their tail and to demonstrate that they are sophisticated. But a lot of that can be a ruse, or an empty effort if you truly don't have the decision makers employing it. And I gotta tell you, it's a lot easier said than done to employ this information and to figure out the right context to put it in because, at its essence, we're dealing with human beings and performers who are more like Broadway actors or Hollywood actors than they are corporate management, or corporate executives, or corporate anything.

"And you've got the vagaries and the human side of it, the relationship side of it, and that always trumps 100 percent, no matter what. It just does. So the analytic components can be additive to a well-run human organization that deals with the relationships and deals with the frailties and everything that goes into this."

Penn noted that the influx of many new technologies in the league was creating a different landscape from the one he was operating in just a handful of years ago. While much of the discussion about analytics involves the communication and sharing of information, the primary building block is the initial collection of the actual raw data, with teams having more equal access to the loads of information being generated.

Where once the advantage was in early adoption of the actual processes to collect data—like the Mavericks and others trying to stop Brian Kopp from bringing SportVU to every team—now the in-house advantages lie in how good the people are at parsing that data, and then how well and creatively you can break it down, communicate it, and then execute it based on your findings.

He also emphasized how fragile the entire process can be, with one misstep—whether it be in computation or interpersonal dealings—able to compromise large parts of the process.

"A few years ago, only Dallas, Houston, and Portland had data points; now the whole league has access to [them], but the cutting-edge folks are to the next phase of data collection," Penn said. "You know, first it's collection, then it's analysis, and then it's communication.

"So those are the three phases of it. It's get the data, [and] figure out how to analyze it in a way that it's helpful, but at every step of this, you have to have [a] communication aspect on the back end or it's useless. And you can have your brilliant stats guy meet with your head coach once the wrong way and say the wrong thing based on some formula that's silly, or all formulas have outliers; coaches are really good at drilling down and finding the outlier information. And then they will . . . a head coach who is busy and under pressure will just flat shut that dude off. He will be effectively useless to him, and that becomes useless data."

Golden State Warriors assistant general manager Kirk Lacob concurs. Lacob, the son of team co-owner and venture capitalist Joe Lacob, has been in charge of ramping up the Warriors' analytics efforts. On one hand, given how far sports use of increasing amounts of data has lagged behind other industries (which Lacob witnessed as his father built his fortune), he is fascinated by how much attention this area is getting in the basketball realm. On the other hand, he understands perhaps better than most that communication is the key to the value of the info.

"We're learning a lot, and people are certainly analyzing the data that's suddenly been dumped on us at a kind of an increasingly rapid rate," Lacob said, "but . . . no matter what data you have and how well you put it together, if it's not used properly, it just doesn't happen.

"It really doesn't matter at all. Because you can have all the data, but if it's not being used for one reason or another—and, in this case, because people who need to use it don't understand it or don't want to see it—it's 'What are we doing the whole thing for?' Because what we're trying to do is narrow the margins on the edges, and, you know, slice off that last little piece of advantage we can find, and if it's too much of a headache to slice that piece, then sometimes it's better to just be more efficient and, you know, take your 5 percent error rate rather than cut that error rate to 2 percent."

Lacob, whose father also was a blackjack player, also knows Jeff Ma, a member of the famed MIT blackjack team that was depicted both in the book *Bringing Down the House* and the movie *21*. He uses analogs from that casino game to describe the NBA team-building process. The goal, per Lacob, is to keep refining your strategy as you learn more and more about the environment you're in, and then be ready to "increase your bet" when the situation is favorable for you.

Of course, in basketball, you're not just playing against a dealer (and the house). There are twenty-nine other teams in the same market for players or assets, so Lacob said, at times, team-building can be more like a blackjack tournament, where you are competing against other players with various strategies, but a lot of the final result comes down to who hits their big moves at the end. Having that kind of mindset is helpful because, as Lacob notes, a team can position itself extremely well, or get lucky and be in a seemingly advantageous position, but the cards—or, in this case, the draft class or the player performance—don't end up rewarding you.

An example of this is the Cleveland Cavaliers, who, after having won the draft lottery in 2011 and nabbing blossoming star point guard Kyrie Irving, won it again in both 2013 and 2014. The 2013 pick, though, came in a draft where there was zero consensus as to who the best player was, or whether any of the players in the draft would be difference-makers as pros. The Cavaliers tabbed forward Anthony Bennett, who was dreadful in his rookie season in Cleveland. The following May, after beating the odds yet again, future star Andrew Wiggins was waiting for them at No. 1. The Cavaliers subsequently packaged both Bennett and Wiggins to the Minnesota Timberwolves for standout forward Kevin Love after luring LeBron James back as a free agent, so what was initially a good luck/bad timing outcome in 2013 became much more favorable after they repeated the trick with better timing.

Lacob also noted that the San Antonio Spurs have benefited over many seasons from having the same management and coaching personnel in place, as well as their top players, so the Spurs' communication across the entire franchise is more refined than any other team in the league. Given Golden State had a new coaching staff in 2014–15, with rookie head coach Steve Kerr at the helm, figuring out the proper dynamics of communication were even more crucial, and this was something the franchise really focused on from the outset of the season as Kerr's staff looked to build on the fifty-one-win success of prior head coach Mark Jackson. Every team approaches this in its own way, but with the Warriors, the front office wants to empower the coaching staff to feature as the lead voices.

"To me, it's important to talk to the people who are actually going to do the work," Lacob said. "So what does that mean? It's the players, the coaches—the coaches have a direct line to the players, [so] in the front office, we never want to get in the way of that. I mean, look, there's, I'm sure, some teams [where] that information should be conveyed directly from the front office, maybe that's how they believe it [should work]. We don't. We think the coaches are the ones working every day, [so] we as management do not have any interest in talking to players every single day about this stuff.

"We want there to be one voice, because it's the voice of nineteen on the court, when things matter. So the coaches are the ones delivering this message to the players. How can we best deliver this message to the coaches in a way they can understand? And, you know, we really pride ourselves on trying to find that balance, and it's a very delicate balance. We've struggled with it at times, no doubt; we'll be the first to admit that. But I think we found a pretty good spot, and now we have a new coaching staff, who we're working really closely [with], and one of the things we kind of told them from day one was, look, let's find out what you're comfortable with, what each guy is comfortable with, and [though] we want to share what we want to give you, we also want to hear what you want to see, and let's kind of try to find a happy balance between that."

Lacob also concurred with what the Raptors' Rucker said in terms of it being harder than you would imagine to discern exactly what analytics is doing for you on a night-to-night, or even month-to-month basis. When you're dealing with small edges that you're trying to make slightly larger over time (and sustainable), it can be difficult to isolate individual things happening, even as you believe the entirety of the operation is working to win you a possession here, or a quarter here, or steal one extra game there.

"A lot of times even [with] data, you look for, 'Does there seem to be incremental improvement somewhere?' And, you know, then we have to test out whether it's randomness or not," Lacob said. "But you're really not going to see the full effects for probably—on most things—for a couple of years. And, you know, for game-to-game stuff, it might be over a course of a couple months. You do have to let randomness play out, and you do have to take that kind of variability and kind of test it out and see—how big are the variants here? But, no, sometimes we won't really know, and so, we're making a bet. Absolutely, we're making a bet on our future."

There may be no bigger bets in the NBA than player acquisition, and the most expensive ones come from the free-agent market. There, a player's current team usually has an advantage in terms of being able to offer extra years and guaranteed salary, and all thirty teams are jousting in a controlled market for very limited amounts of talent. When you layer in individual team systems and coaching preferences and agent/franchise relationships and everything else that goes into whether one team has a chance with a choice free agent, you shouldn't then be surprised to learn that while analytics has a very crucial role in targeting players, it can't have nearly as much impact in terms of what price you end up paying for the player, regardless of what his "valuation" is.

As explained by multiple front-office people, player acquisition is a binary exercise: you either get a player, or you don't. As such, while you may value a primary free agent as a "$10 million player," the open market—and possible advantages to the current team in terms of contract size—often create market dynamics that drive a player's cost up beyond his perceived value. At that point, teams need to evaluate whether that cost can fit into their salary structure, and how badly they want this specific player versus secondary options. A lot of the buzz every summer, and now especially with the salary cap rising so much and so quickly over the next couple of seasons, is that a guy is "overpriced" when he's signed. For certain decisions, though, that's a more favorable outcome than missing out on the player altogether.

"Very infrequently would you think about 'let's not give this player this much money because of some analytical nuance,'" Penn said. "The talent is so scarce, and the opportunity to get talent is so infrequent, that almost always you gotta go grab the talent when you can. So, the numbers would play into the overall feel of who's the right talent and who's the right target, but very rarely would you get into parsing out some detail, some point of the analytics, and say, 'No, we're only go to pay x, not x + whatever percentage.' That's more of a straight-up negotiation thing; 'this is our guy, let's get this done.' That's what we used to do. We'd pick our target, and the analytics would help us shape who our target is, but then we would spend as aggressively as we could within the rules to get the deal done."

The related complication is that timing within a club's development is a huge factor. There may be a free agent that you really like, but he doesn't fit with your other key pieces. It's not a rotisserie or daily fantasy team where you simply have to fit pieces in within a salary structure. You have a partially completed puzzle, and you're constantly evaluating what pieces you need and what are available along with what the cost considerations may be. In the end, analytics may suggest a piece isn't exactly perfect, but if a player comes available at the right time, and you can afford him, you may need to pull the trigger anyway.

"You can have all this theoretical analysis—we did this, we analyzed the last ten or twenty [teams], for the last ten years of finalists—and we looked at the way they were built with their cap structure," Penn said. "Was it two great players? Was it three great players? Where did they invest in what positions? And what that ended up outputting was a really interesting study for a sports management class, but it's completely impractical because you never really get a blank slate, and you never really get the opportunity to go out and build like that. You sort of, by circumstance, bump into or arrive at whatever talent you got, and then you have to build around whoever that is. 'Best player available' is a phrase used a lot."

⁓

Of course, the players are the main actors that make your analytics decisions look good or bad. And while there are a good number of players in today's NBA that take analytics output seriously, there's still probably no better overall case than Shane Battier.

Battier, who retired after the 2013–14 season after a thirteen-year career, became the player face of the analytics movement after a lengthy Michael Lewis *New York Times* feature in 2009 unveiled a lot of the information that showed Battier to be a really valuable piece of winning teams even though his personal statistics were never particularly impressive.

"I was fortunate enough to play in an era that the analytics were able to explain and give . . . more validation than if I had played ten years earlier," Battier said. "From college ball all the way to the analytics movement, I was always described as a glue guy. And the hustle guy—a guy who played hard. It's a nice way of saying he's an unathletic guy who helps the success of the team. Basically a proxy for 'glue guy.'

"And, really, with the Michael Lewis article that came out about me, it was the first time that someone could explain—and Lewis did an amazing job—to explain what I did and why I was an effective basketball player, even though even most basketball pundits couldn't put a finger on exactly what I did to positively impact the game. I was always part of winning teams and championship-winning teams, but my numbers were never overly sexy, my skill set obviously was not overly sexy, but I was always on the floor when it mattered, and more often than not, my teams won."

As widely reported in recent years by the sports media, the Houston Rockets are involved early in a lot of the deeper analytical thinking in the sport. And in Battier's case, Morey and the Rockets smelled out his hidden value before anyone else. In a 2007 *Houston Press* column on Morey's methods, Jason Friedman wrote that when the Rockets' brass were conducting a self-analysis prior to the 2006 draft and seeing who they could acquire to fix some of the issues, Battier "stood out like a Mensa member at a Paris Hilton party."

The Rockets went on to trade the No. 8 overall pick (and forward Stromile Swift) to the Memphis Grizzlies in exchange for Battier, which drew predictable howls, especially since UConn's Rudy Gay had dropped in the draft and was available at that spot. It's probable that even Battier didn't understand why the Rockets had given up that kind of asset to acquire him, but that soon changed. So did the ways in which Battier understood the game, and how he could best deploy his own abilities to further his team's chances of winning.

"I didn't even know what the analytics really, really meant. It wasn't until I got to Houston that I had it sort of explained what my value was to the Rockets' organization, and it gave me a perspective on my career," Battier said. "And even when I was playing before the Rockets in Memphis, I did things that I was taught to do—just be a good teammate, move the ball, block out, make the opponent take a tough shot, run back on defense—all the things that translate into modern-day analytics as the price of winning."

"It really was an amazing experience to play for [Daryl] Morey and Sam Hinkie, who sort of explained their worldview of basketball, and I've always been super-analytic and always tried to look at a situation as it is versus what it's supposed to be or getting caught up in the hyperbole. And the way they drew me into their analytic world—and I don't know who the player was, it might've been Kobe, but they said, 'Hey, do you know who Kobe Bryant is at his core?'

"And they showed me this scouting report on Kobe that he was a dominant right-handed player that finishes and gets fouled and shoots a free throw rate at a legendary level, and they had all the numbers and stats to back that up. And [they] really deconstructed one of the greatest players of all time, instead of traditional scouting reports that say Kobe's got a really good right hand, he's got a pretty good step-back jumper, he's good in the post, all very general basketball terms, but nothing that could really give you an edge as a defender.

"I knew exactly how much better Kobe was going with his right hand versus his left hand, and I knew exactly how much better he was if I kept him—how much chance I had to survive if I kept him—out of the paint versus allowing him to get a paint touch with the basketball. And, basically, a legend [was] deconstructed, and you see what he is. He's still obviously a legend, but you see there are warts and there are flaws and there are strengths that if you could navigate, it gave you a much better chance to dissect a player coming from a defensive perspective.

"And after I saw that, I said, 'Wow, I'm sold. What else you got?' And it really was an education of the analytic way of thinking about basketball, sort of the academic approach, if you will, to basketball in the new millennia."

While Battier's reputation was principally built around his defensive ability and selflessness—Lewis's feature detailed a situation where the Rockets were readying to play the San Antonio Spurs, and Battier suggested to the coaching staff that he come off the bench that game so he could better match the minutes Spurs sixth-man Manu Ginobili, his primary cover, would play—the Rockets also molded Battier into a lethal "3-and-D" wing. Battier shot a searing 42.1 percent from the 3-point line in his first season in Houston, and in his four seasons with the Rockets, he took at least four 3-pointers a game in each of them, and never shot under 36 percent.

Battier came to crave the kind of information the Rockets (and, for his final three seasons, the Miami Heat) could provide, but he was a bit of a rarity then. Even now, the NBA is full of guys who have no interest in seeing their own stats or shot charts, let alone those of players they will be defending. These players have gotten to the league and landed eight-figure contracts doing things their own way, and it will take some time for a larger subset of the players to buy in.

"It's still in its infant stages, to be honest with you. At this point, it's still a fairly academic movement," Battier said about the analytics surge. "It's still a movement that is rooted in the office of the GMs and the personnel directors. Now you have coaches who are trying to implement the data, and are walking along the company line of the analytics-based general managers, but there's still a ways to go before the effect is complete and it reaches the most important people in the equation: the players. There's still a deep rift between the belief in, I guess, what we would say [is] traditional basketball and what that means and what the data suggests as good or bad basketball.

"And the divide is pretty stark even with coaches, especially those of the old guard. Obviously not new, younger coaches who have been exposed to analytics, but the last frontier is players," he said. "As a player, you're taught basketball is almost a primal exercise. It's mano a mano, the strong will survive, and you have to do what you need to do to survive because there's always someone knocking, clipping at your heels, trying to take your job, trying to take your contract, trying to take your roster spot, trying to take your money, and trying to take your life.

"And so when you try to explain analytics and data to a player, they think, 'Whoa, whoa, whoa, basketball is not about numbers, basketball is about being primal, it's about emotion, it's about mental toughness,' and most players don't think there's any link to the data. In actuality, all analytics are are a way to explain all those things: heart, determination, and toughness. And you just have to look at it in a different way."

At the 2015 Sloan Sports Analytics Conference, Battier relayed an interesting story about how in one of his seasons with the Heat, he only took one jump shot that was inside the 3-point arc. He said his consumption of data, understanding what efficient shots were, and what his specific role was on those teams actually hindered him as an offensive player. He would find himself thinking on the court about whether something was a bad shot rather than playing naturally and taking what was available.

That said, knowledge for a player of Battier's skill set can be really valuable, and it's doubly so when the team's coach buys in and is delivering the message. Battier said that a large part of his success in Houston was in the way then-coach Jeff Van Gundy (Stan's brother) would internalize data and then impart that philosophy to his players.

"Jeff is one of the smartest coaches I've ever played for, and he understood the value of a lot of the data, and he would just tell us, 'Look, 2-point dribble jump shots don't [beat] us,' Battier said. 'And he would beat that mantra into our heads: 2-point dribble jump shots don't [beat] us. And if you know the data behind that, you know that that's the lowest-percentage shot in basketball . . . [a] non-paint two, off the bounce. In an elite level, shooters like, you know, Steph Curry is like 46–47 percent. The rest of humanity is a [sub-40 percent] dribble jump shooter. And as a defender, that was my shot to make people take. But when you put it like that, and you create a mantra, and Jeff would say, 'Look, if someone makes a 2-point dribble jump shot on you, it's on me as a coach, I'm never going to yell at you, you're not going to get crushed, it's on me.'

"And that gives you an amazing confidence as a defender knowing that, look, I get it, from an academic standpoint, an intellectual standpoint, and I know I'm not going to get punished for it, yeah, OK, yeah, no problem with a long, off the dribble, 2-point jump shot. It's going to take that sort of simplification from a coach, and that's what makes coaches great coaches. The ability to reach each member of their team. If you start spouting stats like, 'Look, if you got a 3-pointer on the angle at the break of the arc, don't take it, if you can get a [closer] 3-pointer because the percentage is 10 percent better,' all of a sudden, you are being confusing. Say, 'Hey, I will never yell at you if you take a corner 3-pointer,' people get that. And you don't necessarily have to explain why. Sort of like Van Gundy did."

As data-friendly as Battier was (and still is), there's one area where he's still a bit reticent of recent developments: the growing push for biometric data on players. Battier understands from a player's standpoint how potentially harmful this could be. For every instance where a player can stave off injury or find out some predisposition to a potentially lethal condition like Marfan syndrome, there are situations where data could be used against a player, and many don't want all of that personal information in the hands of their employers. There are issues of data security, and the NBPA will have to wrestle with a process that likely will benefit its membership overall but could have some individual cases of collateral damage should info leak.

"I was interested in my own performance," Battier said. "I took very good care of my body for thirteen years in the NBA. I probably drank too much red wine, didn't sleep as much [as I should have], but I was always interested in trying to see how I could find an edge with rest, or recovery, and that is all very applicable and poignant. But I think we are entering a very dangerous time. If you're a player, [it would be] the invasion of privacy. Because when you own information, you can [distort] that information to your own purposes. So that's the danger of where this is all headed.

"I think it's inevitable that teams will be able to collect information via blood, urine, stool, what have you. It can be used for good, but it can also be used for destructive purposes and when—it's sort of the whole big brother question and that allegory that comes into play. How much do people really need to know? And the body fluids and lifestyle choices . . . I'm glad I'm getting out of the game at the right time."

CHAPTER 7

How the NBA's
Best Teams Were Built

We'll look for patterns, we'll look for weak spots, and then we'll determine how valuable those are to us because . . . there's no way you're going to construct a perfect team [that's] perfect in every position. The only way to do that is if there are like five twenty-eight-year-old LeBrons available, and you can't afford to pay all of them, right?

—**Kirk Lacob, assistant general manager, Golden State Warriors**

The 2015 conference finals ended up pairing the top two teams in each conference, which perhaps not coincidentally included four of the more analytically inclined teams in the league. While the Houston Rockets are always discussed at the industry's forefront, both the Golden State Warriors and Atlanta Hawks have built their own strong internal number cultures (helped by key hires with San Antonio Spurs roots), and the Cleveland Cavaliers have gotten more coordinated in this area over the last few years after having previously invested in it with less eventual benefit.

Obviously, you don't need a team of data analysts to tell you that you want LeBron James on your team, but more work is required to sniff out the ceiling of a James Harden, or to build a contender around cores of Al Horford/Paul Millsap or Steph Curry/Klay Thompson. All of those players are now various levels of NBA star, but none came with a pedigree anywhere close to James's when initial big-money decisions were made to build around their skills and complementary natures.

Each of the conference finalists has its own interesting and unique story about how it got there, and the details stretch back well before the 2014–15 season. In many cases, crucial decisions made a number of years ago ended up hitting, and two teams—Houston and Cleveland—also made deft, in-season changes of direction that were crucial to their successes. Here is how each of the title contenders were built, and how analytics helped underscore their team-building plans.

The Golden State Warriors and Chasing Greatness

Golden State Warriors first-year head coach Steve Kerr looked a bit bemused as he casually strode along the midcourt line of the Philips Arena court, making his way toward the media gathered along the sideline. Kerr, a former member of the media himself in between his time as general manager of the Phoenix Suns and his current role with the Warriors, quickly was surrounded by a horde of reporters and TV crews. Everyone was there to capture his thoughts after his team's shootaround ahead of this February 2015 battle of surprise conference leaders between the Warriors and the homestanding Atlanta Hawks.

Normally, media at shootarounds are limited to a small handful of local media members and bloggers who cover the teams playing that night. On this particular Friday morning in Atlanta, though, there were dozens of media members in attendance, running the gamut from local to national entities, with both ESPN and *Bleacher Report* having multiple reporters on the scene.

Warriors–Hawks was a matchup that at the beginning of the 2014–15 season looked as innocuous as many of the 1,229 others on the NBA's master schedule, but it had become a national media event as the two teams, unexpectedly, were well in front in their respective conferences. This meeting was the first of two scheduled meetings between two teams, and, according to Elias Sports Bureau, the first matchup of teams with fewer than ten losses this late in a season since the Cleveland Cavaliers and Los Angeles Lakers faced off on February 8, 2009.

Once Kerr stopped and literally was surrounded by the mass of folks carrying cameras, digital recorders, and notepads, he looked around, and with a chuckle, said "Welcome to the Finals!"

While the hype over a regular-season matchup was a little overdone—even with the Hawks winning a 124–116 thriller that evening—both teams definitely deserved the attention. Atlanta, which had been a thirty-eight-win 8-seed in the East in 2013–14, in part because star center Al Horford was lost to a season-ending injury, had just seen a nineteen-game winning streak end earlier that week at New Orleans. They entered this game having won thirty-four of their last thirty-seven contests, and were firmly in charge in the race to the 1-seed and homecourt advantage in the Eastern Conference playoffs.

As good as Atlanta had been, though (and the Hawks will be discussed in greater detail in a few pages), Golden State was the best team in the NBA all season. The Warriors entered this showdown at 39–8 in the tougher Western Conference, on their way to a final mark of 67–15. They featured the backcourt of soon-to-be league MVP Curry and Thompson, who recently had dropped an NBA-record thirty-seven points on the Sacramento Kings in one quarter without missing a shot.

The Warriors were flexing their muscle well beyond their win–loss record, too. Entering this Hawks game, they had an average margin of victory of over eleven points a game. They finished the season at plus-10.1, the eighth-best mark in NBA history, according to a search of Basketball-Reference.com, which put them in NBA royalty. Every team on that "Plus-10 list" won the NBA championship except the 1971–72 Milwaukee Bucks, who lost in the Western Conference Finals to the Lakers, whose plus-12.3 is the best single-season mark ever.

More impressive was the way the Warriors achieved that success. Golden State was the first team in NBA history to lead the league in both defensive efficiency and pace of play (98.3 possessions a game), and they were only marginally passed late in the season by the Los Angeles Clippers on the offensive efficiency list to keep them from an unbelievable statistical trifecta. When you factor in how many fourth-quarter minutes the Warriors' starters sat out because the team had a huge lead (Golden State's fourth-quarter scoring margin actually was negative for the season), they likely had the league's most potent offense, as well.

Even threatening to lead the league in all of those categories was so rare and imposing that, when asked on Twitter during the season about the name of the award for a team that accomplished it, Houston Rockets general manager Daryl Morey replied, "The Larry O'Brien Award," referencing both the trophy given to the NBA champion each season, and the Warriors' chances of claiming it.

This all helps explain the massive challenge of facing this particular team. Golden State crafted an enormous spread advantage between their offense and their opponent's offense on a per-possession basis, and applied it relentlessly over a huge number of possessions in a game. They could break a team's will both with quick scoring barrages and throttling defensive stretches. As such, it was nearly impossible for inferior teams to stay with the Warriors; either the opponent's offense or defense (or both) would eventually break down under the pressure. Golden State capped off its dominance by being one of the most effective transition teams in the league, both in terms of how often they ran (north of 18 percent of possessions) and in how they scored in transition (around 1.2 points per possession). Easy layups and open transition threes for everyone!

All of this was happening with a first-year coach in Kerr, who had replaced Mark Jackson, who was let go after winning fifty-one games the season before. The club also had managed a summer's worth of speculation about whether to give up Thompson in a deal with Minnesota that would net them standout power forward Kevin Love. Ultimately, Golden State refused to part with Thompson, who management believed was a great complement to the more diminutive Curry, and also to some of the Warriors' other wings. Love eventually was dealt to Cleveland to pair with LeBron James, and Golden State quickly signed Thompson to an extension of four years and $70 million. Now, here they were, the toast of the NBA, with a freewheeling, audience-pleasing style that was bulldozing the rest of the league on a near nightly basis.

"It's been a great transition, obviously made easy by the fact that we have great players who are extremely easy to coach," Kerr said prior to the game. "[We have] high character people, a lot of wonderful people in the organization, so it's been very smooth.

"I knew we'd have a good team because they were already good. They won fifty-one last year and whatever it was the year before, two years in the playoffs in a row. My goal was just really to keep the continuity and continue the growth and improvement. I wouldn't have guessed we'd have this record."

Jackson definitely helped change the Warriors' culture for the positive, but he had, despite semi-regular Curry explosions, made them into a team that was far better on defense than offense. In 2013–14, Golden State finished third in the league in defensive efficiency while ending up just a modest eleventh on the offensive end of the court.

Jackson's inability to unlock the team's offense was one of the major on-court frustrations of his tenure and why it felt like Golden State had hit a ceiling under his command, but it was an unraveling of his relationships within the Warriors that eventually was his undoing. Whether he was in the wrong or not, Jackson had public blowups with two assistant coaches, with Brian Scalabrine being demoted to the Warriors' D-League team in Santa Cruz, and then Darren Erman being fired for secretly audio-recording staff meetings. It wasn't just his immediate staff that had trouble coexisting with him, though. Team owner Joe Lacob, who still maintains that Jackson was the right hire at the time and was what the Warriors needed then, told the audience at a Silicon Valley venture capital luncheon in December 2014 that Jackson's firing was, in part, because "he couldn't get along with anybody else in the organization."

In came Kerr and a philosophy cribbed from the San Antonio Spurs, where Kerr had played for three seasons and won a championship under Gregg Popovich, along with assistant coaches in Alvin Gentry and Ron Adams, who were regarded as among the NBA's best strategists. Suddenly, the Warriors had a whole refreshing new way of thinking, especially at the offensive end.

"Coach Kerr knows that system and [he's] taken a lot of advice from Popovich and coaches on that staff," Curry said, "so you go with what you know to be successful."

While offense is what gets the highlights, though, Kerr insists that his team spends the majority of its time working on defense, and it's on that end of the floor where the Warriors really separated themselves thanks to their personnel. Specifically, as suggested in a January 2015 column by Alex Torres at *Warriors World,* Golden State has used both the draft and the free-agent market to nab a series of athletic perimeter players who all have enormous wingspans. Golden State landed Thompson at pick No. 11 in 2011, got both Harrison Barnes (No. 7 overall) and emerging star Draymond Green (No. 35 overall; a second-round selection) in 2012, added known defensive stopper Andre Iguodala as a free agent in 2013, and brought on guards Shaun Livingston and Justin Holiday in 2014 to round out the group.

The end result is the Warriors have up to half a dozen players with wingspans of nearly seven feet to rotate among the shooting guard, small forward, and power forward positions (or even point guard when Curry's on the bench). This personnel flexibility shows up in the halfcourt, where the Warriors can switch any ball screen and still have a defender capable of moving his feet well enough to defend the handler, and they also are difficult to post up against at any position. The length also really helps in transition defense, as the Warriors don't necessarily have to find a specific cover in the open floor; with multiple guys capable of guarding multiple positions, they just find the guy closest to them as the opponent is pushing up the court.

"Small guys have somewhat taken over the NBA to an extent," Kerr said. "That's where Draymond and Andre and Harrison and Klay have come into effect for us. When we're trying to chase all these quick point guards of pick and rolls, you have to have that athleticism and length and versatility, and I think that's a big part of the way the NBA's played today.

"We're a quick team," Kerr added. "We have a lot of interchangeable parts. We switch quite a bit. We have a lot of rangy, long-limbed athletes. Rebounding can be an issue when we play small, but we have to be on edge and active. When we are, we get to the ball quickly."

Green became the principal catalyst of this group, blending an elite mix of rim protection, post defense, perimeter defense, and wing scoring into a player who quickly agreed to a new five-year, $85 million contract with the team after the 2014–15 season. He's representative of the type of more positionless player that's now thriving in the NBA, and his impact on the Warriors was pronounced.

Per NBA.com's statistics database, the Warriors had a plus-16.5 rating (the net of the team's offensive and defensive points per one hundred possessions) in the 2,490 minutes Green was on the floor, and only a plus-2.5 rating in his 1,456 minutes off the court. On the Warriors, only Curry had a larger spread between his "on" and "off" ratings. Golden State also allowed 102.4 points per one hundred possessions without Green on the floor, which was the worst mark on the team by almost two points per one hundred.

"Draymond just has a knack for being in the right place at the right time, whether it's getting a key rebound or covering guards on the pick and roll, penetration," Kerr said. "He's quick, he's strong, he's really, really intelligent. He just understands angles and schemes. He's really kind of the key to our defense. We have a lot of excellent defenders. I mean, Andre is one of the best in the league and was All-League last season. [Andrew] Bogut's our rim protector. Steph and Klay are excellent, too, but Draymond really ties it all together."

Another significant change under Kerr was the increased appreciation of the physical, rim-protecting Bogut, a seven-footer who missed the Warriors' tough seven-game playoff series loss to the Los Angeles Clippers in 2014. Bogut's presence in the lane in the 50 percent of each game he typically played allowed the Warriors' wing players to more aggressively push up on their men, knowing that if they got beat, at least they could steer the ballhandler into Bogut's path. During the regular season, the Warriors were five points per one hundred possessions better defensively with Bogut on the floor, and his 95.2 points per one hundred possessions "on court" defensive rating was the best on the team.

While teams ultimately will be able to adjust to some of what the Warriors did in 2014–15, this team is far from a one-year wonder. The core is quite young, and the team-building has been fueled, in part, by analytics assessments and an overarching philosophy that seem to be spot on. While assistant general manager Kirk Lacob admits Golden State is not at the top of the league in terms of either personnel or resources thrown at data analysis, the Warriors still have made a series of very prudent—and ultimately potent—decisions.

As an example, Lacob details one of the less-heralded ones, the free-agent signing of Andre Iguodala, a player the team had been after for a long while.

"We'll look for patterns, we'll look for weak spots, and then we'll determine how valuable those are to us because you can't—I mean, there's no way you're going to construct a perfect team [that's] perfect in every position," Lacob said. "The only way to do that is if there are like five twenty-eight-year-old LeBrons available, and you can't afford to pay all of them, right? You actually need ten of them, because you need guys off the bench.

"We came to a head two years ago, where we saw a guy who was available—Andre Iguodala—a guy who we liked for like three or four years," he added. "We thought he did so many things well, and so many of the small things that you could really fit a lot of different pieces around him. He's like kind of the glue, or the base, whatever, that holds a team together. He makes it easier to put guys in different spots because he does so many things."

Iguodala spent the 2014–15 regular season coming off the bench, but became a crucial factor late in the playoffs as a starter (as will be discussed in the Epilogue).

"[When] he became available as a free agent, we decided he was a guy that we really liked," Lacob said. "We thought he fit our timeline a little bit, and we went after him, and that enabled us, I think, this year, to really focus on three or four things that, we thought, based on our analysis, that we really could do better."

A new coach, a few new faces, player development—it all came together better than anyone could have hoped. The result was a truly historic team that navigated a brutal conference with aplomb. While critics like Charles Barkley kept derisively referring to them as a "jump shooting team," in part because of their low free throw rate to go with all the talented guys on the perimeter, the Warriors kept running, kept scoring and kept suffocating opponents. They were the best team in the NBA, and they lived up to that billing on a near-nightly basis in very sexy fashion.

The Houston Rockets: Beyond the Three-for-All

If you only watched one Houston Rockets game from the 2014–15 season, you still would be able to identify their primary offensive calling card: they shot as many threes as they could squeeze off.

Per Basketball-Reference.com, the average NBA team took around 22.4 3-pointers per game. The Rockets exceeded that total in all but four of their ninety-nine combined regular-season and play-off games. They never attempted fewer than twenty in a contest, and launched a season-high forty-six against rival Dallas in a 3-point win on November 22, 2014. On twelve different occasions, the Rockets took at least forty threes in a game, and they made fifteen or more shots from behind the arc an incredible seventeen times.

They set NBA records for most 3-pointers made and attempted in a season. Both shooting guard James Harden and small forward Trevor Ariza each attempted over five hundred fifty threes. Point guards Patrick Beverley and Jason Terry each shot well over three hundred. In all, eight Rockets attempted at least one hundred shots from behind the arc during the regular season.

That wasn't the entire picture of what was going on—the Rockets also were second in the league in free throw attempts, and had the fifth-best 2-point field goal percentage (thanks to taking so few of them and taking most of those close to the rim)—but the visual of threes being coldly and relentlessly launched is what will codify most in the minds of basketball fans. To interpret the Rockets through that extreme lens, though, would be selling their path and their evolution short.

For much of Daryl Morey's tenure as general manager, the Rockets have been the NBA's "almost" franchise—not as much for their relative lack of playoff success as for a series of transactions that either nearly happened and may have made them a legitimate contender sooner, or did happen and undercut their progress. Here's the primary chain of events that eventually led to the composition of the 2014–15 Rockets:

- The seeds were planted as early as 2009, when Morey traded starting point guard Rafer Alston to Memphis for point guard Kyle Lowry.

- In February 2010, Morey acquired forward Jordan Hill from the Knicks as part of a deal that enabled the Knicks to clear cap room for the summer of LeBron free-agency chase.

- In early 2011, Morey traded point guard Aaron Brooks to the Phoenix Suns for point guard Goran Dragic *and* a protected first-round draft pick.

    (The combined Alston/Brooks moves comprise one of the largest trade heists in recent memory. It was a shocking upgrade from two deals where players at the same position changed teams, and Houston nabbed a first-rounder on top of that. Incredible.)

- In December 2011, two crucial things happened—one large, and one seemingly small at the time.

    First, the Rockets were the third team in the infamous Chris Paul-to-the-Lakers trade, which ultimately was nixed by then-commissioner David Stern because the league technically owned the New Orleans franchise at the time and it wasn't felt that the Hornets were getting sufficient value in the deal. Houston would have received the star it was searching for in power forward Pau Gasol, and Dragic would have been part of the group leaving in the deal.

    Later that month, the Rockets released little-known Harvard point guard Jeremy Lin in order to sign journeyman big man Samuel Dalembert, because the three other point guards on the roster had guaranteed deals. Lin signed with the New York Knicks and created the phenomenon of "Linsanity" with his excellent play over a short stretch there.

- In February 2012, Morey tweeted that he had made a mistake in waiving Lin.

- In March 2012, Morey traded Hill to the Los Angeles Lakers and received a first-round pick back as part of the deal.

- In July 2012, Morey traded Lowry to Toronto and received another protected first-round pick. Morey was accumulating assets so the Rockets could try to work a trade for Orlando Magic star center Dwight Howard, who wanted out of Orlando. The team also saw Dragic leave in free agency to sign with Phoenix. Suddenly short on point guards, the Rockets re-signed Lin in free agency through a unique $25 million "poison pill" contract that New York declined to match because of the ramifications on its own cap space.

- In August 2012, Howard was traded to the Lakers in a four-team deal. Morey continued to hunt.

- In October 2012, Morey finally landed his star, working the deal with Oklahoma City that landed Harden. The first-round picks acquired in the Lowry and Hill trades were major parts of the package that went to the Thunder.

- In July 2013, after one disappointing season in Los Angeles, Howard spurned more money from the Lakers and signed with the Rockets. A rumored byproduct of that signing was Houston letting swingman Chandler Parsons out of his bargain rookie deal a year early, which then made him a restricted free agent after the 2013–14 season.

- In July 2014, the Rockets had cleared enough room to land high-impact free-agent forward Chris Bosh from the Miami Heat *and then* re-sign Parsons to a big, market-level deal, which would have given Houston a core of stars as good as anyone in the league. Bosh, though, elected to re-sign with Miami, and then Parsons signed with the Dallas Mavericks after they put together a contract offer that the Rockets felt was too restrictive to match. Instead, Houston signed Ariza as Parsons's replacement, and then acquired the veteran Terry for what was thought would be bench depth.

Whew. Did you follow all of that? That's how Houston came into the 2014–15 season with two stars in hand, but with an overall roster that most NBA observers considered weaker than the one from the season before, when the Rockets were eliminated in the first round by Portland in six thrilling games, thanks to a series-winning, buzzer-beating three from point guard Damian Lillard.

Instead of slipping, the Rockets ended up winning fifty-six games and landing the 2-seed in the Western Conference playoffs for two related reasons: the guys they brought in ended up being terrific fits, and Harden's rise to superstardom was complemented by the rest of the team playing very much like him.

For the season, Harden led the league in total minutes played, was one field goal attempt behind Russell Westbrook for the most shots attempted, and also led the league in free throw attempts by a preposterous margin. Harden attempted more than ten free throws a game in 2014–15, which is outrageous for a guard. While eras are different and game tempos vary, Harden now has two of the twenty-six all-time seasons where a guard had ten-plus free throw attempts per game (minimum sixty games), per a search of Basketball-Reference.com.

Only seven guards in history have at least two such seasons, a list that includes basketball immortals Michael Jordan, Oscar Robertson, Jerry West, Allen Iverson, and Kobe Bryant.

Harden is tremendously clever and versatile in how he drives to the basket, and also is extremely well-versed in enhancing contact to draw foul calls. Mix in his huge number of 3-point attempts, and he's an offense unto himself.

"He can shoot the three, he can drive—he can drive to pass, he can drive to finish, he drives and gets fouled. So you can put him in a multitude of positions which gives you some flexibility," head coach Kevin McHale said of Harden during the season. "We don't have the record we have [right now] if James is not playing at his level.

"I go back to when I came into the league in 1980," McHale added. "It's a players league. It always has been a players league, and it always will be a players league. Guys just have to step up and play. This is the highest level in the world, and the top players are really phenomenal players, and he's right up there with them. So I'm happy for him. He's just taken on every challenge and done great."

Harden also became the offense within the Rockets' offense, almost to an eerie level.

The Rockets' offensive efficiency dropped off to a significant extent in 2014–15 as their shot selection became even more polarized. Part of that is they replaced offense with defense when they brought in players like Ariza, and a good portion of it is they suffered a significant number of lengthy injuries during the season. Howard missed half of the team's eighty-two games. Forward Terrence Jones only played in thirty-three. Point guard Patrick Beverley (another defensive specialist) missed twenty-six games, as did swingman Corey Brewer. Streak-shooting forward Josh Smith arrived midseason and played in fifty-five games.

Yet in the midst of this lineup chaos, even with fatigue dragging down both Harden's and the Rockets' efficiency numbers in the second half of the season, there was nearly perfect symmetry.

BBallBreakdown's Kelly Scaletta illustrated this in an August 2015 article where he showed how Harden, Russell Westbrook, and Chris Paul all fuel their teams in different ways, but their team offensive footprints are largely related to the strengths of their ball-dominant players. The image below, from Scaletta's piece, shows a radial diagram of Harden's offensive contributions by category, with the Rockets' team breakdown mapped over his:

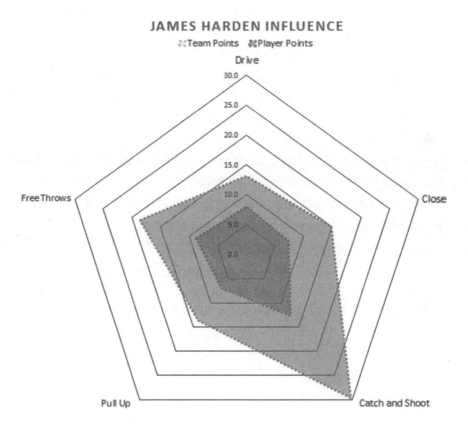

The shapes are nearly identical, which means the Rockets as a whole were basically an extension of Harden himself, despite all of the moving pieces around him as the season unfolded. There is no team in the league that operates more in tune with its primary star. Mix in the much-improved defensive capabilities, especially when Howard was mostly healthy, and you have a better team.

Then there's the chemistry and leadership portion of the equation, some of the stuff that's hardest to measure quantitatively but remains a crucial part of what makes good teams into great ones. In part because of all of Morey's chopping and changing in pursuit of the ideal team, the Rockets' roster hadn't spent very much time together, and a good number of the players hadn't spent a ton of time in the NBA. While the summer additions didn't excite a lot of people from a basketball standpoint (which turned out to be pretty wrong), opinion also undershot the leadership aspect.

"I think a big part of that is Trevor Ariza has come in and helped us, 'Jet' Terry's come in and helped us, I think Pat's maturity—those guys all talk and are all very frank and honest with each other," McHale said about his team's improved chemistry and accountability. "The maturity level of our team, even though we have ten guys with two or less years of [NBA] experience, our team is more mature this year from the Arizas and the Terrys and just their interaction with everybody, and I think that's a big thing. I think that helps James, and James helps us. It's a nice relationship. Everybody's got a part in that."

The Atlanta Hawks and the No-Star System

In a season where the preseason expectations were that Cleveland, reloaded with LeBron James and Kevin Love, would romp through the East, it was another heavily Spurs-influenced team that instead took the conference by storm.

To say no one saw Atlanta's sixty-win season coming would be an understatement. The Hawks, hindered by injuries a season earlier, had limped to a 38–44 record in 2013–14, garnering the 8-seed in the weak Eastern Conference almost by default before taking the top-seeded Indiana Pacers to the limit in the first round of the playoffs. The Hawks were a nice, modestly successful franchise, but hardly looked like a burgeoning powerhouse, even in a watered-down conference that was in considerable flux.

The 2014–15 season was Hawks head coach Mike Budenholzer's second with the franchise after spending nineteen years with the Spurs, the last seventeen as an assistant coach under the legendary Gregg Popovich. Budenholzer brought a lot of the same team-building philosophy and mentality to the job, including his mentor's notable terseness with the media, but he certainly didn't have legends like Tim Duncan, Manu Ginobili, and Tony Parker on his roster, nor the years of continuity that allow the Spurs to not only maintain their culture but also execute so seamlessly on the court.

Things were further complicated over the summer of 2014, when the franchise found itself embroiled in two different racism scandals. First, then-owner Bruce Levenson self-reported to the NBA a text he had sent in 2012 concerning the Hawks' struggles in growing its fanbase. It included Levenson wondering why there was such a high percentage of black fans at Hawks games versus crowds at other NBA venues, and whether the team's in-game presentation, which included heavy doses of hip hop music, was driving away white fans. As the league was in the midst of excising Los Angeles Clippers owner Donald Sterling over racist audio recordings involving a mistress (and Levenson was an outspoken critic of Sterling over that scandal), the Hawks' owner fell on his own sword and agreed to sell his ownership stake in the team.

Soon after, audio tapes of a Hawks management conference call leaked in which then–general manager Danny Ferry was reading from a scouting report provided by a source at the Cleveland Cavaliers that disparagingly described potential free-agent target Luol Deng as having "some African in him, and I don't say that in a bad way other than he's a guy that may be making side deals behind you, if that makes sense." The report also made a comparison to a merchant who sells counterfeit goods, and that Deng "has a little two-step in him—says what you like to hear, but behind closed doors he could be killing you." Ferry soon was suspended indefinitely by the team and ultimately was replaced after the 2014–15 season, with Budenholzer taking over as director of basketball operations and assistant general manager Wes Wilcox bumping up to the general manager role.

Ferry's removal was notable not just because of the way he delivered the report's racist remarks about Deng on a conference call with team higher-ups, but because he had done a quietly outstanding job in building the Hawks' roster. Atlanta wasn't considered a major free-agent destination, but Ferry and his staff made a series of savvy moves in 2013 that were starting to pay off significantly.

- The team elected to match a four-year, $32 million offer from the Milwaukee Bucks for restricted free-agent point guard Jeff Teague, even though Teague's progress had been somewhat halting during his rookie contract after being drafted nineteenth overall in 2009.

- They re-signed shooting guard Kyle Korver, who had been acquired the year before from the Bulls, and who described the trade to the Hawks from conference power Chicago as "a bit of a bummer." Korver re-upped for four years and $24 million.

- They signed athletic-but-raw small forward DeMarre Carroll on a two-year, $5 million deal.

- They drafted German teenage point guard Dennis Schroder at No. 17 overall.

- They also signed versatile power forward Paul Millsap on a two-year, $19 million contract.

Perhaps most notably that summer, Ferry also hired Budenholzer, whom he had both played under and worked with as an executive with the Spurs. Ferry, after his first season as general manager, elected to move on from Larry Drew after three seasons as head coach, even as the franchise had made its sixth straight playoff appearance. There was a perception that the Hawks had run into a glass ceiling as a perennial lower playoff seed, and needed a new approach to bust through it.

The seeds of Budenholzer's approach, cribbed from the space-and-shooting approach fashioned by the latest Spurs teams, started to get planted during his initial campaign in 2013–14, but a season-ending injury to de facto center Al Horford—the team's MVP and a poor man's Duncan in terms of his understated impact on both ends—helped undermine that season. Getting Horford back in 2014–15 was huge, but all of the players having a second season in Budenholzer's system created a multiplier effect that made the Hawks into a surprising force.

Still, the lack of a supposed star was a storyline that was hashed out all season. The Hawks only had one thirty-point scorer the entire season (Millsap scored exactly thirty against his old team, the Utah Jazz) and, perhaps more tellingly, had a seven-game stretch in December 2014 where a different player led the team in scoring each game, and all seven scored at least twenty points. In January, when the Hawks didn't lose a game in the midst of a nineteen-game winning streak, the NBA tipped its cap to the team's construct when it named all five starters as the Eastern Conference Player of the Month.

In sum, the Hawks were an extremely balanced team where no one was sure whether they had the type of player who could single-handedly win playoff games, when scouting, familiarity, and extra rest cut down the advantages of a team with a fluid offensive system like Atlanta's. Because they believed in the system and were getting the results, they were unapologetic about it.

"It's really fun to play on this team," Korver said. "Every time down the court, we all matter, because we play as a group. We all matter every single time. You might not shoot the ball, but you're definitely at least going to set the screen or make the pass or make the cut that opens up whoever it is that's going to get that shot. It just makes us play hard because you matter. Right? When you matter in life, you do a little bit better when you feel like you matter, and we feel like we matter. No matter who's out there, we all matter.

"I mean, it's easier on teams when you have superstars. I mean, they're really good. And you give them the ball, and you say 'make a play.' And a lot of offenses are created to feed off that guy. We don't have that guy, so we have to play a little bit differently. There's different ways to do it, so this is what we do."

It also helped that they had two very unique features: all five of their starters can shoot the three, and they have Korver, perhaps the most uniquely destructive offensive player in the league.

While Budenholzer inherited a top shooter (through the first twelve seasons of his career, Korver had made 43.4 percent of his nearly 4,000 3-point attempts) who was coming off an excellent first year in Atlanta, the new schemes the Hawks began running to maximize his strengths (and ability to help his teammates get shots) created an offensive monster.

Korver made nearly 50 percent of his threes in 2014–15, and many of those came off sub-variations of pick and rolls, with Korver first sprinting from a corner or settling into an action after setting a screen himself and receiving the ball on a handoff or flip. When these actions are run with a big player who can shoot, such as Millsap, Horford, or even with reserve big man Pero Antic, it puts opposing defenses in a huge bind. With many teams also having to try to defend these actions with big men that are not as comfortable guarding in space, there are no good answers.

Korver's constant motion and ability to shoot on the move add another element to the Hawks' success: he compromises defenders who have to track his every move. Per SportVU data, Korver is right at the absolute top of the NBA in terms of highest "gravity" score, meaning that his primary defender leaves him to help defensively less than any other player in the league. Even if Korver doesn't get the ball on a possession, the defense is effectively stuck chasing him around and defending the rest of the Hawks four-on-four, which provides more space and creates additional headaches for the opponent in their defensive coverages.

"He creates so many opportunities," Budenholzer said of Korver. "Really, the interesting thing for his teammates is he creates so much space and it makes it difficult, hopefully, for the defense to make decisions about taking away other options, taking away other opportunities—or if you take that away, Kyle may be free. It's just such a game of space and shooting and attacking the basket and attacking the rim, putting pressure on the defense, and he probably does that, creating opportunities for his teammates because he's such a good shooter. For himself, what he can do in terms of moving without the ball, coming off screens and sprinting in transition and rising up into shops, he's just a very unique—not just shooter, but how he can move and catch and shoot and move with great speed and rise up.

"Probably the last thing I saw offensively was his passing. He's really underrated as a passer. He comes off of screens, they try to take away the shot, he's creating opportunities for other people. I just think he's a really good basketball player that sometimes is mislabeled as just a shooter."

"He's [also] an amazing screensetter," Budenholzer added. "He loves setting screens. He loves getting his teammates open. So when you just kind of put all of that together, it's a big part of how we've built our offense and our identity. He fits. Our other guys fit with him. He fits with them. He's huge, and defensively, I think he's really underrated. His length, his commitment to it, his understanding of rotations, being early to rotations, his work on the defensive boards. He's really a complete player."

Korver was not the sole reason for the Hawks' massive jump, though. Teague, who had more or less plateaued over the previous three seasons as he grew into a starter's role and point guard usage rates, took a huge leap forward. No one advanced metric tells the whole story, but when they all basically show similar levels of improvement with career-best rates, it's telling. In the 2014–15 season, Teague easily had the best PER, box plus-minus, and win shares per forty-eight minutes rates of his pro career. He also was competently deputized by Schroder, who became an important, ball-dominant scorer off the bench on a team that didn't have that much reserve firepower, and also was able to close out games when Teague was struggling or the matchup favored Schroder's penetration skills.

Millsap, already thought to be a value at less than $10 million, may have been the "best" player on the Hawks while Horford, as the team's anchor, rim protector, and nineteen-foot face-up jump-shot splasher, arguably was the most valuable. Arguably, because of the emergence of Carroll, whose offense evolved to such a degree to complement his defending and overall effort that he suddenly found himself among the league's most effective "3-and-D" wings.

"He's one of the ultimate competitors in our league, he plays so hard on every possession," Budenholzer said of Carroll, who subsequently left the club in summer free agency to sign with the Toronto Raptors. "That's probably more important than anyone, as basic and fundamental as it seems, so that stands out. He's been growing as an offensive player. Everyone knows how good a defender he is and how he can impact a game defensively, but his shooting was improving, his ballhandling was improving. You could just see a player who was on the rise."

Also notable was the team's chemistry, which stemmed from a locker room where an unusually high number of players had spent three or more years in college and/or had come from outside the United States. Of the starters, only Teague, with two seasons at Wake Forest, fell short of either metric. Horford (originally from the Dominican Republic) and Millsap each played three NCAA seasons while Korver and Carroll both played four. Off the bench, there was defensive stopper Thabo Sefolosha (Swiss and a noted positive locker room guy), Schroder (German), Mike Scott (four years at Virginia), Mike Muscala (four years at Bucknell), Kent Bazemore (four years at Old Dominion), and Pero Antic (Macedonian). The Hawks also had veteran Elton Brand, another strong locker room guy who had played two years at Duke.

In composite, in a league with a high number of inexperienced and still-developing young American players, the Hawks didn't have any. Instead, their locker room was filled with mature and high-academic types, and you could sense a different vibe from other NBA teams when you spent any time with them. They weren't the only team that seemed to like being around each other, but there was a calmness that was palpable. And while the Hawks didn't go out specifically targeting guys who weren't one-year college players or from overseas, the guys they collected in order to play the style Ferry and Budenholzer wanted ended up being that way.

"We really value guys who are really unselfish, high-character guys, guys with high basketball IQs," Budenholzer said. "I don't like to paint with a broad brush, and if you're one-and-done and have those characteristics, we're interested. If you played in Europe and have those characteristics, we're interested. . . . it's not anything that we categorically don't take, or we only take or anything like that. It's just we have some things that we really value, and maybe it tends toward those kinds of guys. But we have a good idea what we're looking for, and we know how we can hopefully find guys that fit with us."

"We spend more time focusing on, and trying to understand, the character traits," Wilcox added. "That's our focus. Highly competitive, highly focused, hardworking, highly skilled, mentally tough, resilient, curious . . . these are the things that I think we have identified and that we try to add."

The end result was one of the league's most surprising—and surprisingly watchable—teams. The Hawks effectively locked up the

Eastern Conference's top seed so prematurely that they lost a bit of momentum down the stretch of the season, and they weren't helped by a spate of injuries to key players, including the big one—Sefolosha having his leg fractured by a New York City policeman during a police-provoked altercation outside a club in the aftermath of an incident that involved the stabbing of Indiana Pacers forward Chris Copeland. While the Hawks made it to the Eastern Conference Finals, they didn't impress very much on the way there, and then they were taken out in four straight by the Cavaliers, who themselves were shorthanded.

Regardless, 2014–15 was a landmark season for the franchise that, buoyed by new ownership, the resolution of the Ferry situation, and a rebranding as the Atlanta Hawks Basketball Club, was primed to move forward. Despite all the hype about trying to become "Spurs West" with the coaching and management connections to San Antonio complementing an unselfish and measured style of play, the Hawks really developed their own identity in year two of the Budenholzer era. It was fun, it was different, and it was an interesting test case on how to build a championship-caliber team. The fuller answers will be found in the seasons ahead.

The Cleveland Cavaliers and the Seven Faces of LeBron

It's fair to say that no one on the Cleveland Cavaliers signed up for the season they ultimately had in 2014–15.

Head coach David Blatt, who had long excelled at multiple stops in Europe, accepted the job in late June 2014 without knowing whether he was going to have star point guard Kyrie Irving around. Irving was eligible for a five-year contract extension that would tack on to the remaining year of his rookie deal, but there were a lot of rumblings during the 2013–14 season that Irving might look for a way out of town.

On July 1 of that year, Irving, who came to Cleveland via the No. 1 overall pick in 2011 after the Cavaliers fell to a nineteen-win season after LeBron James left for Miami the previous summer, ultimately agreed to stay without knowing what help he was going to get after his first three seasons with the franchise yielded an overall record of 78–152 and no playoff appearances. He had no assurances at the time that James would mend fences with team owner Dan Gilbert and return to his quasi-hometown four years after his departure became very public and contentious.

Since James didn't mention either 2014 No. 1 overall pick/superprospect Andrew Wiggins or 2013 No. 1 overall pick Anthony Bennett in his "I'm Coming Home" essay in *Sports Illustrated* that announced his plan to re-sign in Cleveland, it's safe to presume that he was informed of/approved/requested the Cavaliers' eventual August 2014 trade of the duo as part of a deal to land star forward Kevin Love from the Minnesota Timberwolves. He did not, however, sign up for a season spent finding different ways to motivate Love to fit in better, eventually including a thinly veiled shot on Twitter.

Love surely did not agree to join James and Irving in Cleveland to spend much of the season as a 3-point-chucking glorified decoy in an offense that didn't look much like what Blatt liked to run.

And none of them—coach or players—signed up for the angst, jousting egos, and injuries that required a tireless tamping down of in-house storylines that went public, a midseason two-week injury break/vacation for James, and two key in-season moves to reshape the roster—all as they limped to an underwhelming fifty-three wins and the Eastern Conference's 2-seed behind the Hawks.

From the outset, Irving spoke as if he understood the overall deal, but there were still some gaps in his understanding of how things were about to radically change. He was about to get paid like the face of a franchise, and seemed eager to continue in that role after three years of a slow rebuild, all the while knowing that LeBron—and everything that comes with him—was back in town, and on a short-term contract, to boot. LeBron had realized in Miami as the roster fell apart around him due to age and injuries that he shouldn't lock himself into a new long-term deal. Yes, there were financial considerations involved in his decision to take a one-year deal with a second-year player option, but it also kept pressure on ownership to make sure everything was exactly to his liking.

At the US National Team tryout camp in Las Vegas in late July 2014, Irving told assembled media that he had never wavered on re-signing with the Cavaliers.

"It was just confidence in our management, our coaching staff, the direction we're going, I wanted to be a part of," Irving said. "That was the leading reason why I came back. Just the opportunity we have in Cleveland with things going the right way. Whether or not LeBron was coming back, I was still going to sign. We got it done on that first day, we agreed to terms, and I signed on the tenth, and that's the way it should go. They wanted me to be a part of the organization long-term, and I wanted to be a part of it."

Concerning LeBron's return, Irving added, "At first, you can't believe it. It's more or less . . . I've been watching LeBron for a while now, and now that I'm going to be running alongside of him and be his point guard, it's an honor. Hopefully, we can do great things," but "the only thing that matters right now is what we do out there on the court."

But there's a marked difference between talk and action, especially when you are creating the highly combustible combination the Cavaliers were stirring together. You had a young, budding star who needed the ball in his hands; a six-year veteran standout in Love who was imported from a different losing situation and never had made the playoffs, let alone been tested in the crucible of truly meaningful games; and the world's most talented and demanding player, a basketball savant who was coming back home not just to attempt to nail down Cleveland's first-ever NBA title, but to basically reinvent the entire culture of the franchise he himself had once left.

Bleacher Report's Ethan Skolnick, in a July 2015 feature on how the Cavaliers reinvented themselves around LeBron's personality, provided insight to just how commanding James immediately was after his return to Cleveland. From the outset of the season, James demanded total accountability from everyone in the organization, from management through the head coach through the fifteenth man on the roster. There was an immediate urgency to win.

But it wasn't working, at least at first. LeBron, asked to be the team's best player, leader, and club culture overhauler, was wearing down physically and mentally. Love didn't seem happy or well used by Blatt. Irving was still feeling out his new role on the floor. It was a grind, with an adjustment period that seemed much steeper than when LeBron went to Miami and had to figure out a potent pas de deux with Dwyane Wade.

The Cavaliers started 5–7, then won eight straight games. They headed to Miami for a Christmas meeting with the Heat at 17–10, and then lost there in LeBron's return, with the major talking point afterward being how James connected much more readily on the court with Wade than any of his new teammates. A win at Orlando preceded a desultory twenty-three-point loss at then 6–23 Detroit on December 28, and then LeBron was done playing for a couple of weeks. Mostly without him, the Cavaliers ended up on an eight-game losing streak and bottomed out at 19–20 overall on January 13, 2015.

Statistically speaking, the Cavaliers only had a plus-3.4 net rating (net points per one hundred possessions) in November, and actually had a negative team rating in December and through the first half of January. Then things began to change in a hurry.

A week before the loss in Phoenix that dropped them back below .500, the Cavaliers had swung a three-team trade with the

New York Knicks and Oklahoma City Thunder that offloaded inefficient shooting guard Dion Waiters for mercurial, semi-inefficient shooting guard JR Smith and "3-and-D" wing Iman Shumpert. The move solved a couple of issues for the Cavaliers, as Smith overall was a shooting upgrade on Waiters, and they added defensive depth on the perimeter, too.

The next day, the team acquired center Timofey Mozgov from the Denver Nuggets, providing them with a physical rebounder and rim-protecting presence that the roster, thanks in part to an injury to Anderson Varejao, had sorely been lacking.

The Mozgov trade was expertly tailored by Cleveland general manager David Griffin, and very well explained by ESPN's Brian Windhorst in a January 2015 column. To do it, the Cavaliers carved out enough room to take on Mozgov's $4.4 million salary through a series of barely reported transactions that turned an initial, paltry $1.6 million in cap space into a trade exception worth more than $5 million, all the while only using second-round picks as enticements to get other teams to work with them. It was the subtle kind of masterful cap manipulation that ultimately can be the difference in championship aspirations, and in this case, delivered the Cavaliers what they desperately needed.

It's not quite as simple as saying that the Cavaliers took off from there, but they proceeded to go 34–9 the rest of the way, even while throwing away a couple of late-season games as they rested key guys ahead of the playoffs. In February, the Cavaliers had a plus-8.8 net rating, and they followed that up with a plus-8.3 net rating in March as the revamped roster hit its stride and made them, especially on the offensive end, an extremely formidable force. In fifteen March games, the Cavaliers averaged 111.6 points per one hundred possessions, which would have led the NBA for the season.

The subtext, though, was how their big three were meshing together, and what happened when various combinations of James,

Love, and Irving were on the floor, and that is something that remains a work in progress.

Per unpublished lineup information culled by Jacob Rosen, a writer for Cleveland sports blog *Waiting for Next Year,* the Cavaliers' season-ending numbers when all three stars were on the court—even with all the early on- and off-court drama—were extremely potent. In the 1,441 minutes the trio was together on the court (about 36 percent of the Cavaliers' total for the regular season), the Cavaliers had a plus-13.3 net rating and were very good on both sides of the ball. Those numbers, though, fell precipitously when either Irving or Love went to the bench, with neither a LeBron/Irving nor LeBron/Love combo even reaching a plus-3.0 net rating in a combined 720 minutes on the season.

Somewhat interesting—both in how the roster was bolstered, and as foreshadowing for the playoffs, when both Irving and Love were injured—was that Cleveland was actually quite good when, of the three stars, *only* LeBron was on the court. In 333 regular-season minutes of "LeBron Plus Four Others," Cleveland was a surprising plus-13.1 net rating, and defensively, only conceded 88.2 points per one hundred possessions. The Cavaliers had become a fuller team around LeBron, but they also were finding a scheme that worked when LeBron was the one and only orchestrator.

Management must have noted, because they basically brought back every piece of the 2014–15 team to make another run at it. Irving was already locked up; Love signed a five-year, $110 million extension; and Shumpert inked a new four-season deal for $10 million per year. Cleveland also brought back Matthew Dellavedova and Smith on low-cost deals, and finally agreed to new terms with power forward Tristan Thompson on the eve of the new season. LeBron was always going to come back, and perhaps he reached a detente with Blatt, off a playoff run where the rookie NBA coach worked over more experienced coaches like Tom Thibodeau and Mike Budenholzer.

It's also worth noting that LeBron won titles in his second and third seasons in Miami, and man for man, Cleveland's roster is better than those Heat teams. Expectations heading into 2015–16 were understandably huge, especially after Cleveland survived the growing pains of the initial season of immense change.

CHAPTER 8

No Single Path to Mining Talent

I think there's that pressure when you're a top-ten, top-five pick that you want to come in and put up numbers . . . but once you're in the league six, seven years, you realize that numbers aren't that important. . . . You get the W, that's more important. . . . No one's really going to talk about a guy who averaged twenty and ten on a team that was terrible.

—Andrew Bogut, center, Golden State Warriors

Players can work to push themselves to reach the level of quality required to succeed in the NBA, but it takes more than an individual's skill to become successful. We read every year about supposed "busts" who don't live up to their draft status, but so much of player success depends on the environments in which they land, and NBA rookies don't have much control over that process. The questions persist for any player that's not a franchise-level star, though. Is this the right coach for that player? Does the coach get to stay awhile so continuity can develop? Is the franchise well-run at the owner and management level? Are there quality veterans in the locker room? Are the facilities and services that help players stay healthy up to current standards?

Likewise, there are a wide-variety of talent acquisition strategies (and sub-strategies) that teams can pursue, depending on where they are in the competitive cycle, how much money they have available, and how desirable a location they are for players. While the draft and free agency are the two most direct ways for teams to acquire the kinds of players they want, trades and player development can be even more potent because they often are less impacted by outside market factors dictating who you can have and for how much money.

Good teams find players from all of those avenues, although smart drafting and development is really crucial. Smart players develop and evolve to make themselves as valuable as they can be for as long as possible. The dance goes on and on, with a healthy dose of right time, right place also factoring in. To show the variety of ways teams can find the right players, here are five case studies from the NBA that show the different ways teams can obtain and nurture extremely valuable talent, and how certain players find a way to extend their value in the league.

Andrew Bogut: From No. 1 Overall Pick to Pivotal Role Player

Andrew Bogut is tired of talking about his injuries. There were the two most notable ones—the broken ankle he suffered when he landed on the foot of then-Houston Rockets guard Kyle Lowry, and the dislocated elbow suffered when he was nudged slightly on a fast-break dunk against the Phoenix Suns and landed awkwardly on his arm—but there have also been a broken rib, another long-term ankle "sprain," and the constant assortment of bumps and bruises that an NBA big man suffers when he plays as physically as Bogut does night in and night out.

Bogut considers the vast majority of his injuries to be flukes rather than a byproduct of his favored playing style, but they certainly have had an impact on his career trajectory. He had a promising start to his NBA career in Milwaukee after the Bucks made him the No. 1 overall pick in 2005, maturing to the point where he averaged 15.9

points, 10.2 rebounds, and 2.5 blocks a game with the Bucks in 2009–10. The injuries kept mounting, though, and as they started to impact his shooting and mobility, he had to begin reconsidering his path as an NBA player.

Things didn't start much better when the injured Bogut was acquired by the Golden State Warriors at the trade deadline during the 2011–12 season in a deal for guard Monta Ellis, a popular mainstay who was deemed expendable as Stephen Curry grew into his stardom. At a jersey-retirement ceremony for team legend Chris Mullin the following month, team co-owner Joe Lacob was booed by the Oracle Arena crowd when he attempted to speak because of the fans' displeasure with the trade.

Bogut's recovery from his various injuries was difficult. In an article written by Yahoo's Marc Spears in December 2014, Bogut explained how badly his body had been failing him during the 2012–2013 season, going as far to suggest to his agent that he couldn't play anymore.

So Bogut had a choice to make. He couldn't be a thirty-plus-minutes-a-game player anymore and stay effective and healthy, so he had to recast himself. He had retained his skillful passing ability and his affinity for setting screens, and as the league moved to a drive-and-kick spread offense motif, Bogut's rim-protection skills remained very much in demand. So, he set out to be the best crucial role player he could be, all the while cognizant that some considered him to be a disappointment.

"I've been in the league long enough. I was on a bad team where I put up numbers, and unfortunately had some bad injuries that have kind of changed my game a little bit," Bogut said while sitting on top of an advertising board on the baseline of Atlanta's Philips Arena. "I had two injuries where I was told I probably wouldn't play again, so I'm happy to be out here playing. Obviously, as a No. 1 pick, I haven't exceeded expectations, but I haven't been a bust, either. I've kind of been in the middle, in my opinion. Probably average. I really hit my stride my third, fourth, fifth year, and obviously had some issues. So I don't buy into [the perception] right now."

Bogut's injuries may have been a possible red flag, but the Warriors were pretty determined to bring him in, and his elbow injury provided them the opportunity they needed. According to assistant general manager Kirk Lacob, team management had conducted a study of past Warriors teams as well as what kind of roster combinations were working in the league at the time, and came to the conclusion that they really needed to add a physical screen setter and rim protector to help out their perimeter players on both ends of the floor.

"We basically found that the Warriors never had a center," Lacob said. "They tried to draft one a million times. We need[ed] a center badly, a big guy. And not just like a center, we want[ed] someone very specifically who is a monster defensively, protects the rim, and can pull off rebounds. That's specifically what we went after. I mean, I'm not going to pretend that we didn't get very lucky to get Bogut—a lot of things had to go right, he had to get hurt, they had to want to trade him. That trade was like a twelve-month thing, but it's definitely a guy that we targeted."

Fast-forward to the 2014–15 regular season, and while most of the attention on Golden State was focused on Curry and fellow "Splash Brother" Klay Thompson, or the emergence of multifaceted Draymond Green as the team's very high-quality glue guy, Bogut's defense, picks, and passing from both the high and low post were all enormous factors in the team's success.

Individual player net ratings, or the team's point differential per one hundred possessions when they're on or off the court, can be somewhat misleading and can be impacted by playing fewer minutes, but it's worth noting that Bogut's plus-16.6 "on court" net rating, per NBA.com, was the second-best on the team, just behind league MVP Curry. Bogut also had the team's fourth-"worst" off-court net rating, meaning the Warriors struggled a bit more than usual when Bogut wasn't playing. Additionally, the team's 95.2 points allowed per one hundred possessions while Bogut was on the floor was the lowest for any regular rotation player, underscoring his rim-protecting importance. When Bogut was off the court during the regular season, the Warriors allowed a more pedestrian 100.2 points per one hundred possessions.

Since Bogut only played a bit less than twenty-four minutes a game, it was almost like the Warriors had two separate teams, with very different approaches. That flexibility—whether it was Bogut conceding minutes to fellow bigs Marreese Speights or Festus Ezeli, or whether they went very small, with 6-foot-7 Draymond Green playing the role of de facto center—proved very difficult for most opponents to handle, and was extremely crucial for the Warriors in the postseason.

To Bogut's credit, he didn't really care how much he played, and the team understood his unique value. Lacob said early in the season that, if told that Golden State would have Bogut and Andre Iguodala healthy for seventy-five games apiece, he wouldn't have to ask for anything else in terms of a basis of great expectations for the season. Come springtime, he looked very prescient.

In Bogut's sixty-seven appearances in the regular season, the Warriors went 58–9 (versus 9–6 when he didn't play). In the playoffs, he served crucial strategic roles in some series (like when Steve Kerr switched him onto poor outside shooter Tony Allen in the second round against Memphis, which allowed Bogut to roam freely in the paint and help deter the Grizzlies' excellent inside duo of Marc Gasol and Zach Randolph), and played a total of two minutes and forty-six seconds in the Warriors' final three games in the NBA Finals, when his skill set was not required given the specific matchup with the Cavaliers. That was OK by Bogut, who endured a long and painful road to get to this point and has moved team success well ahead of personal kudos on his priority list.

"We have enough scorers and guys who will get stats," Bogut said, "so [we need someone] setting good screens, getting the rebound, block[ing] shots, protect[ing] the paint, and I predicate the way I play on those things.

"I think there's that pressure when you're a top-ten, top-five pick that you want to come in and put up numbers," he added, "but once you're in the league six, seven years, you realize that numbers aren't that important. To me, they're not that important. To other guys, they are. I think letters are more important to me. You get the W, that's more important to me at this point of my career. No one's really going to talk about a guy who averaged twenty and ten on a team that was terrible."

Khris Middleton: From Trade Toss-In to Leading Role

One of the NBA's most impactful young players was a mere footnote in a trade that happened in the summer of 2013, when the Milwaukee Bucks and Detroit Pistons swapped point guards, with Brandon Knight heading to the Bucks in exchange for Brandon Jennings.

As part of the transaction, Milwaukee also received Ukrainian 7-footer Viacheslav Kravtsov, who had played 224 minutes in his debut NBA season for Detroit (and who was subsequently dealt to Phoenix as part of a trade to obtain veteran swingman Caron Butler before ever playing a minute for Milwaukee), and Khris Middleton, a second-round pick from Texas A&M who had shown some flashes both in college and during his rookie campaign in Detroit (he played 475 minutes in twenty-seven games), but was far from a finished product on either end of the floor.

Two years later, some advanced metrics considered him to be one of the best players in the NBA.

ESPN.com's real plus-minus (RPM) is best described as a next-generation attempt to refine an already-complicated metric called regularized adjusted plus-minus (RAPM), which was a calculation that tried to determine just how much of a positive impact individual players had on team performance on both offense and defense. These calculations were improvements on the original adjusted plus-minus calculations, which were a rough approximation of how many points better or worse a team performed while a player was on the floor, adjusted for his teammates on the court with him.

For the 2014–15 season, the real plus-minus leaderboard doubled as a who's who of NBA greats. League MVP Stephen Curry led the category, followed by LeBron James (the best player in the world), James Harden (league MVP runner-up and a first-team All-NBA guard), Anthony Davis (the next huge thing), and Kawhi Leonard (a destructive two-way force for the San Antonio Spurs). Of the top nine players on the list, four made first-team All-NBA for that season, and three more made second-team honors.

At number ten overall was Middleton.

Furthermore, if you round up Middleton's offensive RPM score of 1.97 to 2, he was one of only seven players in the league with a rating of 2+ on both ends of the floor.

Moving on to ESPN's wins above replacement player (WARP) calculation, which attempts to calculate how many wins a player is worth over an average player, Middleton finished ninth overall, once again only trailing eight of the sport's best players (everyone on the RPM list besides Sacramento's DeMarcus Cousins, who was sixteenth in this metric).

No one metric is the gospel, but it's indisputable that Middleton emerged as one of the sport's bright young talents through a combination of hard work, player development, and a positional switch that helped unlock everything he has to offer on the court.

"When I came into the league, everyone looked at me that I was going to be a better defender, and that's how I earned my way to play—towards the end of Detroit and [in 2013–14 with Milwaukee], just playing defense and playing as hard as I can," he said while icing down his knees after the Bucks' morning shootaround at Denver's Pepsi Center.

"I think [positional certainty] has [helped] in a way. I felt like I had a pretty good year [in 2013–14] at the small forward position, but at the two-guard this year, I'm able to use my length a lot more. A lot of threes now are my size, so being able to guard smaller guys, it's helping me at the defensive end and the offensive end."

In a 2013 writeup for SB Nation's *BrewHoop* site examining the trade with the Pistons, Eric Buenning actually sniffed out Middleton's upside potential, writing that he "*might* have the potential to become a rather nice 3-and-D type, with a little more versatility on offense. Middleton developed a rep as a guy who could get his own shot while [at] Texas A&M, which he should be able to get off over most small forwards. The question is whether he can find reliability in his stroke from distance, which tailed off during an injury-plagued junior season in 11/12," but what's happened has blasted through the ceiling of that projection.

Middleton started to emerge as a small forward on the 2013–14 Bucks, playing around thirty minutes a game and doubling his scoring output from his rookie season while knocking down 41.4 percent of his 3-point attempts, but the Bucks' decision to switch coaches to Jason Kidd ahead of the 2014–15 season initiated a move of Middleton to the shooting guard role. There, he was able to use his 6-foot-7 frame and nearly 7-foot wingspan to disrupt smaller players' shots while still having the athleticism to guard them in space. In 2014–15, Milwaukee often used Middleton as their primary defensive stopper as well as a leading source of offense on a team that didn't have a ton of reliable options on that end of the floor.

"He's grown in the right direction for us, both offensively and defensively," Kidd said. "He's not just a shooter. We've asked him to guard the best wing player, and he's stepped up to that challenge. He's as good as they come.

"I don't know if [his work ethic is] better [than the previous season]—this is the first time I have been around him—but he works extremely hard. He's up for the challenge of being pushed, so as a coach, that's nice to have a player that you can get on and he responds in a positive way. He's a quiet kid. We're asking him to talk a little bit more. Sometimes, he is talking, but maybe we want a little bit more. We get greedy as coaches when you see something, but the guys respect him, and again, he's playing at a very high level."

Middleton's development has earned him the respect of his teammates, as well. The well-traveled and well-spoken Jared Dudley (who subsequently signed with the Washington Wizards as a free agent in the summer of 2015) was Middleton's teammate for Middleton's first two seasons in Milwaukee, and even in that timeframe he saw the evolution of a hard worker into a very complete player—one who earned his minutes and then his expanded role.

"Defense a lot of times is hard, there aren't a lot of people who want to play like that and grind all the time," Dudley said about what Middleton brought to the Bucks upon his arrival. "Khris realized the more defense he plays, the more minutes he's going to play, where that would be more offensive production."

On offense, Dudley added, Middleton "has a really unique game where he is really good from seventeen to twenty-two feet, one dribble and he can pull up. He's added the post game. He's a big two-guard, so he can shoot over most two-guards in the NBA, especially since more NBA teams are going 2-point guards nowadays. He's improved his ballhandling to where we throw the ball to him now in transition, but I think in our system, we find guys, and guys know he can knock down shots, so guys will turn down a good shot for a great shot in finding him."

Milwaukee didn't waste any time making sure it locked down its emerging star for the long term. In the summer of 2015, the Bucks signed the restricted free agent to a new five-year, $70 million extension. Given Middleton's desirable two-way talent and the market conditions spurred by the forthcoming massive growth in league revenues that will lift the league's salary cap by approximately $40 million over two seasons, the deal was regarded as a terrific bargain. Meanwhile,

Knight, the cornerstone of the original trade that landed them Middleton, was moved in the middle of the 2014–15 season to the Phoenix Suns in a complicated multiteam deal that sent Philadelphia 76ers point guard Michael Carter-Williams to Milwaukee.

Ultimately, the Bucks made the 2015 playoffs as the No. 6 seed and were a significant thorn in the side of the favored Chicago Bulls, finally losing the series in six games. Then, in free agency, the team signed forward Greg Monroe from the Detroit Pistons to provide additional low-post scoring and rebounding. With a new arena on the way and smart, wealthy new ownership of the club in place, the future as of this writing looks very bright in Wisconsin. Middleton sees the team's potential much like he once did his own: predicated on defense, with the potential for the offense to emerge from that building block with a lot of hard work.

"Every day, we work on defensive principles, how to close out high hands, force a player one way," he said. "We work on that every day, so it definitely helps during games. I think [everything] starts with our defense. We got a lot of young guys, but we have a lot of size and athleticism to cover a lot of positions, so once we get stops a lot and get steals, we're able to run a lot. Once you force turnovers, it's hard for the other team to stop you on the fast break."

James Harden: From Huge Potential to Star to Superstar

In 2012, the Oklahoma City Thunder found itself in the midst of a fascinating and unusual NBA problem: they had drafted *too* well a few years earlier.

Five springs prior, the franchise (then still in Seattle) grabbed the University of Texas's skinny freshman scoring machine Kevin Durant at No. 2 overall after the Portland Trail Blazers made the ill-fated choice of Greg Oden, whose NBA career never really got off the ground thanks to a series of debilitating injuries. A year later, the team picked UCLA guard Russell Westbrook at No. 4, believing he could transition to the point guard spot as a pro. At No. 24 over-all in that same draft, the Thunder grabbed athletic Congolese big man Serge Ibaka, who pretty much instantly was a rebounding and shot-blocking fiend, and held his rates as his minutes increased.

Then, in 2009, the Thunder had the No. 3 overall pick and some-what surprisingly used it on Arizona State sophomore James Harden, who was a sensationally efficient scorer on decent Sun Devils teams but there were some questions about how his level of athleticism would translate to the pro game. Harden improved steadily in his first three NBA seasons, ultimately becoming the NBA's Sixth Man of the Year in the 2011–12 season as the Thunder's primary scorer off the bench while veteran Thabo Sefolosha started at shooting guard to provide a valuable defensive presence between Westbrook and Durant.

Over that three-year period, the Thunder absolutely nailed three straight high-lottery picks as well as a late first-rounder, and now, coming off an NBA Finals defeat to the Miami Heat in 2012, they had a problem on their hands. The club already had tied up Durant, Westbrook, and Ibaka to contract extensions worth around $200 million combined, and now Harden, a year away from restricted free agency and coming off a gold medal with the US Olympic team, also needed to get paid. Complicating the decision was the additional strain of a third budding star starting to feel his own oats, with re-ports after Game 1 of the Finals against the Heat (which the Thunder won for their only victory in the series) detailing how Harden was complaining about his minutes and shot attempts. He felt the verbal wrath of veterans Kendrick Perkins and Derek Fisher in the locker room afterward.

In the end, Harden's fate came down to $6 million. The Thunder, capable of offering a four-year, $60 million extension to Harden per the terms of the collective bargaining agreement at the time, first of-fered in the neighborhood of four years and $52 million, and finally ended up at $54 million. According to reports, they also gave Harden an hour to decide whether to take it. General manager Sam Presti was concerned that offering Harden every available dollar would (a) cost the Thunder significantly more in luxury tax penalties (a sliding tax scale based on how much, and for how many years, you would be over the salary cap); and (b) would hamstring him in terms of making additional moves to round out a roster where the sixth man was making $15 million a year.

Plus, he had a Plan B. As detailed by Yahoo! NBA insider Adrian Wojnarowski in an October 2012 column about the situation, Presti communicated to Houston general manager Daryl Morey that the Thunder would trade Harden to the Rockets if he didn't agree to the deal.

That's what happened, and Harden quickly inked a five-year max extension with the Rockets worth almost $80 million. The Thunder, unwilling to let Harden reach restricted free agency the following summer, were unable to offer that magnitude of a deal to Harden because they had already used their "designated player" tag on Westbrook to sign him to a five-year extension.

Opinion on the move from the Rockets' perspective was far from unanimous at the time. It was a lot of money and years to tie up in a player who had only started five games in three seasons, and hadn't played more than twenty-seven minutes a game in his first three seasons. There were questions about whether Harden's scoring ability would translate as a No. 1 option when he didn't have Westbrook and Durant on the floor with him.

This is where analytics came into play. Morey and the rest of Houston's management team saw Harden's star potential because, when you dug deeper into what he was doing in Oklahoma City, advanced stats suggested it was very possible.

As ESPN Insider's Tom Haberstroh expertly broke down right at the beginning of Harden's time in Houston, Harden had very compelling numbers on the rare occasions he was on the floor without either Durant or Westbrook. In 460 total minutes, he was scoring

32.6 points per thirty-six minutes on the floor (a normalization rate used to approximate a full game for many top-end starters) while also averaging 6.2 assists and 4.7 rebounds per thirty-six. He was able to handle a much greater shot volume, and his free throw attempts rate nearly doubled.

Haberstroh went on to explain that this wasn't just a case of Harden racking up these numbers against the benches of opposing teams; they were similar when he faced starters in these situations. Now, 460 minutes over eighty-two games is not a ton to go on, but these numbers were extremely promising for Harden's potential to be a No. 1 option.

That educated guess has panned out in spades for the Rockets, who identified an underutilized talent, paid a legitimate price to trade for him, and allowed him to become a star. From his first moments in Houston, Harden exploded. He averaged 25.6 points, 4.8 rebounds, and 5.9 assists per game over his first two seasons as the Rockets' clear primary star, and his numbers barely changed from the first season to the second, even when the team signed perennial All-Star center Dwight Howard as a free agent ahead of the 2013–14 season. Harden made third team All-NBA in his first season with the Rockets and then made first team the next, cementing his growing reputation as one of the game's best players.

Still, the Rockets didn't make it out of the first round of the playoffs in either season, and there was one looming issue that was holding Harden back from perceived superstardom: he was considered a *really* poor defender.

With any flaw (or strength), the social media/video era can make you look much better or worse by quickly mining and sharing visual examples of your most egregious moments. Harden was one of Basketball Twitter's favorite punching bags for his foibles on that side of the ball, which more often than not involved a lack of effort and/or attention as a play was unfolding. Perhaps the most egregious example was against Turkey in the 2014 FIBA Basketball World Cup, when Harden completely lost track of his own man at the 3-point arc while he watched another Turkey player drive right past him off the dribble and then find Harden's man with a simple pass for a game-tying three, but there are numerous others that can be found with a YouTube search of "Harden defense."

It wasn't all that much better in the NBA, where whatever (somewhat imperfect) defense-specific advanced metrics you examined confirmed what your eyeballs led you to believe. From the 2010–11 through the 2013–14 seasons, Harden's *best* defensive box plus-minus was 0.1. The other three seasons, he was below (and in one case, *well* below) the –0.3 mark that is considered to be the theoretical replacement-level for that statistic, based on work done by Jeremias Engelmann, who created ESPN's real plus-minus calculation.

Per a December 2014 column from *ESPN The Magazine*'s Jordan Brenner, Harden was in the league's eleventh percentile during the 2013–14 season in terms of scoring against him in isolation (one-on-one) situations. His overall defensive rating—an approximation for personal responsibility for points allowed per one hundred possessions—for his last four seasons before 2014–15 hovered between 105 and 108, which is subpar. While much of Harden's defensive problems were attributed to a lack of concentration, or how much effort he was putting in on offense, or the flaws of his teammates, there's really no way around it: he was a weak defender for most of the first five years of his career.

His improvement on that end of the floor was a leading storyline for both Harden and the Rockets in 2014–15, and was part of the reason Houston finished as the No. 2 seed in the Western Conference and Harden was runner-up to Steph Curry for the league's MVP award.

"On the ball, I was pretty good. It was just help-side defense, ball-watching, letting my man cut backdoor," Harden suggested about his struggles in past seasons, in an article I wrote for *The Cauldron* in December 2014. "Small things like that that are very noticeable, so this year I've eliminated most of those things."

Much of the attention was paid in the first two months of the season, when both the Rockets and Harden were *really* improved on that end of the floor (despite rim-protector Dwight Howard missing a large number of games), but even a regression in the second half of the season (with fatigue being a legitimate issue for Harden) didn't dampen the progress the team and its star made overall defensively. The Rockets improved from 106.3 points allowed per one hundred possessions in 2013–14 to a much stingier 103.4 in 2014–15. Harden posted the best defensive box plus-minus and defensive rating of his career, which brought him up to being a competent defender overall.

"He's really gotten better and that's a credit to him," Houston head coach Kevin McHale said, talking about Harden's defense at a mid-season shootaround in Denver. "He's battling on every possession, he's getting in there, he's doing a lot of little things. The big thing is, it hasn't affected [him on the other end]. Believe me, there are days there he is tired. We put a lot on his plate, and we understand that, but he has an unbelievable tank for the game of basketball."

On his favored end of the floor, Harden continues to get better while carrying one of the highest usage rates and workloads in the NBA. Harden in 2014–15 "used" (meaning a made shot, missed shot, assist, or turnover) 31.3 percent of Houston's possessions when he was on the court, which was the sixth-highest rate in the NBA. The five players ahead of him all missed a decent chunk of the season through injury, though. Harden played 2,981 minutes, missing just one game all season. He led the league in total minutes played, and was second to Chicago's Jimmy Butler in per-game average. Given all that, Harden's 118 offensive efficiency rating was outstanding.

In short, Harden had the best offensive season of his career paired with his best defensive season, which at the level he plays on offense makes him an all-world talent. He came up short to Curry both in the

MVP voting and in the Western Conference Finals, which Golden State won 4–1, but in many other seasons, Harden would have won multiple trophies with his level of play. Harden wouldn't have developed the same way in Oklahoma City with two other ball-dominant stars playing heavy minutes, but he still resonates as the one who got away from a Thunder franchise that, in part due to injuries that Harden may well have helped mask, hasn't reached the heights of that 2012 season ever since.

Nikola Vucevic: Growth of a College Stats Monster

Nikola Vucevic did not take the traditional blue-chipper path to NBA success. A native of Montenegro, Vucevic came to the United States to play his senior year of high school basketball under the tutelage of a friend of his father's, and landed at University of Southern California, far from a basketball power even with its Los Angeles location and membership in the big-money Pac-12 Conference.

Vucevic was forced to miss the first eight games of his freshman season while the NCAA worked through some eligibility issues, then made twenty-three appearances for a Trojans team that slipped into the NCAAs as a 10-seed, all but three off the bench. He didn't even average 3.0 points per game that first season, but did convert an eye-catching twenty-six of forty-two shots from the field when he did look for his own offense, and he rebounded on the defensive glass very well for a limited-minutes freshman.

The following year, Vucevic moved into a starting role and increased his gross outputs dramatically. He nearly tripled his minutes per game to thirty-two a night and pushed his usage rates up from around 13 percent as a freshman to 20 percent as a sophomore, and that resulted in a quadrupling of his per-game scoring average and his gross rebounds per game going up by three and a half times. More notably, he converted on 55 percent of his field goal attempts and his per-minute rates either held or increased significantly pretty much across the board. Vucevic made the successful conversion from role player to significant contributor as a starter without much impact on his effectiveness.

Then, as a junior, he upped his minutes even further and vastly increased his usage rates again, as he became the primary offensive option for an NCAA tournament team in 2010–11. Carrying a heavy possession load of above 25 percent, Vucevic still converted 54 percent of his 2-point attempts, became a legitimate 3-point threat (making 35 percent of his eighty-three tries that season), and continued to inhale rebounds, especially to close out opponent possessions. He finished twenty-first in Division I that season, with a defensive rebounding rate of 26 percent. Over his three seasons, his shotblocking rates increased slightly year-over-year, as well.

Vucevic declared for the draft after that season and was picked sixteenth overall by the Philadelphia 76ers, playing one season for them before being included in the disastrous Andrew Bynum trade, with Vucevic's rights going to the Orlando Magic. Vucevic made 208 starts for Orlando over his first three seasons there, and was developing into a very productive NBA big man, with the same types of strengths—efficient, high-usage scoring, and defensive rebounding—that he displayed in college. In his first three campaigns with the Magic, Vucevic never shot worse than 50.7 percent from the field, and he averaged between 8.1 and 9.1 defensive rebounds per thirty-six minutes.

In 2014–15, taking advantage of more touches in better spots thanks to some of the spread pick-and-roll sets Orlando figured out made best use of its personnel, Vucevic posted his highest-ever offensive efficiency rating (a 109), offensive box plus-minus (the first time he'd ever been in positive territory in that category), and a PER that equates to a very good NBA first option. The Magic's offense fell off by nearly three points per one hundred possessions when he was on the bench, a figure just below that of Elfrid Payton and Victor Oladipo, the team's starting guards. Vucevic's frontcourt teammates weren't surprised.

"First, he just needs to stay healthy. Other than that, he can do whatever he wants. He's a [expletive] monster. Good gracious, almighty," teammate Channing Frye said. "I think for us, we just have to give him the room to operate and make sure we're running sets for him, but I told him 'You're going to get tired getting that ball.' I'm OK with me shooting one shot and he shoots ninety. For us to win, we have to continue to feed him and go to him. We need to work through him."

The defensive end has been more of a struggle. With expanded minutes and offensive responsibility on the offensive end, Vucevic posted a career-worst 106 defensive rating in 2014–15, per Basketball-Reference.com, and he was middle of the road in overall on/off splits because of the relative defensive weakness. According to *Nylon Calculus's* Seth Partnow, who calculated estimated "points saved" for big man rim protectors for the 2014–15 season, Vucevic was toward the bottom of the league with a 53.7 percent field goal percentage allowed around the rim, and a -1.25 points saved rate that put him below so-so defenders like Greg Monroe and uncomfortably in the proximity of porous Oklahoma City Thunder big man Enes Kanter. Part of this is Orlando never really figured out the right big man to pair with Vucevic—Frye helped space the court, but the defense was poor; Kyle O'Quinn (who moved to the Knicks in the summer of 2015) was better defensively but more limited on the other end; and small ball with Tobias Harris wasn't sustainable over huge minutes, either.

So, yes, Vucevic still has some flaws, especially at the defensive end, but should it be a surprise that what he showed offensively in college is panning out in the pros? If you believe independent research, it shouldn't be.

In 2009, Jon Nichols, now part of the analytics team for the Cleveland Cavaliers but at the time a writer for Basketball-Statistics.com, posted a piece where he ran some simple correlations on different stats categories for successful college players who went on to make the NBA. He discovered that shotblocking rates were the stat that translated from college to pro the best, with a full 92 percent of a player's NBA shotblocking explained by his performance in that category at the college level. Similarly, rebounding had a correlation of 0.8927. Other than assists per minute, no other stat category was all that close to shotblocking and rebounding as a projectable statistic. A 2015 column from Neil Paine and Zach Bradshaw at *FiveThirtyEight* suggested that among the most telling individual stats that translate are 2-point shot attempts per minute, offensive rebounding rate, and usage rate. Whichever ones tend to suggest future success, Vucevic was delivering in them at the college level.

That said, even Vucevic knows he's not yet the finished product in the NBA.

"I think I'm still early in the process. I have a lot of room to improve. A lot of room to get better," he said after a game in Brooklyn against the Nets. "I have improved every year I've been in the NBA. I've added a lot of stuff to my game to help me. I think that playing more years, getting more experience, all the stuff that I do will become easier for me. I'm still early into my career, so I have a lot of room to grow.

"You see playing all of these games against different guys, you see what you did well, you see the takeaways of what you can add onto that," he added about how he's gone about improving his game. "A countermove or something. A lot of it is just you watch other players against whom you play, and if you like something they do, you try and see how you like it. A lot of it is just trying and getting a feel for something and seeing how you like it, if it fits your game and if it helps your team."

In a league where a growing premium is put on bigs who can face up and shoot, it was a bit curious that former Magic head coach Jacque Vaughn never fully explored pushing Vucevic occasionally out past the 3-point arc, given his junior season numbers at USC and a relatively strong positive correlation between college 3-point percentage and the pros. In his first four NBA seasons, Vucevic has been used mostly as a post scorer, a seemingly lost artifact now in a league with occasional 6-foot-7 "centers" and more-than-occasional slash-and-kick offensive styles that often tend to bypass traditional big men on the block.

Vucevic, at least during the 2014–15 season, didn't seem that interested in evolving that part of his game, though.

"I'm not going to make it a big part of my game, because it would take away from the other stuff that I do," he said about 3-pointers in a January 2015 interview with *Grantland*. "But I'm capable. I shoot them pretty well in practice. Maybe I could make it a bigger part of what I do without taking away from other things. Who knows? But playing inside is always going to be my focus. Maybe we can run a play for me to shoot a 3 sometimes, just as a surprise."

Vucevic is an interesting test case. It's not often in the modern era that NBA teams get three seasons (including two as a major contributor) to evaluate a big man with raw talent like his, but his path to college excellence is one worth considering. It also will make the future development of someone like Charlotte Hornets lottery pick Frank Kaminsky, the 2015 college Player of the Year whose college numbers and development trajectory were even more impressive than Vucevic's, worth watching. The Hornets were widely discussed after the 2015 draft when reports surfaced that they may have declined a package of four current and future first-round picks from the Boston Celtics for the No. 9 spot where they selected Kaminsky.

Thanks to varying levels of competition and systems to often go with small sample sizes at the college level, translation of production there to the pro game is still a work in progress. Vucevic's best college performance comparables, according to Ken Pomeroy's site, were a bunch of mostly nondescript, non-NBA players, while Kaminsky's are a solid bunch of future NBA pros. One thing seems pretty certain, though: the new 76ers management team likely is angry at its predecessors. Tony DiLeo and his staff saw the potential in Vucevic, but didn't have the organizational patience or foresight to see it out after his rookie season.

Channing Frye: Survival Through Evolution

It's extremely difficult to make the NBA. It's even harder to stick around for any length of time. Of the 450 or so players in the league in any given season, maybe 10 percent of them—if even that many—can be considered "stars." The rest of the league revolves around those players, with each franchise trying to find the proper mix of second bananas and role players to form a cohesive and successful team. As a player, if you're not going to be a star, you need to very quickly figure out what your primary role is going to be. Those who do can carve out lengthy, lucrative careers.

Channing Frye is an excellent example. Frye was originally a lottery pick, take No. 8 overall by the New York Knicks in 2005. He had a very credible rookie season, providing 12.3 points and 5.8 rebounds a game in only twenty-four minutes an outing. Frye struggled defensively like many young big men do when they get to the NBA level, but he shot nearly 48 percent from the field and over 82 percent from the free throw line, showing off a nice face-up touch and athleticism on the offensive end, especially considering he had played a more traditional post game in college at Arizona.

Things went downhill in his second season in New York, as Frye, far from a dominant rebounder or shotblocker at 6-foot-10, was proving to be a poor fit next to groundbound center Eddy Curry. His averages and per-thirty-six rates dropped across the board, with the *New York Times* writing that Frye "hardly developed in two seasons as a Knick and has been little more than a midrange jump-shooter." On draft night in 2007, Frye was part of an exchange of problem players with Portland, with disgruntled point guard Steve Francis heading to the Trail Blazers in exchange for rugged power forward Zach Randolph.

Frye didn't realize a rebirth in the Rose City, though. In his two seasons in Portland, his minutes and per-game averages continued to wobble, and in his second year there, his shooting percentages dropped below even those of his disappointing sophomore campaign in New York. Now four years into his career, Frye quickly was reaching a crisis point. As a free agent, he signed a two-year, $3.8 million contract with the Phoenix Suns, with the second season a player option. Not that Frye was struggling to make ends meet, but in the first year of his second NBA contract, he was making the lowest salary of his career. That's not the way things are supposed to work, and Frye knew things had to change. He was willing to adapt to save his NBA viability.

In Phoenix, Frye morphed into an early prototype of the "stretch" bigs who are now so profoundly important to offensive spacing in today's NBA. In his first season with the Suns, Frye made an astounding 172 3-pointers (after making just 11 the previous season in Portland) while shooting 43.9 percent from the arc, which was the sixth-best success rate in the league that season.

"When I was in college, I was a post-up guy," Frye said. "Came to the league and figured out that just wasn't going to ride, so I started to develop other parts of my game. So it's a combination of what team you're on, and what the coaches want you to develop, and what you can do on a nightly basis."

Where once his specific skill set was considered a weakness, he worked with the staff in Phoenix to extend what he was good at, with profound results.

"I think you kind of see it," Frye said about what parts of his game were going to continue to work, and what he needed to develop in order to stay effective. "Certain things for me, it was like 'face up and shoot a jumper,' and then over the course of the year, they put smaller guys on me, and then they put bigger guys on me. And then it was like, 'OK, how can I continue to be effective, drawing the guy away from the hoop and going farther and farther back?' And finally in

Phoenix, they were like 'We want you to shoot this. This is the shot. Practice this. This is what you're looking for.' So I just developed into what I am now.

"It's really more of a routine [in Phoenix.] 'We need you to do this. This is what we need you to do to be effective.' Coach would be in film, and be like, 'This is what we want you to do. Can you do this on a nightly basis, and how can we tailor this toward what you're good at?'"

Frye declined the cheap second-year option on his contract and, in the summer of 2010, when the Suns were poised to lose power forward Amar'e Stoudemire in free agency, he re-signed with the team on a five-year, $30 million deal that included a $6.8 million player option in the fifth season.

In 2010–11, Frye took an incredible 5.7 threes a game, and connected on 39 percent of them. With additional minutes, he set career highs in both scoring (12.7 points) and rebounds (6.7) per game, while also converting on 48 percent of his 2-point attempts. He never was quite that good again as a Sun, and actually missed the 2012–13 season with an enlarged heart diagnosis, but in his final season in Phoenix, in 2013–14, Frye made 37 percent of 432 3-point attempts. In three of his four seasons with the Suns, Frye attempted at least 53 percent of his shots from behind the arc after maxing out at just 12 percent in his second season in Portland.

After his rookie contract, Frye knew he needed to adapt in order to survive in the league, and the huge adjustment he made not only kept him in the NBA, but made him a very significant amount of additional money. Not every player, though, is willing or capable of such a transformation.

"Some people, they get told what their role is, which is I think sometimes easier. Some other people, it's just by playing a game and finding something they're really good at, and understanding that's their niche and growing from there," said then–Philadelphia 76er wing Luc Mbah a Moute, who kept himself in the league because of his prowess as a defensive specialist and solid locker room presence.

"I think that the mistake some of the young players make sometimes is they come into the league and they don't know what their niche is. I think it's something you got to recognize: it's always what your niche is and growing from there, expanding your game from there."

Frye leveraged his success in Phoenix in the summer of 2014, when the Orlando Magic, desperately in need of some perimeter shooting to complement big man Nikola Vucevic and athletic-but-not-dead-eye guards Victor Oladipo and Elfrid Payton, lured Frye to the Magic Kingdom with a four-year, $32 million offer.

His first season with the Magic didn't go as well as expected as the Magic under coach Jacque Vaughn struggled with any kind of offensive continuity. Frye shot the three well for the first two months of the season, but was a really low-usage player. As his possession usage ramped up, his shooting dropped off before recovering some toward the end of the season, but for the entire season, he cut down on his 2-point attempts drastically. In his first year with the Magic, Frye took a full 73 percent of his shots from behind the 3-point arc, making over 39 percent of them.

Still, Frye's is a story of NBA survival and evolution. Once on the verge of fading out of the league, Frye reinvented himself with the help of a prescient staff in Phoenix, and that has been worth at least another $50 million in guaranteed compensation. Frye clearly understands the necessary mindset and the potential value of being someone like him in the current NBA.

"A lot of these guys coming out, they're the superstars and the go-to guys," Frye said. "Everyone wants to be the Jordans and the Kobes and the Kevin Durants, but sometimes teams will pay for the Nick Collisons, for the Ben Gordons, for the Channing Fryes. That's just the thing, and that goes back to the idea of who you think you are, and attaching yourself to what's going to keep me in the NBA and getting those nice paychecks."

CHAPTER 9

The World's Most Perfected Player

One of the things about Korver that's really unbelievable is that he averages about thirteen points per game, but you go into the game and you have to treat him like he averages thirty, or else it could be thirty. I think that's where he presents a whole lot of challenges. He presents a whole lot of challenges in his cuts, how much attention you give him off the cuts, how much he opens up for everyone else. He's a really good player.

—**Brad Stevens, head coach, Boston Celtics**

The creation of perhaps the deadliest 3-point shooting stroke in NBA history spawned from an impromptu tennis session at a Caribbean beach resort about four years ago, when during an All-Star weekend trip to the Turks and Caicos Islands, Kyle Korver wanted to get some exercise.

"I had a hip problem, and I got a cortisone shot right before All-Star break, so I decided to rest for a couple of days and then do something on it," Korver said. "So I went to this resort and there was a tennis court there, and there was a pro, and I was like, 'I played tennis in high school, what if I just play some tennis for a little bit?' It wasn't anything dramatic. I hit balls with them for forty-five minutes, just to move and do something outside. It was amazing.

"Two hours later, my elbow was completely swollen. My right elbow, it was just horrible. I couldn't move it. It just felt so tight and stiff. And I was like, 'Oh, no. I'm going to have to go back to Chicago and explain to Thibs [head coach and known taskmaster Tom Thibodeau] that I can't play because I hit some tennis balls.' Do I make up a new story? I told the trainer I had swelling, I was sore, I couldn't shoot, I could hardly bend it. Had it drained, got a cortisone shot, tried to play the next day, because I was not going to miss a game because I played tennis.

"But I couldn't shoot it like that. I couldn't shoot a 2-point shot for almost two weeks, but I could shoot a three, but my elbow had to be completely straight. This mattered, it had to be there," Korver said, showing his elbow tucked in straight and positioned lower than he had previously held it when he began his shooting motion, "and then it wasn't all the pressure on my [elbow].

"I was using more than just that part," Korver said, pointing to his right forearm, "and it felt so weird, but I think I shot 80 percent for threes for two weeks." [It was actually 26-for-56, for 46.4 percent, over his next fourteen games.] "I was like, 'This is so strange. Why?' But now, what is one of the things I think about every day while I'm shooting? This matters if it's there [showing his elbow completely aligned with his forearm], and here [showing the elbow flared out, a fraction off-center]. I now feel it when I shoot. If I miss it, I felt that my elbow was a half-inch out."

This tale is not to suggest that Korver suddenly became a great shooter out of nowhere. He was a top marksman in college, and had annually shot between 38 and 43 percent from the arc as a professional prior to arriving in Atlanta in 2012. Since then, though, Korver has completely redefined and raised his ceiling as a player through a comprehensive mix of accumulated experiences, highly refined practice, advanced data and film work, and off-court training and lifestyle choices that have both healed his body and emboldened his mind. The total body of work—along with a tennis session—has transformed a competent NBA role player into a regular headliner who has evolved into one of basketball's most disruptive offensive players.

Kyle Korver is not the best basketball player in the world, but he is the most *perfected* player.

∽

You cannot become great without a solid base to work from, and Korver definitely had that. Long before he was regularly knocking down threes, he was already immersed in a family basketball culture unlike many others.

Korver spent his early years in Los Angeles (before a middle-school move to Iowa) and spent many a night watching Pat Riley's Showtime Lakers with the rest of his family, all of whom had established (or went on to) some level of basketball excellence themselves. Korver is the oldest of four brothers, and all of them played in Division I in college. Additionally, his father, mother, and two uncles all played in Division III at Iowa's Central College, and his mother once scored seventy-four points in a high school game. According to a 2013 feature from *Atlanta Journal-Constitution* Hawks beat writer Chris Vivlamore, it was Korver's mother who provided him with the piece of lasting advice that initially made him into a good shooter.

"She said, 'Kyle, if you look at the front of the rim, you hit the rim,'" Korver said in that column. "'You look at the back of the rim, you hit the back of the rim. Look just over the front of the rim, and the ball goes swish.'"

Having so many family members capable of playing quality basketball meant that, from a young age, Korver had ample opportunities to be in gyms, around pickup games, and on the periphery of simple shooting practices on backyard courts. He would regularly watch his uncle play in high school, and would rebound for older relatives when they practiced. Per Vivlamore's column, Korver wanted to belong on the floor with them, so when he first evolved to shooting the ball with one hand, he did so left-handed (even though he's a righty) because he could send the ball farther at that time with his off-hand. It wasn't until a year later, after a relative asked him what he was doing, that he started shooting right-handed. Over the years, every family holiday gathering featured five-on-five games, and the way the games unfolded had a lasting impression on Korver.

"When I was growing up, when we were playing—me and my uncles and my dad and a ton of cousins, we would play basketball all the time," Korver said, recalling those formative times after a February 2015 game against the Golden State Warriors, one in which Korver missed a wide-open corner three after good ball rotation. "We would all say 'Extra pass! Throw the extra pass!' I love it. That's how I grew up appreciating basketball. The team that threw the extra pass, that team was going to score. The extra pass should never be missed, it seems like."

Korver eventually matriculated at Creighton University, where he played in a total of 128 games over his four seasons. After first blossoming as a sophomore, Korver went on to win Missouri Valley Conference Player of the Year honors in both his junior and senior seasons. Over the course of his Bluejays career, Korver connected on 371 of 819 3-point attempts (45.3 percent) from the old nineteen-foot, nine-inch college distance, establishing himself as a top perimeter threat.

Despite his solid size and college accolades, though, Korver didn't have the prototypical athleticism or ballhandling desired of wing players and slipped all the way to No. 51 overall in the 2003 NBA Draft. His pro career then got off to a rather ignominious start. As detailed by Zach Lowe in a July 2014 column on *Grantland*, the (then) New Jersey Nets selected Korver and then traded him to the Philadelphia 76ers for cash considerations that ended up covering the Nets' summer league team expenses, as well as a new copy machine for the Nets' team offices. It wouldn't be the last time that a team unloaded Korver for virtually nothing and then ended up regretting it.

Korver's time in Philadelphia was up and down, with numerous coaching changes bringing different approaches to how Korver would fit into the 76ers' plans. His rookie-year coach, Randy Ayers, wanted Korver to develop more of a mid-range game to complement his 3-point capabilities, but things quickly changed the next season, when former Boston Celtics head coach Jim O'Brien took over the team.

As Lowe describes in his column:

> In the team's very first practice, Allen Iverson ran a two-on-one fast break with Korver filling the wing. Iverson dished to Korver behind the 3-point arc. Korver took two dribbles, nailed a 17-footer, and waited for the applause.
>
> O'Brien was livid. He screamed for Korver to look down at the 3-point line. O'Brien told him that if Korver ever passed up another open 3-pointer, he would remove him from the game. Korver remembers one thought flying through his head during O'Brien's tirade: this is awesome.

Korver went on to lead the NBA that season, making 226 threes (a total that still stands as his most for a season) while shooting a crisp 40.5 percent from the arc. That season reinforced in Korver that he could play in the NBA, but the ongoing situation in Philadelphia, with its constant flux and questionable facilities, was not conducive to him thriving. Then, midway through his fifth season in the league, he was traded to Utah in a deal that included its own bit of flukish good fortune.

In December 2007, Jazz guard Gordan Giricek got into a verbal confrontation with head coach Jerry Sloan during a timeout in a game in Charlotte. Sloan, who was very successful and very old-school, predictably didn't react well to the incident, sending Giricek to the locker room and then sending the guard home for the following three games for the insubordination. Giricek never played another minute for the Jazz. Two weeks later, he and a conditional first-round draft pick went to the 76ers in exchange for Korver, who for the first time since his Creighton days, had the structure and support he craved.

"It was very different [going] from coach to coach [in Philadelphia] to 'this is what it is and you are part of a team,'" Korver said. "We [had] practice at 10 a.m. every single day, no matter what time we got in the night before, and we practiced. And Deron Williams played forty minutes last night? He practiced hard at 10 a.m. every day. It was just a whole different approach.

"And I think that was the first time that—I've always been a gym rat, or whatever you want to call it, want to be in there, want to play, love the game, think about it all the time—but that was, it was just a different approach to the NBA. A more professional approach. I had a couple of good vets my first couple of years in Philly, but [in Utah] there was a team full of guys who were committed to the team, and we wanted to win a championship, and we believed we could win a championship. We had the Lakers back then. Those Lakers were good, but we really thought that we could beat them."

But while Korver's mind was being put at ease by the Jazz's straightforward approach, his body didn't cooperate. His three seasons with Utah, while still decent performance-wise, were undermined by a series of injuries, including one where, according to Korver, the tip of his knee cap broke off, causing him all sorts of extended pain and soreness. Fortunately for him, though, the Jazz were the first NBA team to contract with P3 for movement testing and refinement. It started with a small set of players including current Hawks teammate Paul Millsap, and eventually evolved into the team sending all of their players down to Santa Barbara for a week, where they got personalized training plans. In Korver's mind, the workouts there probably saved his career, because for the first time in years, he had some hope of feeling healthy enough to improve.

"It was between getting to a spot where my body was pretty broken, going to P3, and then for a short period of time—it's like when you know that, when you see the light at the end of the tunnel, or you know that something will get better if you do the work, you're so much more willing to put in the work," Korver said about his buy-in with P3's methods. "Especially when you are down, you are broken, and especially in basketball. I felt, if I do this, I can get back to playing how I want to play basketball again and not have to worry about which move I can't make, or which turn I can't make, or that just totally you become robotic.

"And that's what I felt like I was becoming. I couldn't turn on my left leg, I couldn't pivot certain [ways]. It was hard for me to think about expanding my game, because I'm trying just to turn and pivot on my left leg. Anyway, so between being in a bad spot, finding P3, and then seeing the progress, I just got really excited and I really dove into it."

The initial process of breaking down an athlete's movement and then rebuilding it can be humbling for a player. Korver already was an established NBA player working on a multimillion-dollar contract when he first crossed paths with Marcus Elliott, with movement motions that had been ingrained since his high school days. Plus, Korver is not a stationary jump shooter; he moves at high speeds around screens, and twists and pivots quickly and forcefully to release his shots. Elliott wanted to alter a number of things in the way Korver moved and trained after P3's motion capture systems and analysis determined that there were enormous problems with the way he was doing it.

"It was really funny," Korver said, "because Marcus was standing there with a couple of guys, and I'm just standing there listening to it all, and he's like, 'Yeah, he's horrible at this, and there's none of that,' and I'm like, 'I'm standing right here!' You feel really bad because they're just [talking] like you're the worst athlete of all time, how are you even still together? That's obviously not what he was saying, but that's really what I was at the time.

"But I remember looking at one of the videos—they showed one of the camera angles, [and] you see your jump—and this was a big thing for me, seeing my movements, because I'm a visual person. A lot of people are."

Korver then demonstrated how one of his knees was bowing in every time he went up for a shot.

"I almost threw up," he said, about seeing the video. "I was horri-fied at my own mechanics. I got chills. I'm like, 'I've been doing that every time I jump?' But if I'm going to make a big jump, that's the exact movement I make. Even when I shoot [now], my [right] foot is kind of turned in, everything just kind of feels like good to me, so I have this weird turn. Well, that's going from your foot all the way up into your knee, into your hip, and then your back."

Like any training method, P3 is not a magic elixir. The changes in motion and strengthening have to occur over a period of time, with very dedicated exercises and effort required to first implement and then to retain the changes. So while Korver was encouraged by the process and by Elliott's expertise, he still wasn't moving like he wanted to on the court, and at one point during the 2008–09 season, he seriously contemplated whether he could even continue his career.

"When you're playing and you're hurt, basketball's not as much fun—and that's why we play, because it's fun," Korver said. "And when it just becomes about trying to set up yourself for later on in life, making enough money, putting in enough years—that's not a good driving force. So, my knee, some . . . things I could play through—they weren't keeping me out—but it was just hard to play and it was a lot of work every day to get something to go.

"I couldn't work on certain things at practice, and you're not shoot-ing between games because your elbow hurts or your wrist hurts or whatever it is, and then you're not playing as well as you want to. Then with my knee, I just couldn't do it, and we had a hard time figuring out what it was. Is it tendinitis? We tried these little things here and there, and things would get better, try a tape-job and it helps out a little bit, and then all these things, [but nothing really helped].

"I remember sitting in my hotel room in Orlando and just thinking, 'I don't know if I want to play anymore.' It's not that I don't love basketball, it's just my body hurts, [and] I don't feel like I can be very good. If I'm not going to be good, I'm not going to keep on trying to do this. And then slowly after that point—there were a lot of things that mentally, spiritually, [helped on] a lot of different levels—but I started to play a little bit better."

Korver missed the first chunk of the 2009–10 season due to injury, but managed to connect on a searing 53.6 percent of his 110 3-point attempts after he worked his way back into the rotation. That summer, the Jazz elected to let Korver go in free agency, in part because they wanted someone who played better defense. Somewhat slighted, Korver elected to sign with the Chicago Bulls and Thibodeau, who is widely recognized as one of the NBA's foremost defensive experts. It was in Chicago where Korver started to round out his overall game. He had to if he wanted to play.

"He's by far the best defensive coach I'd ever had up until that point," Korver said of Thibodeau, who helmed the Bulls until he was let go after the 2014–15 season. "Everyone talks about team defense, but no one teaches it like he does. And no one makes you repeat the drills and the footwork and everything like Thibs does. It's a lot of work. You go to Chicago and you work. And you get better, but you put in work on the defensive end and a lot of it builds habits.

"Everything got broken down into exactly where I'm supposed to force my man, exactly where my feet are supposed to be when I'm guarding him, exactly when I'm gonna push on my man, and when I'm gonna release. Like, everything got broken down so small, and then you could focus on the details and not a bigger concept."

Thibodeau's approach to teaching defense was similar to how Korver thought about shooting, where he broke down his approach into micro-checkpoints rather than worrying about his shot as a whole entity, or the results of his shots. Korver feels that if he's sound in his approach, the results will follow, and it's a process that undergoes frequent refinement as Korver continues to tinker with his shooting technique. In a January 2015 *USA Today* feature by Jeff Zillgitt, Korver detailed an updated 20-point checklist that determines whether he feels right or not when he releases a shot.

During our initial conversation, which happened a couple of months before Zillgitt's article ran, Korver expounded on his approach, how he needs to think about shooting, and why Thibodeau's approach really catered to his pre-established way of thinking about his game.

"I don't even care if the ball's going in," Korver said. "I want to get to the spot where my mechanics feel right, because if they feel right, the ball's going to go in. If I shoot it the way I want to shoot it, I believe it will go in every single time. When I miss, I feel like it's because something was off, and why do we have a shooting slump? Why does that happen? Most of the time, it's because your body is—something is wrong, and my body is out of alignment. I have something nagging, something going on.

"What feeds the rhythm? What feeds out of the rhythm? Those become focuses, not just on shooting and getting eight in a row to go in—and it's the same thing on defense. Defense, with Thibs, everything got broken down so much smaller and to the littlest detail. And I need details in my game. I can't go out there—like, a lot of great players can't be good coaches because they don't know what they did, they just did it. A lot of guys don't know how they do it, they just figure it out, they just do it. But I can't do that. I need to know exactly why something is happening or why I'm pushing someone where the help is supposed to be, and where the rotation's supposed to be, and why my shot isn't going in. I want to know it all—why my knee hurts. I like that stuff."

Korver was on some excellent teams in Chicago, but the Bulls were undermined on more than one occasion by injuries and never won the NBA championship they believed was in their reach. The quality of those Bulls teams, though, was why Korver was upset when Chicago traded him to Atlanta at the 2012 trade deadline instead of picking up his $5 million option for the 2012–13 season. The Hawks, at the time, were a modestly successful franchise with a fairly moribund fan base in a city that typically struggles to support pro teams outside of the NFL's Falcons.

In his first full season in Atlanta—Larry Drew's third and final season in charge of the Hawks—Korver became a starter for the first time since 2005–06, when he was still with the 76ers, and was excellent, connecting on 45.7 percent of his 414 3-point attempts while posting a career-best effective field goal percentage of 62.1 percent. Then came the fateful summer of 2013, where the Hawks elected to go with Mike Budenholzer as head coach and made a series of personnel decisions. One of the less heralded ones, but now among the most crucial, was getting Korver to re-sign on a four-year, $24 million contract.

It's also when everything truly started to come together physically and mentally for Korver, who annually moves his family to Santa Barbara for the summer so he can regularly work out at P3. Beyond the continued motion refinement work that was easing the pain in his knee and allowing him to move more freely, a lot of P3's training work focuses on specific strength and explosiveness improvements tailored not only to your sport, but to the specific role you play within it.

Korver is not a dynamic athlete by NBA standards, but he doesn't have to be. As Elliott says, given what Korver's role is, "It doesn't matter if he can [vertical] jump forty inches. It matters if he can get to twenty-four inches first," because that's the height of his jump-shot release, and Korver just needs a fractional amount of space to let fly.

So instead of working to improve Korver's vertical leap max, Elliott and Korver worked on improving Korver's vertical "quickness."

They also worked on pushing the limits of Korver's mental strength, in part through an annual, one-day exploration of pain called a *misogi*, a type of Japanese purification ritual. Basically, the goal was to come up with a physical challenge that seemed impossible, and then do it in order to push through mental and physical boundaries. In that first summer, Korver, Elliott, and others paddleboarded twenty-seven miles from Santa Barbara to the Channel Islands out in the Pacific Ocean. Korver had never paddleboarded before the attempt, but got through the adventure by micro-focusing on perfecting his strokes while blocking out the fatigue, pain, and potential danger.

In 2014, the *misogi* of choice was an underwater 5K "run," with the group taking turns picking up an eighty-five-pound rock at the bottom of the ocean, running as far underwater as they could with it, and then dropping it for the next "runner" before surfacing and treading water until it was their turn again. In 2015, the plan was to run repeatedly up a stairwell in a Los Angeles skyscraper until they reached the total vertical height of Mount Everest (29,035 vertical feet), pausing only to take the elevator back down to the ground floor before immediately heading back up the stairs for the next stage of the climb, but Korver was not able to partake because he was recovering from injury.

Overall, Korver says he felt better at thirty-three years old than he did at twenty-three, and the combination of a fitter Korver and the arrival of Budenholzer proved to be extremely potent. As detailed in Lowe's column, Budenholzer's designs on a free-flowing, 3-point-heavy attack mapped very well with Korver's constant needs for movement and tinkering—with some growing pains attached. In their first season together, Korver often would end up freelancing on plays that would wind up with multiple Hawks standing near each other, ruining the set's spacing. Still, Budenholzer pretty quickly understood what he had with Korver, and he started crafting creative offshoots of standard NBA actions to best unleash his new weapon with space to operate.

The Hawks started running what approximated as pick and rolls, but included short pitches from the big man setting the screen to Korver rather than Korver initiating the action, since he is not a particularly refined dribbler. The pitch instead of a handoff or Korver having to dribble himself sometimes provided Korver with enough space to immediately squeeze off a catch-and-shoot three, but over time, Korver also has built improvements into his game that allow him to take a dribble or two off that action and find a pass (back to the screener or kicking out to the other wing) or even pull up in the lane for an occasional floater.

When opponents started sniffing out these actions, the Hawks then started running counters to them, often involving a smaller guard in the post and/or Korver actually setting a screen to help unsettle the defense before the main action ended up being run. And he kept burying shots, making 47.2 percent of 392 3-point attempts while bumping up his 2-point field goal percentage a bit and also getting to the free throw line a touch more often, where he made himself into a 90-plus percent shooter. He wasn't *the* key to the Hawks' 2013–14 offense, but he was a guy opponents quickly realized they absolutely had to start keying on.

"One of the things about Korver that's really unbelievable is that he averages about thirteen points per game, but you go into the game and you have to treat him like he averages thirty, or else it could be thirty," said Boston Celtics head coach Brad Stevens. "I think that's where he presents a whole lot of challenges. He presents a whole lot of challenges in his cuts, how much attention you give him off the cuts, how much he opens up for everyone else. He's a really good player, as we all know."

A good part of Korver's excellence comes from his rigorous pre-game routines. He says he's not superstitious about what he does to get ready for games, but he continuously tinkers with his regimen to best prepare him for the types of movements and shots he's going to get in a game.

Each game night, Korver was assigned to be in the final pregame shooting block, and had half of the court to himself. Before he stepped onto the floor, he would undertake a lengthy stretching and movement routine, using a variety of poles, exercise bands, and advertising signage boards to work through a series of muscle-loosening, static stretches, and resistance movements before he even takes a shot. He then spends the remainder of the period going through a sequence of plays that attempt to simulate where he will get the ball in games and what options he will have.

So, Korver will come full speed off curls, catch inside the arc, and drive for a layup. He'll use the same motion and pull up for a floater. He'll shoot some free throws. He'll take some catch-and-shoot threes from the corner. He'll interact with multiple coaches to set and receive screens, and simulate pick and rolls and pitches to him, finding his range with one sweet arc after another. Everything is done with pace and purpose, mimicking how the Hawks want to play, and this sets Korver up for another night of relentless movement and catch and shoots off the dead run that stretch and bend even the better NBA defenses in really uncomfortable ways.

"We were talking about it before [the game]," said New Orleans Pelicans wing Ryan Anderson, himself a quality 3-point shooter, after losing to the Hawks in Atlanta. "Ninety percent of their plays could end with an opportunity for him to score, so even though the ball's not in his hands, he's always a threat.

"You have to watch out for screens. There's some guys like Ray Allen, Reggie Miller, guys in history . . . those guys commanded as much attention as him. There's not a lot of guys [like that] anymore, guys coming off screens looking for a shot, guys always active coming off pindowns, or guys in transition you always have to be aware of. That's dangerous in this league now because it's [about] such stretched-out offense. You want to get those quick buckets, and you can really hurt a team with those huge dagger threes."

In Korver's second season under Budenholzer, with big man Al Horford back in the fold and other Hawks like Jeff Teague and De-Marre Carroll blossoming around him, he stretched the limits of NBA history, nearly becoming the first player to have a "50–50–90" field goal percentage–3-point percentage–free throw percentage season. (Golden State Warriors head coach Steve Kerr actually reached that summit in the 1995–96 season, but didn't make enough field goals or free throws for it to "officially" count.)

Korver had to settle for a (rounded) 49–49–90 campaign, still one of the greatest shooting seasons in NBA history, making 221 of his 449 3-point attempts. His 3-point shot chart on NBA.com looked like a minimalist painting, with all five regions outside the arc bathed in the sweet light green color of outperformance, and his marksmanship attracted the attention of the league's best players.

"The numbers he's putting up this year, shooting over 50 percent, that's crazy," said Golden State Warriors guard and future league MVP Stephen Curry ahead of the teams' first meeting of the 2014–15 season. "I think I've had—Klay [Thompson] can say the same thing—stretches of the season where you feel like you are on fire, and I haven't touched that 53 percent number or whatever. It's pretty remarkable to keep that going. I think he's made some big shots, as well. You enjoy it when you see another shooter do what he does."

Korver's "worst" area from behind the arc was the left wing, where he "only" made 40 percent of his 90 attempts (which was still six percentage points above league average from that quadrant). From three of the five zones around the arc, Korver shot at least 15 percentage points better than the league average, converting nearly half of his attempts from straightaway and from deeper on the right wing while the league barely makes a third of its attempts from those regions. Given how often Korver is shooting, especially after sprinting around a screen, his success rates are astounding. He was even more lethal from the shorter right corner, where he knocked down thirty-three of his fifty-eight tries for an effective field goal percentage of 85.3 percent.

For perspective on that last figure, Los Angeles Clippers put-back and pick-and-roll lob dunk specialist DeAndre Jordan converted 72.7 percent of his "restricted area" field goal attempts in 2014–15. Players with similar profiles, like the Phoenix Suns' Brendan Wright and the Dallas Mavericks' Tyson Chandler (now also in Phoenix after signing as a free agent in the offseason) were at 75.1 and 72.2 percent, respectively, per the SportVU data available on NBA.com. So, incredibly, a Korver right-corner 3-point attempt was worth considerably more in expected points per shot (1.706) than an array of dunks and putbacks from the league's most efficient big man rim finishers (between 1.444 and 1.502, for the three big men above). You sometimes hear an announcer yell that an open shot is "like a layup" to a great jump shooter, and in this case, that was true—and then some.

Because the Hawks had effectively wrapped up the Eastern Conference's top seed so prematurely, there wasn't a lot riding on their stretch run of games, and the team tried to stay sharp and healthy beyond anything else. As such, conversation more frequently turned toward Korver's run at history, as he had spent much of the season over the necessary benchmarks.

The chase, as it was—along with some roster shuffling and the relative lack of meaning in the games they were playing—may have affected Korver a little bit. Acknowledging that players "have to speak to the media every day," he copped to being aware of where he stood, but "if you're going to think about that, there's a chance you're going to start shooting tentatively. You know what I mean? You're not going to shoot [as freely]." Korver said his late-season drop-off that pushed him just below the thresholds was more a case that his shooting elbow started flaring up down the stretch of the season than any pressure to maintain some round-number benchmarks. Korver ultimately had surgery on that elbow over the summer (along with surgery for an ankle injury caused by Cleveland Cavaliers guard Matthew Dellavedova when he somewhat controversially rolled up on Korver's leg during a loose-ball scramble during the conference finals).

Regardless, 2014–15 was Korver's third straight season shooting at least 45 percent on at least 200 3-point attempts, tying him with two-time league MVP Steve Nash for the most such seasons in a career. There have only been thirty-four instances of that combo since the NBA first installed the 3-point arc in the 1979–80 season, and Korver's shooting way more than most others on the list. All three of Korver's qualifying seasons included at least 392 3-point attempts; Nash never tried more than 293 in any of his 45-percenters.

And, for the record, it was Korver who received the advice from Kevin Durant about his heels, and he did end up sticking with the approach to better shot-loading.

"It's really good advice," Korver said from Santa Barbara, where he was back preparing for the 2015–16 season. "It's all about just feeling strong, feeling loaded, and lift up with your legs. Yeah, [it's] definitely one of the things that I think about [when I'm shooting]." Korver said it took him awhile to really get comfortable with staying more solid through his heels, but "it's like the story with my elbow, though. You feel like you're doing it right."

After the Hawks' regular-season success, the end of the campaign didn't go as expected. Hampered by an increasing number of injuries to key players, and perhaps having lost their sharpness during the insignificant final stretch of the regular season, the Hawks made hard work of a series with the mediocre Brooklyn Nets, were helped significantly in the second round when Washington Wizards star point guard John Wall injured his hand, and then were whitewashed in four straight by LeBron James and the Cavaliers in the Eastern Conference Finals.

Nonetheless, at an age where most players are fading, Korver finally had arrived, feeling healthier than he had in years, playing better than he ever had, and impacting the NBA in ways that very few others are capable. The once-reluctant Hawk now loves being in Atlanta, and the Hawks fans have embraced "Threezus" as one of their favorite players. Three decades after Showtime influenced him at the very start of his path to the NBA, the way Korver is playing—and how he's made himself into what he now is—is setting an all-around example for future players who want to reach their absolute personal max.

"What I love about Kyle is what I loved about Steve Nash and Grant Hill," said Kerr. "There's sort of an intellectual approach to the craft, not just a physical one. It's not about just going out and practicing a bunch of shots. It's thinking about how to get better, preparing your mind, it's challenging yourself with different routines, different activities to search out what helps you the most. I've read a little bit about Kyle this year, doing so many things to improve himself, and the guy's a pro. He's great for the league, and obviously great for the Hawks. He's a hell of a player."

The Warriors Come Out to Play

The 2015 NBA Finals between the Cleveland Cavaliers and the Golden State Warriors featured two major storylines that are incredibly relevant to this book, but neither may have surfaced if not for the dramatic ending of Game 1 in the series.

In that contest, the Cavaliers—sizable underdogs on the road in Oakland—had a wonderful chance to win the game on their final possession, but LeBron James missed a makeable driving layup and, after the rebound kicked out toward the right corner, guard Iman Shumpert was fractionally short on a catch-and-shoot fling that looked good when he let it go. The game went to overtime, and early in the extra session, Cavaliers star point guard Kyrie Irving went down with a knee injury. The Cavaliers ended up losing that game, and Irving never played again in the series.

With the Cavaliers' other standout, forward Kevin Love, already having sustained a shoulder injury in the team's first-round playoff series against the Boston Celtics and also declared out for the remainder of the playoffs, Irving's injury left the Cavaliers with LeBron and a cast of role players. Shorthanded Cleveland suddenly looked extraordinarily overmatched against the best and deepest team in the league, which had hurt opponents all season with its shooting and interchangeable personnel, and after the Cavaliers missed their chance to steal Game 1, most NBA observers expected the series to last five games, if that many.

Then a funny thing happened: the Cavaliers won Game 2 on the road. Then they went home and won Game 3, as well. Beyond the shock of the unexpected back-to-back wins, it was James's role in how those games unfolded that created the series' first major discussion point.

To be certain, a lot of things beyond the best player in the world carrying his team had to go right for Cleveland, given how short on firepower the Cavaliers were. In Game 2, the Warriors' Stephen Curry shot a woeful five of twenty-three from the field, Cleveland big man Timofey Mozgov destroyed Andrew Bogut and the other Golden State bigs with a seventeen-point, eleven-rebound statement, and backup Cleveland point guard Matthew Dellavedova made some huge plays down the stretch of the 2-point overtime victory. In Game 3, Cleveland's "Delly" poured in an improbable twenty points while Warriors forwards Draymond Green and Harrison Barnes shot a combined two for eighteen from the field as the Cavaliers won by five.

But the two wins were mostly about LeBron—who played 96 of the 101 total minutes—and how Cleveland head coach David Blatt orchestrated the Cavaliers' approach, slowing the tempo of the contests against the league's most up-tempo team down to an absolute crawl.

Time and time again, LeBron brought the ball up the court, pounded the dribble, and then tried to attack out of isolation sets. Sometimes, he scored (he had thirty-six points in Game 2 and forty in Game 3, albeit on twenty-five of sixty-nine combined shooting). Sometimes, he passed (he had nineteen combined assists, even though his teammates didn't make many shots in Game 2). And if he missed, Cleveland was in good shape positionally to get back on defense and defuse any Golden State fastbreaks.

It was the most prudent (and perhaps only) approach for the Cavaliers, as they were constituted. It also was a strategy that had some quantitative merit. Remember that, somewhat surprisingly during the regular season, Cleveland had been quite good when it only had LeBron on the court without either Irving or Love, and most of the success in those (admittedly small-sample) situations came on the defensive end of the floor. The Cavaliers held opponents to just 88.2 points per forty-eight minutes in those situations, which was seven points better than the defensive per-forty-eight rate with all three stars on the court together. The trouble (understandably) came when LeBron also was off the court, leaving Cleveland without any of its stars. Understanding that many of those situations likely came later in blowouts, so the data could be skewed by game situations, Cleveland dropped to a -5.6 net per forty-eight minutes, and only scored 95 points per forty-eight minutes with only its role players on the court.

Basically, Blatt realized that the lineups with James could compete with Golden State, at least on the defensive end. He also knew the Cavaliers would be mostly incapable of scoring against the league's most efficient defense when James sat. So, the plan became James playing as many minutes as possible, and hoping that gorging on isos and floor balance would limit the total number of possessions in the game and put Cleveland in position to steal wins down the stretch.

All Blatt needed was for James, essentially, to be inhuman.

That's not hyperbole. During the series, ESPN Insider's Tom Haberstroh penned a column about a gathering of elite sports scientists who ostensibly were at a conference to swap the latest in athlete maintenance techniques but ended up being transfixed by the NBA Finals, almost unable to comprehend the stress "load" that LeBron was carrying for the Cavaliers. Haberstroh spoke with Michael Young, the owner and founder of Athlete Lab Sports Performance Training Center in North Carolina, about what Young was seeing in LeBron's effort.

But the two-day workshop was overrun with talk of, and concern for, LeBron James. The worry begins with a baseline level of "stress"— that's their term—surrounding all NBA players. Sports science has exploded in recent years with evidence that factors like mucked-up sleep, air travel and densely scheduled games put players in jeopardy. The NBA is elite in all categories.

"It's unfathomable to go across the country from Cleveland to San Francisco—at the very least a five-hour flight—and then play 50 minutes in a game the next day," Young says. "You don't see that in any other sport. The travel stress alone can be debilitating.

"And then you add to the fact that basically it's a one-man team at this point, and the mental and physical burden—it's just overwhelming," Young says.

Young remembers watching Game 3 while the trainers geeked out over the stamina of James, who was coming off two straight overtime games, including fifty minutes in Game 2. This was the party where people were dying to know LeBron's heart rate variability scores—measuring his bodily stress levels. There was speculation about his OmegaWave outputs, a measure of neurological fatigue.

But mostly they just wanted to know how he could keep going at all.

As it turned out, James couldn't. Or at least not quite at the same superhuman level as the first two games Cleveland played without Irving. But after Game 3, with the Warriors down 2–1 and already having ceded homecourt advantage, no one yet could accurately forecast what LeBron had left in his tank. Golden State had not played anywhere near its own ceiling and looked frustrated by the slowness of the games. The Warriors needed to change their approach and unlock their upside, or risk being one of the biggest upset victims in NBA Finals history.

Enter Nick U'Ren, a twenty-eight-year-old special assistant to head coach Steve Kerr, who provided the second major analytics talking point of the series, and very well may have saved the Warriors.

U'Ren started working for Kerr in 2007, when Kerr was the general manager of the Phoenix Suns, and stayed with the Suns through two additional regimes before Kerr, having taken the Warriors job before the 2014–15 season, brought U'Ren over to Golden State. U'Ren was not officially a coach or a scout for the Warriors. He was more of a consigliere for Kerr, helping him keep his schedule, being in charge of the music that played during Warriors shootarounds, and assisting with the execution of team outings, in addition to doing some video work for the team.

Like the rest of the Warriors' players and staff, U'Ren was frustrated by how Cleveland was pushing Golden State around and making the series a slow, physical slog. Per multiple reports, U'Ren went back a year to find the basis for what turned out to be a truly inspired idea, recalling how the San Antonio Spurs replaced Tiago Splitter in the starting lineup with Boris Diaw, who both defended LeBron and added more shooting and spacing on the offensive end.

U'Ren suggested to assistant coach Luke Walton that the Warriors insert Andre Iguodala, their best perimeter defender and a reasonable 3-point shooter, into the starting lineup in place of center and rim-protector Andrew Bogut in an effort to help slow down LeBron while also trying to speed up the pace of the series. Walton then communicated the idea to head coach Steve Kerr, who sneakily implemented the change in time for Game 4.

After Cleveland jumped out to a quick 7–0 lead, the Warriors stabilized, found their footing with more athleticism and shotmakers on the floor, and with Iguodala playing more minutes to help limit LeBron on the offensive end, the Warriors rolled to a series-tying victory. Afterward, Kerr very publicly credited his young assistant for the clever gambit.

From that point on, the series was basically over. Golden State won Game 5 at home by thirteen points and, despite a last-minute semi-scare in Game 6 thanks to some late Cleveland threes, closed out the series on the road to win the title. Bogut ended up playing less than three total minutes in the final three wins while Iguodala ended up being named the Finals MVP.

The whole Golden State scenario was a microcosm of what this entire book is about. Thanks to savvy talent identification and player development, Golden State had the roster with which to quickly change gears. Thanks to James tiring after carrying such a momentous workload, the Warriors regained the extra margin for error their talent suggested they should have. And thanks in large part to a junior staffer, they found a possible solution, vetted the idea among the coaching staff, decided to go for it, communicated the idea to the players, changed their starting lineup and approach, and won three straight high-pressure games. That whole chain set a very significant bar for information sourcing, communication, and implementation under pressure.

It also validated the decision the Warriors made at the beginning of the season, the one where assistant general manager Kirk Lacob said that situations involving this type of specific on-court information would be a coach-driven enterprise, since the coaches were the people who were with the players every day. That let the players get comfortable with the flexible thinking of Kerr and his staff. It allowed Bogut to be OK with a strategic demotion in the biggest spotlight. It positioned Iguodala to be prepared to excel in a huge spot. It helped the Warriors be the league's best team all season, and win the 2015 NBA championship that was rightfully theirs.

NOTES

Prologue

3   **Game for the 2014–15 season:** Ethan Sherwood Strauss, "Klay Thompson's Six New Lethal Moves," ESPN.com, January 9, 2015, http://espn.go.com/blog/golden-state-warriors/post/_/id/199/klay-thompsons-six-new-lethal-moves.

8   **Data-related employees:** Mark Cuban Companies, "Our Companies: Synergy Sports Technology," http://markcubancompanies.com/index.html#/synergy; Mark Cuban Companies, "Our Companies: Catapult," http://markcubancompanies.com/index.html#/catapult.

Chapter 1

10   **Sold in that era:** Louis Guth, "Investing in a Pro Team: Expensive But Worth It," *New York Times,* July 6, 1980.

13   **Contract with the Houston Rockets:** Alexander Wolff, "Searching for a Promised Land," *Sports Illustrated,* August 30, 1982, http://www.si.com/vault/1982/08/30/624378/searching-for-a-promised-land.

13   **Into Guth's offensive formula:** Louis Guth, "Basketball by the Numbers: Free Agents, Computers, and the NBA," *N/E/R/A Topics,* 1984.

15   **"It'll be a better show":** Mark Perner, "The Sixers Trade for Moses Malone," Philly.com, March 8, 2013, http://articles.philly.com/2013-03-08/sports/37564051_1_moses-malone-sixers-fan-lee-fentress.

15   **Lakers in Guth's model:** Louis Guth, "76ers' Wins and Offensive Rebounds Projection (as described in N/E/R/A Topics)," *Sports Illustrated,* September 13, 1982.

16   **Conceded "per possession":** Frank McGuire, *Defensive Basketball* (Englewood Cliffs, NJ: Prentice-Hall, 1959).

20   **Success in that era:** David Leonhardt, "Mavericks' New Math May Be an Added Edge," *New York Times,* April 27, 2003, http://www.nytimes .com/2003/04/27/sports/pro-basketball-mavericks-new-math-may-be -an-added-edge.html.

20   **Shooters, actually worked:** Dean Oliver, "Research Topics," APBR_ analysis, February 10, 2001, https://groups.yahoo.com/neo/groups /APBR_analysis/conversations/messages/1.

23   **Approach with two centers:** Ibid.

23   **Any of his data:** Ibid.

26   **Coaching and management thinkers:** Chris Ballard, "Measure of Success," *Sports Illustrated,* October 24, 2005, http://www.si.com /vault/2005/10/24/8359337/measure-of-success.

Chapter 2

30   **2012 Sloan Sports Analytics Conference:** Yu-han Chang, Rajiv Maheswaran, Aaron Henehan, and Samantha Danesis, "Deconstructing the Rebound with Optimal Tracking Data," 2012 Sloan Sports Analytics Conference, March 1, 2012, http://www.sloansportsconference.com /wp-content/uploads/2012/02/108-sloan-sports-2012-maheswaran -chang_updated.pdf.

30   **Visually unique ways:** Rajiv Maheswaran, "The Math Behind Basketball's Wildest Moves," TED, TED2015, March 17, 2015, https://www .ted.com/talks/rajiv_maheswaran_the_math_behind_basketball_s _wildest_moves.

32   **What a computer tells them:** Brett Pollakoff, "Stan van Gundy Questions Integrity of Advanced Statistical Data at MIT Sloan Sports Analytics Conference," NBC Sports, March 1, 2014, http://nba .nbcsports.com/2014/03/01/stan-van-gundy-questions-integrity -of-advanced-statistical-data-at-sloan-sports-analytics-conference/.

36   **Or a similar carrier:** Seth Partnow, "Industry Q&A: Garrick Barr, CEO, of Synergy Sports Technology," *Nylon Calculus,* February 12, 2015, http://nyloncalculus.com/2015/02/12/industry-qa-garrick-barr-ceo -synergy-sports-technology/.

37   **Cross-sport technology phenomenon:** Synergy Sports Technology, "Our Championship Team," http://corp.synergysportstech.com /nba-video-database.

41   **Movements of soccer players:** Eric Fisher, "STATS LLC Buys Tel Aviv-Based Optical-Tracking Company SportVU," *Sports Business Journal,* December 2, 2008, http://www.sportsbusinessdaily.com/Daily

/Issues/2008/12/Issue-54/Sports-Media/Stats-LLC-Buys-Tel-Aviv
-Based-Optical-Tracking-Company-Sportvu.aspx.

44 **During the 2009 NBA Finals:** David Aldridge, "SportVU Cameras Shift Focus of What's Possible with NBA Stats," *NBA.com,* November 11, 2013, http://www.nba.com/2013/news/features/david_aldridge/11/11 /morning-tip-sportvu-cameras-in-arenas-problems-with-nets-qa-with -paul-george/.

45 **Product called MySynergySports:** William Bohl, "A Synergy Elegy: Goodbye, You Confounding Old Friend," *Hardwood Paroxysm,* October 3, 2014, http://hardwoodparoxysm.com/2014/10/03/synergy-elegy -goodbye-confounding-old-friend/.

Chapter 3

48 **Book determined independently:** Kevin Pelton, "The Great Analytics Rankings: NBA," ESPN, February 23, 2015, http://espn.go.com/espn /feature/story/_/id/12331388/the-great-analytics-rankings.

50 **DNP as "old":** Kelly Dwyer, "Tim Duncan Missed Sunday Night's Game Because He's 'Old,' Officially," Yahoo! Sports, March 26, 2012, http://sports.yahoo.com/blogs/nba-ball-dont-lie/tim-duncan-missed -sunday-night-spurs-game-because-081218158.html.

51 **"Best interests of the NBA":** NBA, "San Antonio Spurs Fined $250K by League," NBA.com, Press Release, December 3, 2012, http://www.nba .com/2012/news/11/30/spurs-fined-announcement/.

52 **More minutes than average:** Ian Levy, "Gaming the NBA Season," *The Cauldron,* November 24, 2014, https://the-cauldron.com/gaming -the-nba-season-6ba2a7fd6ca7.

59 **Against the Chicago Bulls:** Marcel Mutoni, "The Philadelphia Sixers Met with Angry Fans About Tanking," *SLAM,* November 25, 2014, http://www.slamonline.com/nba/philadelphia-sixers-met-angry-fans -tanking/.

59 **Vote were announced:** Ken Berger, "The Sixers' Nonstop Badness Puts Tanking in the Spotlight," CBSSports.com, November 26, 2014, http:// www.cbssports.com/nba/writer/ken-berger/24841864/the-sixers-non -stop-badness-puts-tanking-in-the-spotlight.

60 **Carter-Williams wrote. "Nope":** Pablo S. Torre, "The 76ers' Plan to Win (Yes, Really)," *ESPN The Magazine,* February 19, 2015, http:// espn.go.com/nba/story/_/id/12318808/the-philadelphia-76ers-radical -guide-winning.

66 **"Forcing up a bunch of threes":** Eric Pincus, "Byron Scott Wants Lakers to Average 10 to 15 Three-Point Shots a Game," *Los Angeles Times,*

October 8, 2014, http://www.latimes.com/sports/lakers/lakersnow /la-sp-ln-byron-scott-lakers-three-pointers-20141007-story.html.

69   **Closer to the Rockets' strategy:** Stephen Shea and Christopher Baker, *Basketball Analytics: Objective and Efficient Strategies for Understanding How Teams Win* (Lake St. Louis, MO: Advanced Metrics LLC, 2013).

70   **Also ranked very highly:** Stephen Shea, "Introducing Moreyball Efficiency or Why the Warriors Are Favorites to Win It All," Basketball AnalyticsBook.com, February 11, 2015, http://www.basketballanalytics book.com/2015/02/11/introducing-moreyball-efficiency-or-why-the -warriors-are-favorites-to-win-it-all/.

71   **Italian defensive soccer strategy:** Jason Concepcion, "Embrace the Dark Side: How the Rockets Became the New Bad Boys," *Grantland*, November 19, 2014, http://grantland.com/the-triangle/houstonaccio-morey ball-rockets-efficiency-fun/.

Chapter 4

76   **Couple of decades ago:** Mike DeCoursey, "John Calipari: The Salesman," *Sporting News*, September 2, 2015, http://www.sportingnews .com/calipari/salesman.

77   **Manage the whole process:** Ben Roberts, "Kentucky's Director of Analytics: Who Is He, Why He's Here and How He Is Helping the Cats," Kentucky.com, December 23, 2014, http://www.kentucky.com/welcome _page/?shf=/2014/12/23/3608832_kentuckys-director-of-analytics .html.

80   **Lexington were over:** John Calipari, "We May Never Platoon Again, But Players Will Always Come First," *CoachCal.com*, May 5, 2015, http:// www.coachcal.com/34612/2015/05/we-may-never-platoon-again-but -players-will-always-come-first/.

96   **Low-post scorer Jahlil Okafor:** Barry Jacobs, "How Data Help Refine Duke Approach on Court," *Charlotte Observer*, December 14, 2014, http://www.charlotteobserver.com/sports/college/mens-basketball /article9245507.html.

96   **Attempted off the dribble:** Wylie Wong, "March Madness 2015: Duke University Leads College Basketball's Data Revolution," *EdTech*, March 18, 2015, http://www.edtechmagazine.com/higher/article/2015/03/ march-madness-2015-duke-university-leads-college-basketball-s -data-revolution.

Chapter 5

106 **"I've never seen anybody do":** Mark McKown, quoted on "Dr. Marcus Elliott," P3, http://www.p3.md/team/marcus-elliott/.

112 **A large number of NBA teams:** Chris Ballard, "Want to Avoid Injury? NBA Teams Are Looking to Marcus Elliott for Answers," *Sports Illustrated,* December 23, 2014, http://www.si.com/nba/2014/12/23 /marcus-elliott-p3-nba-injury-injury-analysis-data.

114 **Recover from injuries:** Michael Schwartz, "The Secret Behind the Phoenix Suns' Elite Training Staff," *Valley of the Suns,* April 5, 2012, http://valleyofthesuns.com/2012/04/05/secret-behind-phoenix-suns -elite-training-staff/.

117 **Prolonging his career:** Ian Thomsen, "Weekly Countdown," *Sports Illustrated,* March 28, 2008, http://www.si.com/more-sports/2008/03/28 /weekly-countdown.

119 **Catapult devices during the 2014–15 season:** Ken Berger, "Warriors' Wearable Weapon? Devices to Monitor Players While on Court," CBSSports.com, June 3, 2015, http://www.cbssports.com/nba/writer /ken-berger/25203846/warriors-wearable-weapon-devices-to-monitor -players-while-on-the-court.

Chapter 6

128 **Among Kings officials:** Video: "Draft 3.0: The Sacramento Kings' Radical Plan to Crowdsource the NBA Draft," *Grantland,* June 24, 2014, http:// grantland.com/features/sacramento-kings-2014-nba-draft-crowd sourcing/.

135 **Two seasons of college ball:** Ben Alamar, *Sports Analytics: A Guide for Coaches, Managers and Other Decision Makers* (New York, NY: Columbia University Press, 2013).

138 **Moving around the court:** Zach Lowe, "Lights, Cameras, Revolution," *Grantland,* March 19, 2013, http://grantland.com/features/the-toronto -raptors-sportvu-cameras-nba-analytical-revolution/.

143 **"Communicator to me with it":** Baxter Holmes, "Drew Cannon, 23, Bringing Analytics to Celtics," *Boston Globe,* July 9, 2013, https://www .bostonglobe.com/sports/2013/07/08/celtics-hire-year-old-analytics -guru-drew-cannon/Iv9Ua8NB5gQTVbRh0I8uSN/story.html.

155 **Were never particularly impressive:** Michael Lewis, "The No-Stats All-Star," *New York Times,* February 13, 2009, http://www.nytimes .com/2009/02/15/magazine/15Battier-t.html?_r=0.

156   **"Member at a Paris Hilton party":** Jason Friedman, "Rocket Science: Daryl Morey Brings Hard-Core Statistical Analysis to the NBA," *Houston Press,* October 31, 2007, http://www.houstonpress.com/news /rocket-science-daryl-morey-brings-hard-core-statistical-analysis-to -the-nba-6540549.

Chapter 7

166   **Warriors' chances of claiming it:** Daryl Morey, @dmorey, Twitter, February 5, 2015, https://twitter.com/dmorey/status/563562941442576385.

168   **Anybody else in the organization:** Diamond Leung, "Warriors Co-Owner Lacob Lists Reasons For Firing Mark Jackson," *Bay Area News Group,* December 5, 2014, http://www.mercurynews.com/warriors /ci_27078013/warriors-co-owner-lacob-lists-reasons-firing-mark.

168   **All have enormous wingspans:** Alex Torres, "Warriors Are Redefining Defense with Position-less Approach," *Warriors World,* http://www .warriorsworld.net/2015/01/20/warriors-are-redefining-defense-with -position-less-approach/.

176   **James is not playing at his level:** Andy Glockner, "In Defense of James Harden," *The Cauldron,* December 18, 2014, https://the-cauldron.com /in-defense-of-james-harden-73211071b4b0.

177   **Their ball-dominant players:** Kelly Scaletta, "More on Player Scoring Types: Team Impact Charts," BBallBreakdown.com, August 7, 2015, http://bballbreakdown.com/2015/08/07/more-on-player-scoring- types-team-impact-charts/.

179   **Having "some African in him":** Daniel O'Leary, "Audio of Hawks GM Danny Ferry Saying Luol Deng Has 'a Little African in Him' and All-Star Is Two-Faced Surfaces," *New York Daily News,* September 11, 2014, http:// www.nydailynews.com/sports/basketball/audio-hawks-gm-racist -comment-luol-deng-surfaces-article-1.1937107.

187   **Plan to re-sign in Cleveland:** LeBron James (as told to Lee Jenkins), "LeBron: I'm Coming Back to Cleveland," *Sports Illustrated,* July 11, 2015, http://www.si.com/nba/2014/07/11/lebron-james-cleveland-cavaliers.

189   **His return to Cleveland:** Ethan Skolnick, "A Team Transformed: Inside LeBron James' First Season Back with the Cavaliers," *Bleacher Report,* July 10, 2015, http://bleacherreport.com/articles/2517134-a -team-transformed-inside-lebron-james-first-season-back-with-the -cavaliers.

190   **Windhorst in a January 2015 column:** Brian Windhorst, "How Did Cavs Land Timofey Mozgov?" ESPN.com, January 8, 2015, http://espn

.go.com/nba/story/_/id/12136574/nba-how-did-cleveland-cavaliers
-get-timofey-mozgov.

Chapter 8

195   **He couldn't play anymore:** Marc Spears, "Warriors Andrew Bogut Likens Restoring Cars to Caring for Battered Body," Yahoo! Sports, December 18, 2014, http://sports.yahoo.com/news/warriors--andrew-bogut-likens-refurbishing-cars-to-caring-for-battered-body-020928090.html.

198   **One of the best players in the NBA:** Charles F. Gardner, "Khris Middleton's Rise Brings Stability to Shooting Guard," *Milwaukee Journal-Sentinel,* March 2, 2015, http://www.jsonline.com/sports/bucks/khris-middletons-rise-brings-stability-at-shooting-guard-b99453986z1-294770201.html.

200   **Trade with the Pistons:** Eric Buenning, "Examining the Other Parts of the Bucks-Pistons Trade," BrewHoop.com, July 30, 2013, http://www.brewhoop.com/2013/7/30/4573324/examining-the-other-parts-of-the-bucks-pistons-trade.

204   **Column about the situation:** Adrian Wojnarowski, "Inside Look at James Harden's Trade to Rockets," Yahoo! Sports, October 28, 2012, http://sports.yahoo.com/news/nba—inside-look-at-james-harden-s-trade-to-rockets-28301609.html.

204   **Either Durant or Westbrook:** Tom Haberstroh, "Is Harden Really a No. 1 Option?" ESPN Insider, November 6, 2012, http://insider.espn.go.com/nba/story/_/id/8599109/nba-james-harden-no-1-option.

206   **Created ESPN's real plus-minus calculation:** Daniel Myers, "About Box Plus/Minus (BPM)," Basketball-Reference.com, accessed November 11, 2015, http://www.basketball-reference.com/about/bpm.html.

206   **In isolation (one-on-one) situations:** Jordan Brenner, "The Truth About James Harden's Defense," *ESPN The Magazine,* December 22, 2014, http://espn.go.com/nba/story/_/id/12041846/the-truth-james-harden-defense.

206   *Cauldron* **in December 2014:** Andy Glockner, "In Defense of James Harden," *The Cauldron,* December 18, 2014, https://the-cauldron.com/in-defense-of-james-harden-73211071b4b0.

207   **"Tank for the game of basketball":** Ibid.

207   **Big man Enes Kanter:** Seth Partnow, "Rim Protection 2014/15," *Nylon Calculus,* April 2015, http://nyloncalculus.com/stats/rim-protection/.

210   **On to make the NBA:** Jon Nichols, "How Do NCAA Stats Translate to the NBA?" Basketball-Statistics.com, March 2009, http://basketball-statistics.com/howdoncaastatisticstranslatetothenba.html.

211 **Rebounding rate, and usage rate:** Neil Paine and Zach Bradshaw, "Projecting the Top 50 Players in the 2015 Draft Class," *FiveThirtyEight*, June 19, 2015, http://fivethirtyeight.com/features/projecting-the-top-50-players-in-the-2015-nba-draft-class/.

212 **2015 interview with *Grantland*:** Zach Lowe, "Q&A with Orlando's Nikola Vucevic: On Theme Parks, Nicknames and More," *Grantland*, January 28, 2015, http://grantland.com/the-triangle/qa-with-orlandos-nikola-vucevic-on-theme-parks-nicknames-and-more/.

213 **"Midrange jump-shooter":** Howard Beck, "Knicks Trade Francis, Frye for Portland's Randolph," *New York Times*, June 29, 2007, http://www.nytimes.com/2007/06/29/sports/basketball/KNICKS-WEB.html?_r=0.

Chapter 9

219 **Made him into a good shooter:** Chris Vivlamore, "The Making of a Sharp-Shooter," *Atlanta Journal-Constitution*, February 14, 2013, http://www.ajc.com/news/sports/basketball/family-center-korver-becoming-one-nbas-best-shoote/nWPNs/.

220 **Machine for the Nets' team offices:** Zach Lowe, "An Offense unto Himself," *Grantland*, July 29, 2014, http://grantland.com/features/kyle-korver-nba-atlanta-hawks/.

226 **When he releases a shot:** Jeff Zillgitt, "Kyle Korver vs. Perfection," *USA Today*, January 31, 2015, http://www.usatoday.com/story/sports/nba/hawks/2015/02/02/kyle-korver-vs-perfection-atlanta-three-point-shot/22693565/.

231 **Attention of the league's best players:** NBA, "League Player Stats," NBA.com, http://stats.nba.com/league/player/#!/shooting/?Season=2014-15&SeasonType=Regular%20Season&DistanceRange=By%20Zone&sort=Restricted%20Area%20FG%20PCT&dir=1.

Epilogue

237 **Carrying for the Cavaliers:** Tom Haberstroh, "LeBron James' Unfathomable Workload," ESPN.com, June 14, 2015, http://espn.go.com/nba/playoffs/2015/story/_/id/13071387/lebron-james-unfathomable-workload.

239 **To be a truly inspired idea:** Lee Jenkins, "Meet Nick U'Ren: The Warriors Staffer with the Idea to Start Andre Iguodala," *Sports Illustrated*,

June 12, 2015, http://www.si.com/nba/2015/06/12/warriors-steve-kerr
-nick-uren-andre-iguodala-andrew-bogut-nba-finals-cavaliers.

239   **In time for Game 4:** Marc Spears, "The Mystery Man Behind the
Plan that Helped the Warriors Win Game 4 of the NBA Finals," Yahoo! Sports, June 12, 2015, http://sports.yahoo.com/news/the
-mystery-man-behind-the-plan-that-helped-the-warriors-win-game
-4-of-the-nba-finals-080509364.html.

BIBLIOGRAPHY

Alamar, Ben. *Sports Analytics: A Guide for Coaches, Managers and Other Decision Makers.* New York, NY: Columbia University Press, 2013.

Barry, Rick, and Jordan Cohn. *Rick Barry's Pro Basketball Bible.* Los Angeles, CA: Bonus Books, 1994.

Bellotti, Robert. *Basketball's Hidden Game: Points Created, Boxscore Defense, and Other Revelations.* New Brunswick, NJ: Night Work Pub. Co., 1988.

Heeren, Dave. *Basketball Abstract 1991–92.* Englewood Cliffs, NJ: Prentice-Hall, 1991.

Hollinger, John. *Pro Basketball Prospectus.* Herndon, VA: Potomac Books, 2004.

James, Bill. *Baseball Abstract.* Lawrence, KS: Self-published, 1977.

Manley, Martin. *Basketball Heaven 1990.* New York, NY: Doubleday, 1989.

McGuire, Frank. *Defensive Basketball.* Englewood Cliffs, NJ: Prentice-Hall, 1959.

Oliver, Dean. *Basketball on Paper: Rules and Tools for Performance Analysis.* Herndon, VA: Potomac Books, 2003.

O'Neal, Shaquille, and Jackie MacMullen. *Shaq Uncut: My Story.* New York, NY: Grand Central Publishing, 2011.

Paine, Neil. "Linear Weights: Ranking the Formulas." *Basketball Prospectus,* January 2, 2012.

Pelton, Kevin. "The Great Analytics Rankings." ESPN.com, February 23, 2015. http://espn.go.com/espn/feature/story/_/id/12331388/the-great-analytics-rankings.

Shea, Stephen, and Christopher Baker. *Basketball Analytics: Objective and Efficient Strategies for Understanding How Teams Win.* Lake St. Louis, MO: Advanced Metrics LLC, 2013.

ACKNOWLEDGMENTS

There are a great many people without whom this book would not have been possible.

I owe initial gratitude to my literary agent, Eric Nelson, who patiently and professionally critiqued a number of ideas for a nonfiction basketball book before we hit upon this one. He and Sydelle Kramer, who took over my account at Susan Rabiner Literary Agency when Eric returned to the editorial side of the business, have been invaluable with their advice and support. Likewise, I am grateful to Perseus Books and Da Capo Press for believing in the project. My editor, Dan Ambrosio, was incredibly positive and patient throughout the whole process with a first-time book author.

Of course, no book can exist without its subjects. I was fortunate to connect with a large number of incredibly smart, interesting, and talented people, all of whom have tremendous passion for basketball and/or technology.

I'd like to thank the many NBA teams and their media relations staffs that provided significant access to their players, coaches, and management. Notables include Raymond Ritter and Matt de Nesnera from the Golden State Warriors; Garin Narain, Jon Steinberg, and Jason Roose from the Atlanta Hawks; Chris Clark from the Sacramento Kings; and Chris Wallace from the Philadelphia 76ers. A special thank you goes to Tim Gelt of the Denver Nuggets. Living in Denver, I was able to use the Nuggets games as a home base through which to gain access to many other NBA teams, and Tim spent the entire year being extremely helpful and supportive of my presence during what was a difficult season for the franchise. Also, thanks to Craig Miller at USA Basketball, who helped arrange access and information regarding our junior and senior national teams.

For the off-court pieces of the book, I want to specifically thank Rajiv Maheswaran, Garrick Barr, Brian Kopp, Marcus Elliott, Michael Clark, and Paul Robbins for spending significant amounts of time with me on the phone and in person, which allowed me to more fully understand the businesses they have built around technology and science that help drive ongoing player and team performance. Where we currently are is remarkable, and I'm so excited to see where everything goes next.

There were additional people who were extraordinarily helpful, providing tremendous insights and soundchecks on the ideas and structure of the book. I'd like to specifically thank media colleagues Zach Lowe, Matt Moore, Jay Bilas, Fran Fraschilla, Jeff Goodman, and Luke Winn for their wide-ranging perspectives on basketball across all levels of the sport. I also must thank Steve Hellmuth, the NBA's director of technology, who was remarkably insightful during our conversations and very interested in the project. The NBA is in great hands with him leading the ongoing innovations.

I also received tremendous support from a number of individuals who assisted in the information-gathering and writing processes. There is no way this book would have happened without the transcribing work of Lucy McCalmont and Jacob Rosen. Lucy, especially, was remarkable in both her enthusiasm and production. Additionally, thanks to Seth Partnow for being available throughout the writing process and for vetting chapters as they were completed, providing terrific insights as to how they could be improved.

To all of the basketball players, coaches, and team officials who participated or just let me watch you perform, thank you. Getting to immerse myself in your world was fascinating. The sport is in very good hands.

On a personal level, I want to thank Jamie O'Grady, cofounder and editor in chief of *The Cauldron,* the national sports publication we launched right before I signed the deal for this book. There were months along the way when I had to dedicate most of my time to the book, and Jamie carried the operation in my stead. It's been a blast working with him and building something really cool. I also advise you never to write a book while trying to launch a startup. It's insane.

I'd also like to thank Sandy Padwe, my sportswriting professor at Columbia School of Journalism, who had faith in a raw writer who was changing careers from consulting, and *Sports Illustrated*'s Tim Layden, who helped me vastly improve my first longform feature at SI.com. That piece made me believe that, someday, I could write a book.

Lastly, I owe tremendous gratitude to all parts of my family.

My mom and dad remain as proud of me now as when they were raising me. I've always been fortunate to have a loving and supportive nuclear family that includes my terrific sister, as well.

My best friend, Raj, is like the brother I never had, and is one of the most passionate NBA fans I know. Thank you for more than a quarter century of laughs and sports discussions.

My three children are my shining lights, and they all give up a lot of time with me, as my work often happens at night or involves travel. I am excited to have more "dad time" with them now that this book is finished.

To my wife, Gina, I don't have enough words to express how lucky I am to be with you. Beyond everything you do for our family while juggling your own terrific career, your love, support, and belief in me are remarkable. None of this—this book, this career, this life—would be possible without you. I love you.

INDEX